YOU ARE NOT ALONE

In an increasingly complex and difficult world, individuals are more prone to a greater array of problems and anxieties than ever before, problems that can interfere with our happiness and stifle our path to fulfillment. But now, with a concise and compassionate approach, Dr. Rubin shows us how to overcome these troubles by sharing our common questions on the family, ourselves, our relations to others, and by providing wise and practical answers.

"An awareness of a commonality of problems will help us all to break the vicious cycle of anxiety that starts when we think a problem is ours alone. May this sharing, this awareness, teach us 'not to worry.' "

—DR. TED RUBIN

Pinnacle books by Theodore Isaac Rubin, M.D.

The Thin Book by a Formerly Fat Psychiatrist
One to One
Not to Worry (with Eleanor Rubin, M.S.)

NOT TO WORRY

The American Family Book
of Mental Health

BY
**THEODORE
ISAAC RUBIN, M.D.,**

& ELEANOR RUBIN, M.S.

PINNACLE BOOKS NEW YORK

Portions of this book appeared originally in *Ladies' Home Journal* in
slightly different form.

NOT TO WORRY

Pinnacle Books edition, published by special arrangement with Viking
Penguin, Inc.

Viking edition published in 1984
Pinnacle edition/March 1985

ISBN: 0-523-42425-6
Can. ISBN: 0-523-43413-8

Printed in the United States of America

PINNACLE BOOKS, INC.
1430 Broadway
New York, New York 10018

9 8 7 6 5 4 3 2 1

To the teachers and students
of the American Institute for Psychoanalysis of
the Karen Horney Psychoanalytic Center

Table of Contents

Introduction

IN WRITING FOR magazines and books over the years I have received a great many questions from people of all ages in all parts of the country. Though we are, each of us, unique, it never ceases to amaze me just how many questions, anxieties, and experiences we all share. I believe there is comfort in sharing: I have put together this book in order to share those questions and my responses to them. I hope that clarification of some of the most common problems encountered in our emotional lives may help to reduce worry and anxiety. You may overtly identify with some questions, while others may raise your consciousness. In either case, an awareness of a commonality of problems will help us all to break the vicious cycle of anxiety that starts when we think a problem is ours alone. May this sharing, this awareness, teach us "not to worry."

Q: I am curious about the letters you receive. Do you get many? Are they all from women? Could you tell us which problems seem to be the most prevalent in our country, and is there any one symptom that is most common? What causes it?

A: Yes, I do receive a great many letters from all over the country and this gives me a wonderful opportunity to touch base with many people. Most of the letters are from women, but I also get some from men, a number from adolescents, and even some from very young children. If we use my mail as a barometer, the problem that seems to prevail most is poor communication in families. Family members are frequently at odds and have great difficulty talking to one another on an effective level. This is especially true of husbands and wives but also pertains to children and parents as well as brothers and sisters. Some of the saddest and most upsetting letters I receive are from teenage children who feel that they can't talk to their parents—that is, really talk and say how they feel. Some of them say their parents don't listen. Others are afraid their parents won't understand their problems and will respond punitively. Some feel that their parents won't take them seriously. Some say that their parents are too busy fighting each other.

I think most psychiatrists would agree that depression is currently the most common symptom for which people seek psychiatric treatment. Generally, this may be due to the fact that expectations of ourselves, our mates, our children, and our friends, in a world that has become increasingly complex and difficult to deal with, are exorbitantly high. This leads to bitter disappointment and much repressed rage—at ourselves or others for "failing," at the world for "causing" that failure—which are expressed as depression.

NOT TO
WORRY

Part One

THE FAMILY

THE TRADITIONAL FAMILY unit is under siege. The nuclear family today is often a single-parent household. Even within this framework there are variations: sometimes the single parent is one parent; sometimes parents alternate, with the children drifting back and forth between households. Another variation has the children remaining fixed while the parents replace each other every six months. In other cases the grandparents are obliged to continue parenting their grandchildren as well as their adult child. Oftentimes the extended family becomes very large when divorced parents remarry and each new marriage adds new family members to the original split unit. Obviously most people still feel strongly about family and traditional values since these new configurations use the nuclear family as a model.

The "traditional" nuclear family and the newer version both share a multitude of concerns and problems. These include:

Should we have children? When?

How do we deal with in-laws? Older parents?

How can we prepare a child for separation, school, and divorce?

Can we prepare ourselves for separation from children?

What about a career and marriage?

What happens when an older parent remarries?

Are the new mores a threat to the nuclear family?

What would society be like without the family?

These are some of the issues facing the family today, and the family—however it defines itself—must grapple with the answers.

Human children, unlike animal offspring, are totally dependent on adults for their well-being for many years. Bringing up children in other than a nuclear unit, imperfect though that unit may be, has so far proved to be less than successful. We know this from studies of institutionalized children and of *kibbutznik* children in Israel: these studies indicate that though physical and intellectual development were adequate, a full range of emotional development was lacking in these children.

Chapter One

MARRIAGE

Avoiding Honeymoon Hazards • Married Sex • Infidelity • Divorce

MARRIAGE, THE ULTIMATE commitment, is public acknowledgment that two people intend to share their lives and bond their love. It is a legal commitment of their responsibility to each other, to their offspring, if any, and to society.

Often in the excitement of courtship and wooing, couples fail to spell out their needs, wants, and expectations of marriage to each other. Partners who go into marriage with unrealistic expectations and illusions concerning the roles and responsibilities of each are bound to get into difficulty. This difficulty is often dealt with in several ways:

1. A quick divorce.
2. Having a child.
3. Living together in "quiet desperation."

A wise couple will, from time to time, reassess their expectations about self and marriage. In so doing they try to arrive at mutually acceptable, realistic priorities that can lead to a happier union.

Avoiding Honeymoon Hazards

Many serious difficulties in marriage can be traced to the earliest days of the relationship, some to the time just before the marriage. But there are others that come about during, or because of, the honeymoon itself. Of course many problems are the result of personal difficulties in relating and communicating that are only accentuated and exaggerated by the honeymoon experience. But there are many cases in which the honeymoon turns out to be a traumatic event that leaves emotional scars that could have been avoided.

The most important factor to understand is that every relationship is highly individual—each relationship develops at its own rate and in its own unique way. This means that every couple is in a different stage of their developing relationship at the time of their honeymoon. Some know each other very well. They know each other's values, idiosyncrasies, preferences, tastes, vulnerabilities, motives. They know what they have in common. They know their differences. A certain amount of mutual trust has developed. Some even share common goals, interests, and a common emotional language—mainly the ability to convey successfully what and how they feel to each other.

But some people start a honeymoon with very little relating experience between them. They hardly know each other and in some cases, aside from initial mutual physical attraction, have little or no idea whether they share any common ground. There are also some people who have never had a close relationship with another person; there are those who have never been away from home on their own, or who have never had a sustained, close time in another person's presence.

Obviously people vary enormously in their maturity, general sophistication, education, sexual experience, knowledge, and attitude toward the opposite sex, as well as in their compassion, patience, tolerance, and teaching ability. (This last factor is extremely important if one member of the couple is fairly sophisticated or mature.) It is rare that both people start a relationship at the same level of erudition in all areas of life. Knowing this, and having a willingness to teach or learn from our partners from the very beginning, enormously enhances the possibility for a constructive and fruitful relationship to develop and to evolve.

But when two people are suddenly on their own, alone together, the stress of sudden intimacy may cause problems. Here are a few points to remember in dealing with them:

1. No person or couple should feel that they must comply with any particular honeymoon practice as prescribed by society, convention, family, or friends. In short, they can do what they like!

2. A honeymoon must *never* be considered a test of any kind! This means it must not be seen as a test of love, compatibility, sexual interest, sexual ability, mutuality, or anything else.

3. The honeymoon must not be overinvested with importance. If it turns out to be disappointing, do not make it a self-fulfilling prophecy about the entire future relationship. It is a special time—but it is only one of thousands of times a relating couple will spend together.

4. Most disappointments in honeymoons derive from exorbitant expectations of sustained highs. The couple expects instant, deep, and perfect communication; sexual perfection; constant excitement. They idealize each other and expect their relationship to have a sustained air of romance. Most honeymoons directly follow weddings in which bride and groom are the focus of great attention and excitement by a great many people. We can readily see the loss of emotional "charge" that follows when a young couple are suddenly alone, away from home, and no longer the focus of attention by others. Expectations must be tempered in advance if disappointment and letdown are to be avoided.

5. Remember, it takes time to get to know each other—time, patience, and education. Instant telepathic communication and mutual understanding do not take place between people. This means that in addition to taking time, we must talk and tell each other our feelings, likes, and dislikes if we want to be understood and if we desire mutual satisfaction in any area, sexual included. One of the most destructive notions people have is, "If he (she) loves me he (she) should know what I want or like without my having to tell him

(her). Telling spoils it.'' The honeymoon is a good time to begin the all-important constructive practice of talking— *really* talking. This means openly conveying feelings and preferences.

6. Not everyone wants a honeymoon and there is no law that says that a couple must have one. But if two people decide not to have one they must not recriminate later or feel that they have been deprived.

7. A couple must entitle themselves to have whatever kind of honeymoon they desire. It is best that they plan this together, much as they would a vacation. Individual preferences as regards distances from home, length of time, kinds of activity should be considered. Some young people, however much in love, may initially feel too lonely to be far away from places and people they know. They must not be pressured to jump precipitously into situations totally unfamiliar to them because of their new marital status. Marriage neither signifies nor produces instant maturity. Some couples even prefer to go away in the company of other honeymoon couples. If this dilutes stress, there is nothing wrong with it.

8. For some couples the delay of a honeymoon to a future date may well be constructive. They may have health problems, financial strains, or other matters needing attention—or they may just want to wait until they feel more comfortable alone and away.

9. The honeymoon must not be seen as an indicator of what one's sexual relationship will be like for a lifetime. A satisfying sexual relationship takes time to develop—we can't expect a honeymoon to effect instant mutual sexual understanding or gratification. Only time, patience, and verbal communication can do that! Nor should sexual activity be imposed as a honeymoon command. There are no prescribed rules about how frequent it should be (or about anything else, for that matter). Whatever friends and relatives say about it should be discounted.

10. The honeymoon must under no circumstances be used to externalize or to project difficulties one feels toward

one's partner. In other words, do not blame him or her for any anxiety felt! It is normal and most common for people to feel anxious following an act signifying commitment to each other, but don't get into the habit of mutual blame. Anxiety in any area requires mutual support, aid, caring, and understanding. The honeymoon is a good place to begin.

Q: My brother, who is fifty-four years old, is about to marry a "girl" who is only twenty-three. This is his second marriage. His first wife was much younger than he was, too. Why are some men attracted, and why do some get attached, to women or girls much younger than themselves?

A: In part, society contributes to these relationships by accepting older man/younger woman combinations even as it condemns older women/younger men liaisons. But the individuals involved play the greatest part. In some cases, very young women are mature beyond their chronological age, and so they seek relationships with older men. I've known at least several couples in which the younger woman was much more mature—intellectually, emotionally, and culturally—than her older husband. There are also those cases in which two people have so much in common, and communicate so well, that age plays a relatively minor role in their lives.

Some men are bored with life and want to play Pygmalion or father; they think they can reawaken muted feelings by reliving old experiences vicariously through the senses of a young woman for whom everything is fresh and new. Some men prefer relating to younger women because they feel threatened by women who are more complex and experienced. There are men who have a need for mastery and who feel that it is easier to manipulate and to impress younger women. Many men who are terrified of old age choose relationships with women much younger than themselves in an attempt to identify with youth and to put off the inevitable. There are older men who are drawn to young women largely for purposes of actual physical care—they are looking for benevolent nurses. There are men who seek younger women primarily as a function of vanity and poor self-esteem, in or-

der to impress people with their continuing ability to be attractive. These men see young women as both ego- and
status-enhancing.

Q: Do you think a marriage can work in which the woman
is seven years older than the man?

A: Yes! But everything depends on the people
involved—on their ability to relate, to communicate, and to
struggle for mutual understanding. The level of maturity of
the people in question is important. Their degree of liberation from conventional dicta and stereotypes is relevant
since continued self-consciousness about age differences
can be destructive.

Q: Why are so many articles written about what a woman
can do to save her marriage? Isn't there anything men can do
to save their marriage, or has society dictated that the wife is
the sole savior of a relationship?

A: Women read those articles and men don't! Most men
feel that interest in family articles is a feminine thing; it
takes a man of considerable maturity to put childish and confused notions of masculinity behind him so that interest in
these kinds of problems does not constitute a threat.

As to whether a wife can be the ''sole savior of a relationship''—it takes two to tango, and unless both partners are responsible and motivated, a marriage will be no marriage at
all. However, because neurotic male pride and immaturity
so often get in the way, the woman may have to take the lead
in talking things over and getting help if necessary.

Married Sex

Q: The first two years of our marriage our sex life was
terrific—everything I'd ever expected love to be. But for the
past year my husband has gradually lost interest in me and in
sex. I've tried everything to turn him on, believe me, but
nothing works. He says the problem is simply that he's too

tired all the time. I'm tired, too—of pleading and arguing with him. I know he works hard, but not that hard. And the doctor says nothing is wrong with him. Last week I accused him of seeing another woman, which he denies (and I believe him), and we had our biggest fight ever. What can all this be about?

A: It is only recently that sex therapists have come to recognize loss of sexual interest as a sexual dysfunction. Indeed, loss of interest may well be a more serious problem than impotence, premature ejaculation, inability to achieve orgasm, or anything else. Unfortunately, this "symptom"—and many workers in the field regard it as a symptom—is much more common among married couples, of all ages, than was previously suspected. And unlike other sex malfunctions, it is not readily amenable to the teaching and training of conventional sex therapy. Loss of sexual interest is almost always symptomatic of underlying disturbances. These may not be sexual at all, even though they are translated into sexual symptoms or difficulties. Let me list several of the most common problems:

1. Boredom with life generally and particularly one's own daily routine in living.

2. Frustrated yearnings, especially thwarted creative desires.

3. Jealousy and envy of one's mate.

4. Emotional depression. Loss of sexual desire is often an early sign of emotional dysfunction.

5. The inability to accept close, sustained, and long "contractual" emotional involvement with another human being. This feeling of "loss of freedom" leads to loss of all desire.

6. Repressed anger, which leads to repression of all other feelings as well. This last one is the most common, and recognition and improved handling of angry feelings usually leads to considerable improvement in one's sex life.

Obviously the problem is complex. It is advisable that analytic consultation take place before it becomes a chronic way of life.

Q: My problem is that my husband and I can't agree on when to have sex. I want to make love at night before we go to sleep, and he wants to do it in the morning before he goes to work. I'm just too tired and busy in the morning and he says he's too tired at night. So lately we've been having sex in the morning and I'm not enjoying it at all anymore.

A: Your greatest difficulty is not your individual preferences but rather the inability both of you have either to capitulate to each other's desires and/or to compromise. Holding one's ground, no matter what, is ruinous to all human encounters and particularly to sexual ones. I think it would be wise to talk out your time preferences, letting each other know why you feel the way you do. It would then be useful for each of you to make an effort to please the other as well as yourself. Perhaps you may find it satisfying to alternate times and preferences and also to make greater use of weekends. Changes in daily routine as well as frequent short vacations may be helpful. This is especially true where fatigue is a real factor. But *nothing* is helpful if the real goal for each of you is to maintain dissatisfaction and a sense of martyrdom. If either partner desires nothing short of complete compliance by the other, sufficient frustration and rage will ensue to destroy the relationship—sexually and otherwise.

Q: We've been married a short time and though we have sex fairly often, I don't always have an orgasm. I am not dissatisfied and enjoy making love even though I don't always climax. Is this normal?

A: Much too much time and energy are expended in worrying about what is "normal," especially as regards sex. Many people—including men, though this is less common—do not experience orgasm every time they make love. Frequency of lovemaking or of orgasm—indeed, all sexual preferences—are highly individual. What is important is your feeling satisfied and not suffering chronic frustration.

Q: We are in our mid-thirties. My husband likes to look at sexy girls in magazines and he won't avoid X-rated movies, either. I just don't care for them at all. In fact I find most pornography a turnoff. He says I'm narrow-minded and constricted. I say he's immature. What do you think?

A: I think it's largely a difference between men and women. Men like to "see." They are voyeuristic and "turned on" by sexy sights. Women need emotional investment, exchange of feelings, closeness, caring, and warmth to be turned on. This does not preclude certain sights from being stimulating on occasion to women, but generally this is how it is. Thus most pornographic movies, magazines, and so on, are sold to men. These differences, some behavioral scientists believe, are instinctual and basic. Others, like myself, believe they are largely learned and are the results of the different treatment and upbringing of boys and girls from early infancy. In any case, I don't believe these sexual differences indicate either maturity or immaturity.

Q: Must a woman submit to a man every time he wants sex? My husband understands that sometimes I'm just not in the mood, but he just can't let up. When I feel like it, it is great. When I don't, he feels terribly hurt. Can you shed any light?

A: That you use the word "submit" is interesting. Some people in your position (both women and men) are particularly sensitive to what they perceive as coercion and "submission" in all areas of their lives. Sometimes increasing our *real* ability to be self-assertive helps to dilute these feelings. Most people are sexually arrhythmic—which means that they don't always have the same sexual feelings and needs at the same time. Most married people respond to a refusal of an advance as rejection and feel both hurt and frustrated when this happens. Many couples engage in sex when either partner feels sexually needy, on the basis of cooperation rather than submission. While their sexual response may not always be equal, it is not unsatisfactory either. If we understand that people can't always be "perfectly" attuned to each other, but that they can be compassionate about each other's needs, we are more likely to enjoy mutually satisfying responses. People who are frustrated sexually, for whatever reason, do not relate well. If open discussion and mutual accommodation can't take place, many marriages become severely troubled. Before this happens, combined sexual and marriage counseling may be of considerable value.

Q: My baby is two, and my problem seems to have occurred after she was born. I love my husband, but I have no desire for sex. I know I am being deprived of real pleasure and joy, but I don't care. My husband says I don't show love to him. Our marriage is on thin ice now: What can I do?

A: I quite agree with you that your marriage is in jeopardy: very few sexual relationships can survive one partner's complete loss of interest. And I'm sorry you don't care, because your caring and involvement are crucial if any solution to your problem is to be forthcoming. Not caring is sometimes due to chronic depression and self-hatred. The victim may not be fully aware of self-hate or depression but may have gradually embarked on a course of self-deprivation and joylessness if not downright self-destruction as a result of rage against self (which often takes the form of emotional depression). Some women lose interest in sex following the birth of a child because they feel anger against their husbands, anger at unwanted responsibility, anger at loss of freedom, anger at the child (who represents loss of one's own childhood as well as multitudinous responsibilities and cares). Some women never wanted a child in the first place and had a baby only because "it was the thing to do." Guilt about such angry feelings—especially toward a child—often makes acceptance of the anger impossible. Repressed rage is particularly destructive to sexual feelings.

Of course, there can be other contributing factors: fear of

another pregnancy, combined with conflicting feelings about the last pregnancy; the need for adaptation to new responsibilities; and the genuine fatigue of new parenthood can all inhibit and even paralyze sexual spontaneity. But I doubt that your problem "occurred after she was born." The symptom of your problem—lack of sexual desire—may have occurred then, but the root of your problem probably has much to do with your ideas about sex, marriage, children, yourself, your husband, and so on, that you have had from early childhood. I think that a consultation with a qualified analyst is indicated so as to determine what course of action would be best: marriage counseling? sexual counseling? psychoanalytic psychotherapy? psychoanalysis?

Q: My husband and I are in our eighties and until a short time ago we were very happily married. But now X-rated movies have come along to destroy my happiness. My husband, who is retired, leaves the house every afternoon to go to see these films and then comes home and falls asleep reading the paper or watching television. I don't know what this new habit of his is all about, but I feel hurt and rejected. Can you shed any light, please?

A: Your husband's interest in these movies probably has nothing at all to do with his feelings about you. It is more likely due to an attempt to recapture old times and feelings he had when he was a very young man. It may also be an attempt to satisfy a sexual curiosity that has its roots in childhood. Having grown up in an era of sexual inhibition, your husband may feel that going to these films represents rebellion against old taboos and restrictions. This may have more of a freeing and stimulating effect on his *general* feelings than on his *sexual* feelings. Feeling that we are engaging in something outrageous sometimes satisfies an adolescent urge to break out and raise a little dust.

Your husband may also be trying to tell himself and you that he is bored and would like to do something more than the very things he is doing, including falling asleep watching T.V. It may be a good idea to seek new activities and friends that you can both share. Contrary to some misguided popular opinion, no activities, including sexual ones, should be curtailed on the simple basis of age. In other words, our well-being demands involvement, however old we are. Indeed, the older we get, the more we need involvements of all kinds. As we age and gather knowledge and experience, we become more fully developed selves, and this growth requires additional, rather than diminished, nourishment of all kinds. When nourishment is lacking and perfectly healthy people have unwittingly withdrawn from life more and more because they feel this is appropriate to their age, they will, like your husband, sometimes in desperation turn to any kind of synthetic stimulation to compensate for a need for fuller living.

Q: I'm twenty-seven and my husband is thirty-one. We've been married two and a half years. We have a sex problem, which I guess is the reverse of the usual. He has difficulty having orgasms. It takes him a long time and sometimes he just can't have them at all. Should he see a urologist or a shrink? He has no difficulty having an erection, but then nothing happens.

A: Orgasmic retardation and inability to ejaculate is not as uncommon as you think. It is usually an emotional problem, often linked to fear of commitment and emotional involvement. It is often seen in men who have put too high a value on "freedom" from emotional entanglements. Sometimes it is due to repressed hostility and sometimes to unresolved repressed guilt stemming from a much earlier period in life. Some "detached" men have no difficulty with women about whom they have no deep feelings. Some do all right sexually until they marry. Marriage brings on the problem because it represents contractual involvement. Occasionally a man fears heterosexual encounters, but this is often an unconscious fear, although both he and his partner are fully aware of the sexual symptom.

It would be wise for your husband to be checked out by a competent urologist, but treatment by a good psychoanalytic therapist will probably be indicated. It may be particularly valuable to see a psychiatrist who is trained in both psychoanalysis and sex therapy.

Q: I periodically hear about a sexless marriage. Is it possible for two people actually to be happy or to make a reasonable adjustment without physical intimacy?

A: Human beings are capable of a vast array of behavioral adaptations. This means that there is virtually no limit to the kinds of relationships people develop. Happiness is at best relative, and the kinds of living arrangements people make are entirely dependent on the individuals involved. Sustained relationships, even marriages that are asexual, are probably more common than is realized. "Reasonable adjustments" are possible in these marriages—but of course something is missing. And lack of that something must detract appreciably from the potential fulfillment inherent in being human.

Let me point out, however, that there are also many sexually active relationships in which the sexual area presents many problems and limitations. Also, there are relationships in which sexual relating is excellent but all other areas are problem ridden. "Getting it all together" is never easy. *All* relating requires some accommodation. It is never perfect.

Q: I have the feeling that my husband wants sex mainly when he is bored and has nothing else to do. I just don't feel this is a healthy state of affairs. What do you think?

A: I think several things because you raise some very important issues.

1. Confirm the feeling with your husband. Talk it over.

2. Consult a sex therapist if necessary.

3. You are probably very angry, and if you are, I hope you don't repress your anger. I'm sure you prefer your husband to want sex because he wants you rather than because he's bored.

Boredom does not come from the outside. It is the result of neglecting our own inner resources. Unless the individual develops inner resources he will soon become bored with the activity he uses to fight his boredom. Thus, if sex is used to cover up lack of interest in developing real involvement with people, ideas, activities, creative work, social values, political values, or anything else, sex too will become boring.

If we refuse to be more than shallow and superficial, if we refuse to hook activities to real feelings and values, our activities become boring. Sustained interest in sex is almost guaranteed when sex is linked to feelings of love, when it reflects the relatedness and values and goals people have in common. And the reverse is also true. The stimulation addict who uses sex to dispel boredom often seeks partner after partner in a desperate attempt to keep interested and to feel alive. But no variety of partners or positions dilutes increased feelings of deadness. And promiscuity, drugs, money deals, or whatever are not substitutes for deep, meaningful, highly developed and caring relationships.

Infidelity

Infidelity—as breaking marriage vows or relating agreements is known in our culture—causes so much pain that I'm asked about this subject again and again.

There are several reasons for infidelity. One involves the kinds of relationships people have, the others involve the characteristics or problems the people in question bring into a relationship. If we are unhappy with a mate and we seek another mate, this may be a solution. But if we seek another mate because of our unhappiness with ourselves, we will bring that unhappiness into each new relationship and will destroy each in turn.

There are two main kinds of relationships. One is characterized by shallow relating and the other by deep relating. Shallow relationships depend on initial excitement and the stimulation of mutual attraction; on the initial discovery of each other's attributes; on the stimulation inherent in being with a new sex partner, and being thought of as "a couple" by friends. These are self-gratifying relationships. Deep relationships are characterized by surrender of the self to the relationship, by one partner's commitment to the other without fear of missing out on other relationships and without fear of being emotionally drowned or swamped.

Relationships cannot remain stagnant. They either grow or they deteriorate and die. All relationships start on a shallow level. Some go on to become in-depth relationships that have unlimited potential—the possibility for mutual discovery and emotional investment (caring and involving oneself with the other person) is virtually limitless in human beings. But many relationships never get past the barrier of shallowness. Many people can't "let go," can't commit themselves, and are terrified that they will lose identity if they attempt to struggle through to deeper feelings toward another human being. Shallow relating gets used up very quickly. The initial excitement simply does not last. But even people who cannot tolerate deeper relationships need whatever gratification is possible from shallow encounters. Therefore these people must turn from used up relationships to new ones, which may still offer gratification, however momentary. If these people must maintain marriages because of conventional needs, dependency needs, financial considerations, religious scruples, feelings about children, guilt, or whatever, they often turn to extramarital relating for temporary gratification. Since superficial relating gets used up faster and faster, they develop a habit of infidelity that is supported by their search for human emotional sustenance from the surface when it can be found only in the depths.

Some individual problems and difficulties are chronic, lifelong, and make for the kind of relating that almost always leads to infidelity. Others are more acute and short-lived: they are less likely to cause habitual infidelity. Let me list some of them:

1. Actual incompatibility and a lack of intellectual, emotional, and sexual gratification. This is relatively rare. If

the individuals in question have the ability to seek deeper ground with each other, individual differences can sometimes be overcome, however irreconcilable they seem to be.

2. A serious homosexual problem, sometimes on an unconscious level. This too is not very common.

3. Incurable romanticism, in which both partners seek a dollhouse existence—they refuse to struggle through periods of difficulty either in relating to each other or in coping with the world.

4. Immaturity—one partner or the other is unable to make genuine commitments or to take on real adult responsibilities. This is a major and very common problem.

5. Alienation from one's own feelings. There are people who are afraid to feel anything for anyone too deeply. This is another prevalent problem.

6. Poor self-esteem and poor sense of one's own identity, resulting in fear of being swallowed up by the other person if "too much closeness" takes place. This is very common, too.

7. A background, or family orientation, that condones or even promotes infidelity.

8. Extreme male chauvinism, in which one partner views women as nothing more than sex objects.

9. A "little boy and little girl" curiosity syndrome, in which one can never say no to oneself regardless of how destructive the outcome may be.

10. A middle-age crisis, in which the attempt is made to reassure oneself about one's sexuality and attractiveness and to identify with youthful pursuits.

Of course any of these problems can and often do exist in combination. And the person who suffers from their effects is usually not the person with the problem. The response to infidelity in a partner can be from mild to devastating. Much depends on the "aggrieved" person's own self-esteem, maturity, ability to withstand hurt pride, fear of aging or seeming less attractive, and so on.

It is helpful to realize that many cases of infidelity are due to personal problems of the unfaithful, rather than to short-comings of the partner. However, a history of repeated relationships with unfaithful partners may indicate the need for therapy in order to aid one's ability to participate in deeper relationships.

Divorce

Understanding Barriers to Appropriate Divorces

Some time ago I wrote about the high rate of divorce in our country and why divorces took place. But what about disastrous relationships that should end in divorce but don't? Many people have described relationships to me that are fraught with pain, frustration, and loneliness—which in many cases are utterly destructive to everyone involved, including children.

In many cases these are people who do not suffer from exorbitant expectations of marriage and are not immaturely unrealistic about living closely with another person; they have struggled to make a go of it. In some cases good professional help, including marriage counseling and psychotherapy, has been tried—all to no avail. Many of these people have relationships that are doomed from the outset by incompatible values and frames of reference (ways of looking at life, people, activities, sex, and so on); their differences, simply put, are totally irreconcilable. Some came from backgrounds and cultures that are so different that they preclude the possibility of fruitful communicating. They just can't and don't speak the same language and they lack the basic tools of common experience necessary to understand and to gratify each other. This is a kind of incompatibility that is much deeper and more pervasive than sexual incompatibility—and harder to remedy. A great many people caught in these kinds of marriages have personality and character structures that make it virtually impossible to make a life together however much treatment and struggle take place. Unfortunately, many married much too early in life, in some cases blindly and impulsively, and in most cases for all the wrong reasons. And yet so many of these malignant marriages go on and on. Why? What paralyzes these people? Why don't they rescue themselves and each other from marriages characterized by chronic misery?

Most of the forces involved in keeping destructive relationships going exist outside the awareness of the victims involved. And more than one motive or dynamic is usually operative. Any combination of the following may keep people trapped in marriages they'd be better off out of.

1. *The "don't make waves" habit.* Unfortunately, many people prefer the known evil to the unfamiliar, untried good. These people are resigned to keeping things as they are and are terrified of upsetting what they perceive as the long-standing balance of their lives even though that balance may in fact be painful tension. This is often true of people married to alcoholics and to people suffering from other addictions (gambling, drugs, antisocial activities) but is by no means confined to this group.

2. *Terror of loneliness.* This fear largely exists in people who do not have confidence in their own resources and in many who have little or no confidence in their ability to attract and to be liked by other people. Sometimes these are people who show a marked inability to be alone. Even though it is still much easier for men to meet people than women, I believe that this fear is even more prevalent among men than among women.

3. *Fear of hurting the children.* This always exists on a conscious level and is often used as the principal rationalization for sustaining marriage and ignoring all the other reasons to break up. The fact that divorce in most of these cases gives the children a better chance for health and happiness is likewise ignored.

4. *Sustaining the reputation of being a "good mother" or "good father."* This is the unconscious extension of the fear of hurting the children; it is just as prevalent in men as in women, and is often a more powerful force in men. The parent who cares about this is unconsciously more interested

in sustaining his or her own image of being a "good father" (or "good mother") than in the actual well-being of the children.

5. *Fear of failure.* This exists in women but is, I believe, more prevalent in men. Many people, especially men, see the breakup of a marriage as a great personal failure. Many men feel divorce is a blow to their masculine pride and self-esteem. This dynamic produces great stress, self-hate, and depression in men who do not have a full, conscious grip on it so that they can cope with it.

6. *Fear of rejection.* This fear is strong in both sexes but stronger in men who view the breakup of marriage as a rejection by their wives. It is often strongest in men who felt rejected by their mothers. These same men often feel guilty about rejecting their wives, whom they unconsciously see as their mothers.

7. *Fear of sexual inadequacy.* This concern is very strong among men and is an extension of the fear of rejection. Many men are secretly (and not so secretly) afraid that other women will not be attracted to them and that their sexual performance with another woman will not be adequate. Here, too, rejection is frightening—particularly so in men who never felt they had sufficient love and acceptance by their mothers.

8. *Mutual dependency.* When mutual dependency exists, both partners may find each other intolerable but at the same time feel inadequate to cope alone emotionally. These are often people who feel no sense of their separate selves and need each other in order to feel like whole human beings. Just as the disabled hate their crutches, these people often despise each other for the chronic reminders of mutual inadequacy they provide. They may be fully aware of their hatred but unaware of the reason for it. In these relationships the woman often looks more dependent than the man to outside observers, but the reverse is usually true.

9. *Religious scruples, social stigmas, and familial and conventional forces.* These are very common but interestingly may not always exist consciously. There are many

people who see themselves as "emancipated," but in analysis find out that they are inhibited and even paralyzed by unconscious forces that often have roots in early childhood.

10. *Illusion of great romance.* Some people cannot surrender the great emotional investment they have in their "great love affair." This is truer of men than women—I generally find men to be greater romantics.

11. *Dependence on home base.* Many people, again particularly men, are largely dependent on the marriage and family constellation for a sense of identity. Interestingly, business or professional status is often secondary while marriage and family are primary. These men can be tigers in business, provided that their wives (substitute mothers) are back there holding down home base. Many of these men feel that motivation for work and achievement will disappear without this identifying structure, and that without it they will become "paralyzed bums."

12. Many people are terrified of the *economic consequences* of divorce, sometimes in a way disproportionate to reality.

13. *Dependency on pathological relating.* A couple have come to depend on mutual annihilation as a means of feeling alive and stimulated. This characterizes the sadomasochistic relationship obviously equally prevalent in both sexes and often very destructive to children who are drawn in.

Many people cannot extricate themselves without professional help. Contrary to popular opinion, it is often men who need more help than women. This makes things especially tough because men in our society often see therapy as evidence of weakness and as an attack on their masculinity. Many men, for reasons described above, hide all these facts from themselves and come to believe, and to convince others, that it is their wives who find divorce intolerable.

Good therapists do not destroy marriages! They attempt to remedy problems and to help sustain marriages. They are well aware of human limitations and this includes limitations inherent in relating. But there are many relationships that are malignantly destructive and from which the partners should escape. This is often impossible unless the underlying dynamics are revealed and worked through. The analyst who does not do this where indicated is remiss.

Q: Do you agree with me that it doesn't make sense the way men fight so hard for custody of their children in divorce cases? Of course, I am not talking about cases where the mother is actually incompetent. I mean situations in which the wife is a perfectly fine mother. It seems crazy to me that men should fight for custody when they never took care of the kids in the first place and wouldn't be able to care for them if they won. I have two girl friends who were divorced. There was a terrible harangue about the children in both cases. The mothers won but the fathers got very liberal visitation rights. In the beginning the fathers visited the kids very often and spent much time with them. Now they are busy with their own lives, and while they continue with financial support they hardly see them at all. I'd like to remind them of the big battle they waged. I wonder what they would do now if they had won. By this time the kids would probably be a terrible burden to them. What do you think?
A: Unfortunately, very few men have the orientation, background, development, patience, energy, ability, or real motivation to involve themselves with the intimate care of the developing young child. I think that many custody fights are unrealistic and evidence of poor judgment: the result of sick pride, guilt, and a desire for vengeance. Let me point out that children are human beings and human beings are not *owned*, regardless of whom they live with. A father can continue to have a fruitful and constructive relationship and a good effect on children even if he doesn't live with them. Most men in our society do not spend that much time with their children even in a marriage that is going well. To expect to spend even more time with them after a divorce usually causes complications and undue pressure, which leads to a total breakdown in communication. It is best to be realistic about human possibilities and limitations from the beginning. But this is only possible if the welfare of the chil-

dren is of prime importance. This means seeing them as real human beings rather than as possessions to be used as bargaining pawns.

Helping Children Survive Divorce

Let me quote *The New York Times* of June 15, 1976:

> The latest United States government statistics show that the divorce epidemic is still in full swing and is ever growing. In 1975, the number of marriages ended by divorce or annulment exceeded the million mark for the first time in history. There was almost one divorce for every two marriages last year.
>
> This is an era in which many Americans are far more concerned with their rights than with their responsibilities, and also a time when little premium is put upon patience or accommodation to less than ideal situations.

It is obvious that the population of children of divorced parents increases in multitudes, just as the number of divorces does. These statistics don't seem to inhibit parents from having children, nor do children inhibit them from seeking divorce. I am not suggesting that sustaining a highly destructive marriage is good for the children involved. It is not! But—I believe—many people do give up too easily. Even with the most "civilized" divorces and with "caring and devoted parents," children suffer the consequences of misplaced guilt, mixed loyalties, and internal emotional conflicts just about all their lives. In situations in which the breakup is harsh, or even vindictive and sadistic (as all too often occurs), children often feel much confusion about their identities; they suffer from profound insecurity, chronic anxiety, poor self-esteem, and intense self-hatred. Too often, a divorce involves a battle in which each of the adversaries has a considerable army on his or her side, including friends, relatives, doctors, accountants, and, of course, lawyers. At the height of battle—and these battles sometimes go on for years—the children are often forgotten and have no one looking out for their needs. This is especially true of divorces involving self-pitying, vindictive adversaries who themselves may be extremely immature and childlike.

What can we do to help the children survive emotionally? Let me offer a few suggestions. Of course, these suggestions have merit only if the parents involved, however they feel about themselves and each other, continue to feel that their children's welfare comes first. This requires more than good intentions or lip service because children inevitably know the truth of their importance, or lack of it, in the family constellation.

1. Do not lie! The truth always makes itself known and lying destroys confidence in parental support when it is most needed.

2. Tell them! Do not wait for them to hear about their parents' separation from other people, especially other children.

3. Do not tell them until the final decision has been made! Many people go back and forth before they finally make up their minds. Children's hopes and security are destroyed if they too are forced to take part in shilly-shallying.

4. Do not hold out false hopes for a reconciliation. This destroys morale and confidence.

5. Do not give gratuitous information about the reasons for divorce. Make it as simple and general as possible, especially where very young children are involved.

6. There will inevitably be much anger and frustration on the part of the principals and anxiety and irritability on the part of the children. The children *must not* become victims of any spillover. Their own difficulties during this relatively long period of adjustment (from several months to a few years) require particular patience and support.

7. The children must be reassured that they will continue to be loved, cared for, and supported. They must be told that the current disorganization in no way means loss of parental control over environmental needs, and that it must in no way be interpreted as abandonment.

8. If a child develops untoward symptoms—depression, phobias, compulsions, tics, sleeplessness, a radical drop in school performance, and the like—psychiatric help should be sought at once.

9. While sympathy, empathy, support, and tolerance are in order, radical changes in upbringing can be destructive. These include overpermissiveness, overprotection, and increased susceptibility to a child's manipulations. Consistency is most supportive and must not be sacrificed because of parental guilt feelings.

10. The children must not be used as manipulative pawns in any way, whether for money (as in child support), power bargaining (as in custody or visitation rights), or anything else.

11. Disparaging remarks and discussions involving either parent or his or her family (the child's grandparents) are extremely damaging. This makes a child feel that all of his emotional investments and attachments are dissolving, and causes distrust, mixed loyalties, guilt, internal conflict, and overall insecurity and fear.

12. Adolescent children must not be used as marriage counselors, psychotherapists, confidantes, or surrogate marriage partners.

13. After battles for custody and visitation are over, parents must not forget to exercise these rights vigorously. Too many parents are more interested in attaining rights to see their children than in actually using these rights and seeing them.

14. Children's routines, especially at the beginning of this great change, are best interrupted as little as possible. All major dislocations are to be avoided. Therefore, it is better for siblings not to be separated; schools not to be changed; and the place they live in to remain the same. This is not the time for a child to be sent off suddenly to a boarding school for the first time.

15. Children must be reassured that they are in no way responsible for a parent's departure. This is especially important in the case of girls and their fathers.

16. Introduce new mates and their children only after sufficient time has elapsed for the shock of separation to dissipate; and even then do not expect instant friendship and love to ensue. New relationships, especially of this kind, take time to develop.

17. Make use of the extended family of both parents, especially grandparents, to provide emotional interests, thus contributing to a sense of belonging to a continuing family.

At best, divorce is traumatic for children whatever their ages. Keeping lines of communication open so that children can express their feelings is invaluable. Remember, instant adjustment must not be expected. Reverberations will occur and time is necessary for a solid reorientation to a new family balance and structure to take place.

Chapter Two

THE CHILDREN

Having Children • *Child Rearing*
Schooling • *Problems of the Young*
How Much Are You Contributing to Your
Children's Future Mental Health? • *Bring*
Back the Generation Gap

WHEN IS THE best time to have children—or to adopt them, if such be the case—has today become a more vital question than ever before. This is particularly so since it is becoming increasingly apparent that in many cases both parents will have to work to provide the goods and services necessary for the well-being of the family.

Unfortunately, there are neurotic impingements that complicate practical considerations:

> A baby will keep us from becoming bored.
> Save the marriage, have a child.
> Having a child will help the parents "grow up."
> All our friends are having children now.
> Pressure from parents.

These are certainly all the wrong reasons to become parents.

Having children is one of the finest expressions of marriage. It bonds the parents and contributes joy and love to family life. One must be aware, however, that it is a long-term commitment of nurturing and responsibility, often extending into the time when the child has children of his own.

Having Children

Q: Is there any time that is best to begin to have children? I mean a certain age, or when two people have been married for a certain length of time?

A: No. This is a highly individual issue. Some people may not want children at all. Others desire a large family and want to start early. Most obstetrician-gynecologists feel that young mothers encounter fewer risks, but most "older" mothers do very well, too. Socioeconomic factors have their relevance and emotional maturity is invaluable.

Q: My husband and I have been married for four years and we've been on the verge of a permanent separation—a divorce—at least a dozen times. This time it is very serious. We just can't get along. Would having a baby help?

A: I doubt it. Children often make things even worse. I feel it is a form of child exploitation to use a baby for this purpose and the child often suffers accordingly.

Q: My husband and I have been married five years, and now we're about to have our first baby. I know children drastically change a couple's relationship, and I'm worried. What are some of the ways a baby can affect a marriage?

A: A baby usually affects a marriage in ways related to the unresolved problems the baby's parents sustain from their own childhoods. To put it another way, babies who have babies take on enormous, sometimes unresolvable, problems; while adults (real adults—emotionally) tend to be able to manage this great change in their lives more effectively.

A new baby in a household means a new status quo—and, for a long time, a new emotional center of gravity in the family. A baby always involves great responsibility, work, decisions, restrictions, and attention. Freedom of movement is invariably curtailed. After all, there is little in nature as dependent and needy as a newborn human being. The rewards and satisfactions of taking on this task are enormous, and so are the responsibilities. Emotionally adult, healthy people grow through the experience, and immature, fragile people often have an exacerbation of problems and may require outside help.

The following are areas of difficulty for many people:

1. Some new parents are threatened by the personal attention now focused on the new arrival in the family. His/her presence and needs take precedence over those of a husband and/or wife.

2. People who have unresolved strong feelings of rivalry with siblings may now transfer those feelings to the baby.

3. Highly narcissistic people may view the baby as a double threat: as a rival for attention and as evidence that they are getting older. These are usually unconscious forces but nevertheless create anxiety and irritation.

4. People who have great difficulty with decision making and self-assertion may feel threatened by the demands a baby makes on them in terms of responsibility and decisions.

5. People who have a great need for freedom of movement may feel unduly restricted. This can lead to mutual blame and recrimination without awareness of the source of this irritation.

6. New economic pressures, including crowding and a tighter budget imposed by the arrival of a newborn, are stressful.

7. The increased presence of relatives to see the baby may put stress on the couple.

8. Sexual relations are often affected by lack of privacy and the attention needs of infants.

The arrival of a new baby calls for mutual support and patience with the baby and with each other. It is important for a couple to talk things over openly and to share responsibility and work in the evolution of the new family balance. When difficulties seem unresolvable, professional advice often helps both parents and the new family addition.

Q: My husband had a vasectomy during his first marriage. He is forty-two and I am twenty-eight. I really want to have a child very badly. He is not eager but says if it is that important to me we can have a child. I would love to have my own child with him, but if that is not possible, I was thinking of artificial insemination. But is adoption preferable? What do you think?

A: I think much depends on how both of you feel. It may be advisable for you both to talk it over with a therapist. Some men resent artificial insemination unless they themselves are the donors. This may be possible with your husband. May I point out that a great many vasectomies have been reversed through microsurgery. A good microsurgeon provides a very high possibility for success. However, the issue of whether your husband really wants a baby, even his own, may represent a more serious problem, which is best worked out in advance.

Some Thoughts on Birth and Adoption

Taking a child to be one's own—rather than conceiving and bearing one—is not a simple matter that requires only well-intentioned impulse. Serious consideration is necessary, as is true of having one's own child. Both birth and adoption deserve to be well thought through, for the latter has all the stresses of the former, with some added strains of its own. Adoption of a foreign child who is more than a few years old—a trend we see more and more these days—may well include problems that spring from differences in cultural values and customs. Children who have been grossly neglected and left on their own and who have had little or no parental love and care in their early years will require enormous patience. So-called street children invariably suffer from serious emotional problems, and their adoptive parents will need a good deal of psychiatric counseling. Knowing this in advance is very helpful both in taking this all-im-

portant step and in avoiding disappointment and hopelessness when serious difficulty is encountered.

The most valuable rule of thumb in adoption is "What is
good for the child?"—and this applies to foreign and American children, healthy or sick ones.

In trying to determine what is good for the child, it is important to:

1. Be prepared for a longer initial period of adjustment
for the family and the child as the age of the child at adoption increases from three months upward.

2. Be prepared for competition. The various members
of the family may compete with the new member for your
attention or for the exclusive attention of the new member.
The permutations of competition within a family are endless, and parents are not immune. (This principle equally
applies in the case of the birth of one's own child.)

3. Be prepared to ration your time carefully, especially
at the beginning, so that no one feels left out (including your
husband). The mother of a newly adopted child is usually
eager to have her or him, and is often so grateful at arrival
time that she neglects all other people and areas of her life.

4. Be careful of overprotection. Overprotection is stifling and destructive, but because you may have waited
longer for your adopted baby, you may feel anxious and
overly protective.

5. Be prepared for resentment and even open hostility
on the part of relatives who resent the intrusion of a non-
"blood member" into the family.

6. Be aware that you will have difficulties rearing a
child (we all do). Do not feel guilty when periodic doubts
about your wisdom in adopting a child come to mind. At
times we all would like to get rid of our children—natural or
adoptive!

7. Be wary of unrealistic expectations in many areas:
don't ask yourself, "Is my child's I.Q. high enough to
achieve academic excellence?" "Will he/she be an out-
standing athlete?" Don't tell yourself, "This child will

bring us boundless joy; there will always be laughter in the house, etc.''

8. Be prepared for hostility from friends, neighbors, and relatives. Very few people can accept a sudden change in the status quo with grace or understanding. You may be the recipient of some unpleasantness, especially if the child is older and ''foreign'' in any way.

9. Be prepared to tell your child that he is adopted *before* he is told by a ''well-meaning'' outsider.

10. Be careful not to push gratuitous information on her, but be aware that the child will eventually want to know about her natural parents. It is good to be prepared with some information, not a long dramatization but a simple statement of the facts followed by a warm message from you about your desire for her in particular to be your very own.

I've briefly touched upon what is good for the child—but what about the parents? What is good for them? *Anyone* planning a family, adopted or natural, should ask why they want to have children. Are the reasons worthy—healthy—or neurotic?

People with neurotic reasons often include:

1. Couples who are dissatisfied with their marriage who —feeling their inability to have a child is what's causing problems—decide to adopt a baby to bring them closer to each other.

2. Women who desire fulfillment outside the family but who retreat to motherhood simply because it is familiar and less threatening than an occupation.

3. Families with only one child who decide to adopt another so that the existing child will have a companion.

4. Some families who adopt older children so that they can have a built-in baby-sitter for the younger children and a general housekeeper and servant as well.

5. The young married couple who might decide to adopt a child simply because ''everyone is doing it.''

    6. Anyone who wants to "use" a child to dilute boredom.

    7. Anyone who wants a child in order to feed feelings of authority, power, and importance.

    Healthy reasons might include:

    1. A yearning on the part of parents for the physical and emotional presence of a child to nurture. These people love to be part of the process of healthy human growth.

    2. The desire of a family to share a home and life with another human being.

    3. People's human desire for a stake in the future and for a contribution to the continuance of our species.

    4. Love of people and particularly children and each other.

    5. A desire for family companionship and for the sharing and exchange of all human emotions, including happiness and sadness.

    It is crucial to keep in mind that the introduction of a new member into an existing family unit, whether that family be two or ten, means adjustment. As with any other facet of this business of living, being aware that constant and continuous adjustments have to be made can be of great help. Adjustments do not occur spontaneously or instantly. They require time and struggle. There are always failures and successes, pain and rewards, and a great deal of learning and growing, too, for parents and children alike. The introduction of a new child to a family means a radical change in that family's balance. Adjustment is necessary and this is always the case when we desire the rewards of healthy human growth and change.

Child Rearing

The most important message a child can receive from his parents is that they love him. Parents cannot fool kids! The children know the truth regardless of the words parents use.

Parents who like their kids are tuned in to their needs; aware and respectful of their individuality, their proclivities, and their yearnings; they provide an atmosphere in which feelings and thoughts can be expressed freely and without fear. These parents do not put a price on being liked and do not blackmail or make undue demands as a basis for love. They do not compete with their children, nor do they foster competition among their children. They do not use their children as weapons to fight marital battles, nor do they resort to other forms of exploitation.

Q: My four-year-old son wets his bed almost every night. Is this necessarily a psychological problem?
A: No!

Recent findings indicate that many children wet their beds as a result of a disturbance involving the urinary tract. Quite often there is a narrowing of the end portion of the urinary canal. When this is remedied through the simplest minor surgery, the symptom (bedwetting) disappears. It is important that urological consultation takes place before you undertake psychological investigation. The first should be with a urologist who is familiar with the urinary problems of children. The second, if necessary, should be with a specialist in child psychiatry.

Q: I have been widowed for a few years and I have two children, a girl of eight and a boy eleven. I have been going with a man for a few years and we are very much in love. Because of marital legal difficulties on his part we will not be able to marry for another year. Would it be very traumatic for the children if he moved in? They love him very much and he has become like a father to them. He does sleep over now and then.
A: I think it would be less confusing to them if he moves in than if he sleeps over now and then. If your relationship with him and his with your children are as good as you say, then I can see no harm in the move, unless you live in an extremely puritanical neighborhood where people would stigmatize the

children. But much depends on how you feel with the situation. If you are at peace with the arrangement and relationships are good, then the children will not suffer and may even enjoy having a ''father'' around even if the legal step is still a year away. But if you feel guilty or hostile because of the delay of marriage, this is bound to produce family reverberations and repercussions in the children.

Q: My husband is worried that our eight-year-old son may not be masculine enough. He seems perfectly all right to me and everyone else. He just doesn't have much interest in playing ball and fighting around. But he does have good friends—boys and girls—and seems to get along all right. He spends a good deal of time reading and collecting stamps. He also likes to draw, and I think he may have some real talent. This, too, worries my husband, who thinks that artists tend to be sissyish. What do you think? My husband keeps pushing him to play ball.

A: Interest in competitive sports does not in any way guarantee masculinity, just as it does not indicate lack of femininity in women. Artistic and intellectual interests are likewise no indication at all of sexual identification confusion, homosexuality, heterosexuality, being ''sissyish,'' or the like. Many men who have confused notions regarding gender characteristics and anxiety about their own masculinity or sexuality play out this anxiety through their sons.

Confusion in sexual roles is a complicated manifestation, having its roots in the first few years of one's life and having little or nothing to do with playing ball. Many children who are forced into physical activities they don't like become inadvertently accident-prone and sometimes get seriously hurt.

Remind your husband that good readers and talented people often go far in this world. Few obsessed athletes become professionals. Of course, interest in intellectual activity does not preclude interest in sports, but parental respect for individual proclivities in children is the stuff of future adult self-esteem.

Q: My seven-year-old son has just begun to go to school alone. He is a careful child and there is a guard at the one road crossing he has to make. There is really nothing to worry about but I worry—sometimes I worry myself into a near panic. Is this common?

A: Yes, but the degree of concern, worry, or preoccupation varies. With some people this "worry" becomes obsessive enough to require professional help. Chronic and inappropriate overprotection can be damaging to children. It gives them a sustained feeling and image of themselves of being excessively fragile, vulnerable, and often inadequate. This may contribute to a lifelong lack of self-confidence. Severe overprotection has a stifling effect, not permitting a natural development characteristic of healthy growth. I do not think your worry is of this magnitude because, in fact, you are allowing your son to go to school himself. By the same token, I do not by any means argue on behalf of unnecessary risk, lack of prudence, or overpermissiveness. These, too, can be damaging in both immediate effects and because the child may feel not worthy enough to be cared about.

Letting go—reasonably, appropriately, and prudently—is seldom easy. Many of us see our children as extensions of ourselves—the most valuable, tender, and vulnerable parts of ourselves. When our children give any evidence of being separate individuals after all, we must encourage this endeavor, but it is not easy. For many of us it is the beginning (albeit the very beginning) of all kinds of empty-nest feelings. This is made somewhat easier by our continuing efforts to find new interests and involvements, even as our children go on to pursue new interests as part of their development.

We want the best and safest world for our children and, indeed, for ourselves and all people. But we can only do what is healthily possible. Too much zeal in this direction can be harmful and doesn't work anyway. The environment has never been and will never be completely controllable. We love and we protect and we can try to be reasonable and appropriately responsible, and, if we worry a bit, that's human, too.

Q: I have a young son, fourteen years old, who finds it very difficult to fall asleep. Some nights he doesn't fall asleep until two in the morning. Of course, he's very tired the next day. Can you shed some light?

A: Fourteen is a difficult, transitional age and is often marked by increasing emergence of strong sexual feelings. As a child encounters his emergence into adulthood, he has many mixed feelings involving the desire to comply with and to rebel against parental authority and the desire to retain childhood dependence and at the same time to become independent. This confusion of feelings causes heightened irritability, anger, and restlessness. These are often further enhanced by confusion as to what it is "right" or "wrong" to feel sexually toward oneself or toward one's siblings, peers, and parents. Children who feel particularly anxious sometimes cannot relax enough to sleep, largely because they are full of feelings at night that have not been adequately discharged and experienced during the day. Some children are actually afraid to go to sleep because sleep represents loss of control, and there is a fear that this may bring on unwanted, untrusted, and embarrassing feelings and urges. If insomnia continues, I feel that qualified psychotherapy is needed in order to hasten clarification of information and ideas and in order to help the child discharge feelings properly.

Q: I want to move to the suburbs or to a relatively countrified area because I feel it would be better for the emotional health of our young children. My husband wants to stay in the city. All other things being equal, that is, socioeconomic factors, safety, and physical health, what do you think of the comparative value of each relative to emotional health?

A: I think that it is best not to use the children to manipulate each other. I also think that it is important for children to have parents who are relatively happy with each other and with where they live. Obviously, something has got to give and one of you will have to compromise somehow. Everybody and every condition can never be satisfied at the same time. All "other things being equal," children thrive well in city or country provided relationships in the family are fairly healthy. I must point out that long commutes sometimes cause considerable irritation and also cut into valuable time working parents may otherwise spend with their children. But, if a mother is unhappy with where she lives, the entire equilibrium of the household may be upset, and this can create considerable feelings of insecurity in the children. Yes, there is inevitably a price to be paid for everything, but mutual love, caring, and feeling go a long way in both city and country.

Q: My sixteen-year-old daughter came home several times smelling from alcohol. When I confronted her she said that she just had some punch that had a small amount of liquor in it. Is it really true that there are now teenage alcoholics? Could my daughter have a problem? What can I do?
A: Yes, it is true. There are increasing reports of very young people who are drinking excessively. Much of this starts out as peer pressure, and for some it goes on to become a serious drinking problem. Of course, alcohol addiction is destructive to physical health, emotional well-being, relationships, and functioning generally. For teenagers who drive automobiles, any drinking is very dangerous, at least as dangerous as with adults. Your daughter could have a problem, but you will learn more about if you talk to her rather than "confront" her. I think the greatest help for relatives of people with alcohol problems comes from consultation with Alanon, the organization connected to Alcoholics Anonymous. There is a branch in nearly every community in the country. Psychiatric consultation may be valuable, too, but of course this necessitates cooperation on the part of the patient. In some cases family therapy is very helpful, but again cooperation here is a *must* by all members of the family. Also, it is extremely important that only a qualified fam-

ily therapist is consulted. Help along these lines may be sought through social service agencies such as Jewish Family Service and Catholic Charities as well as county medical societies, local mental health organizations, and branches of the American Psychiatric Association and American Psychological Association.

Q: My thirteen-year-old daughter, Betty Jane, insists on changing her name. This came up about a year ago. At first we didn't take her seriously, but now we realize she really means it. She has no particular name in mind but says she hates hers. When we ask her why, she says she doesn't know. What can this be about?

A: This may well be an indication of dissatisfaction with herself, which may largely be something of which she is not fully conscious. This self-rejection may be focused on her name, which to her epitomizes and symbolizes her identity in all areas. Changing her name may represent a simplistic attempt to change herself and all things she doesn't like about herself. This kind of self-hate sometimes occurs in idealistic and puristic children who develop intolerable guilt when they first become aware of sexual feelings and urges. However, self-hate may be connected with any number of dissatisfactions with self, including lack of popularity with peers, poor performance in school, conflicting feelings toward parents, and so on. It may be a good idea for your daughter to have a consultation with a psychoanalyst who specializes in adolescent psychiatry.

Q: My ten-year-old son has been playing with a boy I don't approve of. This child is smart-mouthed and nasty, but my son admires him and is starting to pick up some of the boy's obnoxious expressions. Should I try to keep these kids apart?

A: This may be a passing phase for both boys or it may be chronic. You might consider speaking to the other child's parents to get an idea what it's all about and to help you in your decision. Talking to your own son about the destructive influence of high suggestibility—especially as regards imitating this particular boy—may be helpful. It may also be helpful and interesting to investigate the source of your son's attraction to this boy and his desire to imitate him. Confusion about aggressive affectations starts very early in life. Also—is his picking up "obnoxious expressions" a way of goading and manipulating you? Unfortunately, some boys get trapped into a kind of competition as to who can be more irritating to parents and all adults and authority figures with whom they come into contact. This, too, may be confused with masculine attributes.

The company children keep is especially important if they are highly suggestible and conforming and less so if they are relatively independent.

Be careful, because prohibitions may make the other boy seem more attractive. It would be helpful to suggest other company and to encourage other friendships.

Q: My young teenage son is very interested in girls and desperately wants to go out with one of a few he knows. He is not ordinarily shy and gets along well with both contemporaries and adults. Since he has always gone to a boys school he has had very little contact with girls. The problem is that he is very frightened and reticent about calling. How can we reassure him? I think he knows that he is good-looking and bright and has a good sense of humor. What is this problem all about? Can you suggest any answers?

A: The "problem" usually involves two factors: idealization and fear of rejection. Boys of this age, especially those who have had very little contact with girls, tend to idealize them. This kind of idealization sometimes takes the form of fear and sometimes the form of criticism and "put-downs" of all kinds in order to dilute the idealization and fear. These boys imbue girls with imagined superhuman qualities that then make them seem unapproachable. This in turn contributes to the fear of rejection: How can a goddess possibly accept an invitation from a mere mortal? This fear of rejection and subsequent embarrassment are prevalent in most people, and especially in sensitive adolescents. Of course, the more we accept ourselves the less we fear rejection from others.

I think discussions with your son about these two factors can be valuable. He must be told that girls are human after all, and he must be acquainted with the fact that girls have the same feelings, conflicts, fears, and so on as boys, including the fear of rejection. Tell him that girls want to meet boys as much as boys want to meet girls. He must also be told that there is no sin at all in being rejected, and that we are all rejected at times with no dire consequences. We must fight against any attacks of self-hate when rejection does take place. All of us are rejected at times, and risking rejection is the only way we can place ourselves in positions necessary for acceptance.

May I suggest that it is usually easier at first to meet and talk to girls as part of a group experience than to start out calling up for a date. Dances of all kinds, sports activities such as tennis, courses and instruction that involve both sexes, work, exchange classes (in which boys schools and girls schools exchange students) can all be valuable. Remember to tell him that girls attend dances and the like for the same reason boys do—in order to meet people of the opposite sex.

Schooling

Q:　My eight-year-old son draws very well and enjoys it very much. He is a bright, lovable child, and I think he is relatively problem-free. He has loved to draw since he was about three years of age. I don't think he's a genius or anything like that, but he does have an eye for both form and color. Some of our friends who know more about these things than we do think he's very talented. Is it wise to steer him in the direction of becoming an artist?

A:　I think the key word is "steer." If steer means to pressure, to coerce, or forcibly to exclude other interests, then the process can be destructive. If "steer" means parental involvement, pleasure, encouragement, and noncoercive interest, then the process is constructive. Your child sounds healthy and happy, and this is indication that trusting your own spontaneity has worked very well for you and for him. Encouraging a child to pursue his own proclivities is vital to his future emotional well-being. This encouragement is delivered in the form of real interest and involvement in the activity in question. But it must exclude pressure, coercion, and the demand for perfectionist performance or any kind of exhibitionist exploitation.

Q: My husband and I have been arguing about the choice of school for our daughter. We are faced with a decision as to what kind of high school to send her to. One school has the reputation of being very traditional and well disciplined. The other is a more progressive school with a good academic standing and a more relaxed discipline. I want to send her to the progressive school and my husband wants the other. Our daughter is a good student and says that she has friends going to both and wants to leave it up to us.

A: It is nice that you have a choice. Your conflict with your husband probably springs from his and your own early experiences with authority and education. This kind of conflict can help you to view all sides before arriving at a decision. Your daughter seems to be unperturbed about either possibility, and since she has friends going to both schools, it appears that both are highly acceptable to her. Unless they have special problems, most children make good adjustments to both traditional and progressive schools.

As a parent, I would visit the schools and see how I feel in each one. If they both fulfill health and safety requirements, I would then go on to consider other aspects. A young person gains much in an environment which in any way enhances her humanity and also helps to develop her individual proclivities. It is valuable if personal guidance is available and if there is a healthy, close relationship between staff and student. Even with the most careful consideration, there are developments in life that we cannot anticipate. The school you choose now may be wrong for your daughter a year from now. You should try to be flexible, and if a decision turns out to be wrong, feel free to change.

Q: I am a high school student and I like science as well as all my other subjects very much and would like to help people. In fact, I really would like to be a doctor. I get very high grades, and my parents want me to go ahead and try. My trouble is that I'm queasy about blood and things like operations. Would it be foolish for me to try to go ahead with it anyway?

A: It would be foolish of you not to go ahead. A great many people feel "queasy" and frightened. Their fear is sometimes based on fear of deep, unfamiliar feelings which operations and blood symbolize for them. But they almost invariably get over these difficulties after initial confrontation with unfamiliar circumstances takes place. In this, as in any other unfamiliar area, at least some minimum period for familiarization and adjustment is necessary. I should also point out that there are many areas of medicine in which surgery plays almost no role at all. This, of course, includes psychiatry.

Q: My youngest son is in the eighth grade and goes to a traditional school. The principal recently gave the boys the option of wearing turtle necks or whatever they want, or shirts, ties, and jackets. We were amazed that all the boys voted for ties and jackets. What possibly gives?

A: Many children relish a traditional approach to life and experience it as safe, predictable, secure, and meaningful. They see participation in traditional institutions as status guidelines and as aids in self-identification. As such, they are reluctant to surrender symbols of tradition for symbols that represent the unknown. This is especially true of children who are reacting to a group a generation in advance of them, who may have been somewhat rebellious and who appeared to them to be chaotic and somewhat lacking in goal direction.

Q: My son is still several months away from applying for college, and he is already in a dither about getting into the college of his choice. How common is this college-application anxiety? He is so afraid of being rejected.

A: Unfortunately, "college-application anxiety" as you call it is exceedingly common. It is largely an offshoot of a malignantly competitive, status-seeking society. Many parents contribute to this kind of college-admission fever with little awareness on their part. This is usually conveyed to children for years preceding application to college by undue preoccupation with future security and status activity of all kinds. Both parents and adolescent peers contribute to college hysteria and to the belief that only certain schools can lead to the good life. With parental backing, just about all young people in our country can go to college, even though it may not be the "college of their choice." More often than not this "choice" is no choice at all, but rather the result of what either family or current peer group (the boy's friends) have decided is the current prestige school. I have actually seen a number of young people in consultations who suffered from considerable anxiety and depression because they believed that failure to get into *the* school relegated them to a second-class status for the rest of their lives. These kinds of prejudiced, perfectionist attitudes and myths are best never developed. But where they already exist they must be diluted and destroyed by confrontation with reality. Your son and other young people so afflicted must, if necessary, be told again and again that many options exist, that these options are excellent, and that one's future does not depend on getting into *the* school. They must also be told, and the parents must believe this or the message will not be effective, that rejections must and do happen in life. When rejections are catastrophic, it is almost always because we view them catastrophically. We must give ourselves the "right to be rejected." Otherwise, paralysis ensues and we

find ourselves unable to apply to college or to any other area
or endeavor in life.

Q: Our youngest son is only eleven years old but says that
he wants to be a doctor. Actually, he has stated this preference for a few years now. He is very bright, excellent in
school, and very interested in all things biological. My
question is, should he be encouraged in this area or should
he be diverted so as to explore other possibilities too? My
husband is a businessman, so it's not a question of identification. But our son is so very young.

A: There is a vast difference between compassionate encouragement and coercive prodding. One involves helping
with the development of a child's interests and proclivities.
The other involves exploitation in order to feed one's own
pride and vicarious living through one's child and ignoring
his needs and desires. Early interests, especially in difficult
fields, do occur in some people and deserve parental interest
and encouragement. This can go on even while openness to
other possibilities is sustained. It is also a good idea to help a
young child who has a special interest to be exposed to other
areas of living, for example, friends, games, music, art, and
so on, so as to avoid becoming too narrowly specialized.
But, one must be careful not to divert or discourage from
primary interests and not to become overly zealous in the development of the so-called all-around person. ''Program-
ming'' children so that they must run from one activity to
another—music lessons, dancing lessons, language lessons,
religious instruction, etc., etc.—leaves little time or energy
for themselves or the chance for real creative possibility and
is ultimately destructive.

Q: My son will be a college freshman at a distant school in
the fall. I have heard that many youngsters have difficulties
adjusting to the first year of college. I'm afraid he may have
difficulty, be unhappy, and spoil his academic standing.
Can I do anything now to prepare him for this adjustment

period? Can difficulties be prevented? Can you help me? Can I help him?

A: Second question first: adjustment is a life process and *cannot be prevented.* If you try to prevent adjustment you will be putting yourself in a situation of frustration and hopelessness. Adjustment is a vital aspect of living. Struggling with new situations is a prime way of learning, growing, and developing valuable self-esteem. Failure is a way of learning too, and it is particularly valuable to learn that we can live through failures at given times in our lives and can come back and succeed at more propitious times.

The preparation for separation and responsibility for self is an ongoing process. Of course it begins in childhood, and some youngsters are prepared for separation by the time they reach the college years. We do not all mature or develop at the same pace, and we must be attuned to our own child's development pattern to be able to assess or to predict his/her adjustment prognosis.

At this juncture in his life you may help your son by having him visit the college for long weekends and sit in on classes so that he can familiarize himself with the geography of the campus and the "feel" of the environment. You and he could discuss guidelines of behavior so that he is not an unwilling participant in drug or sex activity because of peer pressure.

It is of value for both you and your son to realize that options exist. If problems come up he can seek counseling. If necessary he can change schools and neither of you feel "put down" if a change becomes necessary, including one in which he returns home to go to a local school.

Q: I saw a television program recently that was about military school, and some of it alluded to making better men out of youngsters through early tough military training. My husband and I disagreed about this though I couldn't quite put my feelings into words. I just feel it is wrong. I would like your opinion.

A: I feel that the most important qualities both men and women need to develop are those that further their humanity. These are identical for both sexes and include a capacity for openness, tenderness, intimacy, compassion, and humility. These characteristics make "real men" and "real women." I do not see how military school or training in any way enhances these characteristics. I do not believe that military training and discipline help one get in touch with one's feelings or be flexible or be empathetic, all of which create real strength. Military school does perhaps train people to be members of armed forces, but this is in no way "character building." Maturation largely occurs in compassionate households in which family members really care for one another. This creates character, caring, and a sense of responsibility. Indeed, some highly intelligent, sensitive, and creative youngsters suffer irreparable damage when they are subject to callous and arrogant treatment by men who themselves have confused notions of what constitutes manhood, and who are particularly threatened by individuality and anybody who is different in any way.

Q: Our eight-year-old daughter is a charming, wonderful little girl. She seems bright and does very well in school. But she was recently tested by her teacher along with the rest of her school class and only received a 107 I.Q. Does this mean she is not so bright after all?

A: Mass I.Q. exams have little or no meaning. I.Q. exams have relevance—and even here they are limited—only when given individually by an expert in context with other examinations. These other exams—projective tests—are used to determine the state of the person's emotions. Many people with high I.Q.'s become emotionally blocked during tests and consequently test poorly. Only a total battery of tests plus careful interviewing by a child psychiatrist can determine if there is really problematic emotional difficulty or real intellectual deficiency. Your little girl sounds just fine. She may not have been in the mood to take a test. My own feeling is that small children are tested entirely too much and are often unfairly judged by incompetent testers and false results.

Problems of the Young

Over the years I've received a fair number of letters from young people—teenagers and even younger children. These are a number of problems they share and a brief discussion of the twelve most prevalent areas would be of value. As you will see, some of these areas overlap and feed one another, so that it is not unusual for the same child to have several problems at the same time.

1. Depression—These may be passing moods, but many young people and children as young as nine and ten years of age suffer from serious emotional depression. Many complain that parents refuse to take their symptoms seriously. Aside from giving a passing word of reassurance, parents often refuse to talk to them about how they feel. Depression in young people must be taken seriously, otherwise many lives will be lost. Suicide among adolescents suffering from depression is not at all uncommon and even occurs among younger children. Paying little or no attention does not make this most serious problem go away! Professional consultation for young people suffering from depression is at least as important as it is for adults. Treatment is usually effective in preventing serious chronic disturbance and even more dire consequences.

2. Loneliness—This seems to be at least as serious a problem among adolescents as it is for adults. There are many young people who yearn to exchange thoughts, ideas, and feelings with other people, and whose letters indicate a paucity of meaningful friendships and contacts. "I've no one to talk to" is a common statement. This is especially true of shy, sensitive people and for youngsters who complain that there is great difficulty in communicating with their parents. This lack of meaningful, honest, and open talk between parents and child creates a sense of isolation that sometimes leads to the point of despair. Severe loneliness often leads to serious depression, and one feeds the other, completing an all-too-common vicious cycle.

3. *Conformity and peer acceptance*—Many people, in an effort to combat loneliness and depression, seek peer acceptance through compulsive conformity with a peer group. In adopting the value system of the particular group, they often surrender their own values and a healthy sense of individual identity and good judgment. In an attempt to seek synthetic self-esteem through group identification and group approval and admiration, they also act out their anger at parents and what they perceive as adult authority.

4. *Popularity*—The above symptoms, coupled with feelings of inadequacy that lead to the compulsive need to be liked and admired, produce a quest for popularity. This is further fed by our culture, which equates popularity with success and happiness. I receive many letters that are really requests for directions about how to be more popular.

5. *Destructive acting out*—This includes the use of destructive drugs, compulsive promiscuity, prostitution, and all other self-destructive, dangerous activity. Young people indicate that much of this activity starts as a result of loneliness, depression, and a need for peer recognition and popularity. Many people who are particularly self-hating will literally do anything to conform to others' standards in order to be liked. Letters indicate that sexual involvement is often payment for being liked and a reflection of a desire to be asked out again rather than a function of desire.

6. *Being a girl*—I've received a number of letters over the years describing self-hate based on "being a girl." Despite recent efforts, there still seem to be a number of girls who feel that being female in our society is a "put-down." These girls feel that they are born and relegated to second-class citizenship and that their situation is hopeless. This, of course, leads to a basic feeling of hopelessness, frustration, and rage. Unfortunately, our culture (society) still has a long way to go to negate this destructive concept. In some cases there was an indication that parents contributed to this feel-

ing, too, by perpetuating the myth of female inferiority and the concomitant rejection of girls and women as equals.

7. *Macho confusion*—I receive several letters periodically from boys whose writing indicates considerable sensitivity and depth of feeling. Many feel inferior and are self-hating because they do not desire and, in some cases, can't conform to "macho standards" in sports, sex, aggression, and so on. Some are confused because they like art, poetry, and music—"nonmacho" things. Some have difficulty with fathers who want them to be "real" men.

8. *Looks and weight*—There is a preoccupation with looks and particularly with weight. Many teenagers complain about noses and breast size and overweight. I receive many letters from writers who feel that a different nose, or whatever, and particularly thinness, will produce instant happiness forever. This kind of preoccupation with looks reflects lack of intellectual development, fear of aging, low self-esteem, disillusionment, self-hate, and depression.

9. *Unrequited love*—These letters indicate a preoccupation with and overinvestment in a mythical fantasy of a perfect love and melding which would lead to heaven on earth. This fantasy is born of feelings of inadequacy and a need to join with a "perfect self" in an effort to feel whole and adequate. Some of these writers are already in a state of disillusionment and depression.

10. *Sexual confusion*—Many letters indicate that confusion and ignorance about sex are very much alive and unhealthy among our young population. There are still many complaints of an inability to get reliable information from parents. Much misinformation still comes from peers as well as one's own imagination. There is an obvious continuing need for good sex education by well-educated, compassionate, and reliable educators.

11. *Intrafamilial problems*—The most common problem children of all ages—from the very young through adolescence—complain about in this area are 1) favoritism of one sibling over another, 2) parental abuse and exploitation, 3) overprotectiveness, 4) parents who hate each other, 5) al-

coholic parents, and 6) parents who express neither feelings nor thoughts.

12. Shyness and stupidity—Many children equate shyness with "being dumb" and having "no personality." They equate outgoingness and "being the life of the party" with "smartness" and happiness. This unfortunate confusion is often fed by both parents and our culture.

Obviously, many of the problems described above are common to people of all ages. They are, however, often more pressing for young people because if they are resolved at an early age, mild disturbances can be prevented from becoming major problems. But young people are often more intense, volatile, impulsive, and changeable than older people. They also have fewer resources in terms of experience, knowledge, training, and finances. This makes them more dependent and vulnerable.

Many problems can be resolved by increased parental attention and involvement—especially by serious, open, and *nonjudgmental, compassionate talk.* This means talk absolutely free of rancor, judgment, and moral equivocation. Some families cannot do this without professional help. Some problems, however, are more serious and are not "just emotional growing pains" that will go away if no one looks at them or takes them too seriously. Many of these cannot be resolved by well-meaning religious advisers, family doctors, or pediatricians. Some require the intervention of professionals, and, as I indicated earlier, in some cases early psychoanalytic consultation can save lives.

Q: When my little six-year-old son gets very, very angry, which isn't all that often, he sometimes says, "I hate you." Is it possible that he really does hate me even though he is very affectionate most of the time?

A: Yes, he hates you for a moment or two and then his anger passes and he feels otherwise. Being angry for the moment does not obliterate our other feelings, including love. Whatever our age and however we express an angry feeling, getting it out in the open helps make its duration even shorter. When an overtaxed, overpressured, distraught mother says ''drop dead'' to a child, she usually means only for a second or two.

Q: My eleven-year-old son curses and swears on occasion. I'm sure he gets this from his friends because we don't talk this way at home. May I point out we are not particularly prudish and everyone is free to get angry and to express themselves, but I don't like his language. Do I admonish him or just let him talk the way he wishes?

A: Trust your feelings more and your head less. Too many parents are too concerned with intellectual stratagems and theories as regards child rearing. This has blunted their natural, healthy judgment about action vis-à-vis their children. You say that people are free to express anger in your home and that is indeed good. But this does not mean that all rules and good manners are to be suspended in favor of a state of anarchy. How about trusting and expressing your own angry feelings? If you feel offended by your son's language and feel like admonishing him, by all means tell him off and in no uncertain terms!

Q: My seven-year-old boy is a daydreamer, and as a result is doing very poorly in school. His teacher says that he seems to be there one moment and out to lunch the next. Is there anything you can suggest?

A: First, check out his physical condition with your pediatrician. This especially applies to his eyes and ears, and he should have a thorough neurological examination. Lapses in attention may be due to boredom because the work is beneath his level or beyond his grasp, resulting in a sense of defeat and surrender. But lapses may also be due to petit mal episodes, which are a mild form of epilepsy treatable with suitable medication. If he turns out to have no physical problems, it may be a good idea to have a consultation with a good child psychoanalyst who can decide whether or not psychological testing would be of value. It may well turn out that he has no significant problem other than a relatively short attention span, not uncommon in boys this age.

Q: My eleven-year-old son starts to worry about all kinds of imagined illnesses every time he has a holiday from school. We seem to get along well. Is it possible that underneath he really resents us and dislikes being at home? We've asked him this, but he denies it.

A: Some people, and especially children, respond to almost any change in routine with hypochondriacal symptoms. These are often due to anxiety about making adjustments. Your son may feel angry at you even though he doesn't say so, and indeed he may not be conscious of his anger himself. But his symptoms may have another source entirely. Some children, and even some adults, fear vacations because this change of routine demands that they tap their own resources without outside direction. Still others *seem* to fear vacations but really fear becoming addicted to holiday time and are afraid of the difficulty that going back to work or to school will present. This is especially true of children who've had a difficult time breaking away from parents. Re-establishing prolonged closeness at holiday time represents painful breaking away again and reminds them of the initial trauma they felt when they went off to school the first time.

In any case, hypochondriacal symptoms are invariably used to camouflage problems that have no relationship to illness at all. If they persist in your son, you ought to consider consultation with a psychoanalyst who specializes in work with children.

How Much Are You Contributing to Your Children's Future Mental Health?

Ten Vital Questions

1. Do you respect them? This means their opinions, ideas, proclivities, assets, desires. This is very important in terms of future self-esteem. Children learn how to feel about themselves from the way their parents feel about them. This particularly regards constructive aspects of themselves. If you have contempt for them, so will they. If you regard them with respect and appropriate recognition and praise, so will they. This is the earliest basis of self-confidence and provides the inner emotional substance necessary for making the most satisfying use of one's real abilities.

2. Do you set proper limits? Parents must be parents and not children. A gap is appropriate and healthy! Setting limits is absolutely vital to a sense of security. Children feel insecure and anxious and lack confidence in their ability to make realistic judgments when parents fail to set limits. Being poorly educated in rights, wrongs, dos, and don'ts makes a child feel out of tune and afraid. Lacking respect for his parents and himself will make the world seem particularly chaotic and dangerous. Proper limits are neither too lax nor too stringent. Those that are too stringent often lead to destructive rebellion and even criminal behavior. Limits ought to be applied with love; with judicious judgment; with proper regard for a child's sensitivity; with regard for his age, energy, needs, and lack of sophistication. Firmness and consistency are as constructive as even the most subtle and gentle forms of cruelty; ridicule and causing embarrassment are destructive.

3. Are you consistent? The consistency I speak of here applies to the image of your child that you convey to your child. Telling him he is a genius one moment and a blithering idiot the next does little for his feelings of security or sense of identity. Great fluctuations in applied methods of upbringing create confusion, anxiety, and neuroses. This sometimes happens when parents surrender their own spontaneity and suspend their own good judgment in order mechanically and regularly to follow some popular child-rearing fad of the moment. Great divisiveness between parents, especially as regards the child, creates divided loyalty, guilt, and conflict and sows the seeds for future emotional difficulty. Parents need not always agree, but the child must not become the arbitrator in their differences. However they disagree, it is best that they work out their differences between themselves and then present and apply a common consensus to the child.

4. Do you permit and encourage showing emotion? This means encouraging a child to express himself and especially to talk about his feelings and, if he feels like it, to talk with feeling. This is especially true of strong feelings such as love and anger. Both are entirely human and necessary emotional components of human existence. Seeing parents emote and being allowed to emote tells the child that feelings are good and highly acceptable. This prevents repression, inner deadening, and bottling up, all of which contribute to future inability to tap one's resources as well as to depression, explosive rages, and wooden, mechanical behavior. People brought up in what seems to them to be an emotional vacuum become terrified of their feelings and suffer great anxiety and emotional sickness when their feelings are inevitably stirred up by any stimulus.

5. Do you promote acceptance of human realities? This acceptance is the antithesis of perfectionism; it prevents future feelings of hopelessness and self-hate, and keeps us from harboring impossible ideals and exorbitant—and therefore disappointing and damaging—expectations. On a practical level, parents must let children in on the fact that human beings are indeed human and not at all godlike, that the human condition is tough, and that life inevitably has its ups and downs. People—all people—do get jealous, envious, angry, possessive, selfish, lazy, afraid, confused, and hurt. We all fail and succeed. We are all healthy and sick. We all have assets and liabilities. Relationships, work, amusement can be fruitful, may be frustrating, and are never perfect. Learning about human realities as opposed to fantasizing about possible heavens on earth neutralizes self-hatred, hatred for the less-than-perfect human condition and other people, and hatred for one's actual day-to-day existence. Early promotion of human realities, with goodwill and without bitterness and cynicism, ensures future mental health as well as the ability to be happy with what a less-than-perfect world does have to offer.

6. Do you allow appropriate freedom? By this I mean, Do you have enough confidence in and good judgment in your child to permit her independence commensurate with her state of development? I do not advocate overpermissiveness. The child perceives this as not caring, and this promotes not caring about herself. But overprotecting a child is even more damaging. It does not give her ample opportunity to feel like a separate, whole human being. It stifles abilities, blunts assets, and stunts the development of inherent proclivities. It produces morbid dependency and teaches a child to seek dependency relationships. Alas, I have seen so many young women who regard themselves as only fragments of people unless they have men to attach themselves to. This is particularly sad when some of these people are potentially capable and often highly competent whole persons. But they don't see their own value and too often get into disastrous relationships because being alone for any length of time terrifies them too much to wait for and to seek a constructive relationship. Love is important, but it does not provide solutions to all of life's problems. Overprotective parents tend to overemphasize the importance of love in a girl's life, and this inevitably leads to impossible expectations, disappointments, and further feelings of inadequacy. It is in fact very difficult "to let go," and we do take chances even when we let our children cross the street themselves for the first time. But if we *use* and baby them to keep us from being anxious about their safety, then we are helping to stultify and mummify them. There are dangers *out there;* death itself is possible. This is characteristic of life.

But preventing full and appropriate participation in life promotes a living death of parts of oneself over an emotionally crippled lifetime. Of course, I do not suggest exceeding a child's limits. Knowing one's child and judicious judgment are always necessary.

7. Do you encourage and promote family friendship? Members of a family who like one another, relate well, communicate deep feelings, work together, and help one another provide an atmosphere of warmth and security. This enhances feelings of personal strength and a sense of well-being and belonging in the world and among people generally. Parents who encourage competition instead of cooperation among their children and who in any way foster mutual envy, hostility, and vindictiveness are creating an antitherapeutic family atmosphere. Pitting one child against another; establishing a hierarchy of favoritism; using one child's abilities as a standard of performance for another are all destructive activities. Helping each child to appreciate his very own abilities and helping him to share them with other family members enhances a sense of family and personal self-esteem.

8. Are you aware that a child is not an adult? It is of vital importance for parents to realize that children are not grown up and need time to grow up. This requires parental tolerance, patience, and a sense of the particular rate of the maturing process in a child. A child must be encouraged but not nagged and pushed. Each child has his own rate of growth and particular areas that are easy and others that are difficult. Expecting adult sophistication and control from a developing child produces a sense of futility and future feelings of inadequacy and self-rejection. It must be remembered that a young child's neurological system and reflexes are not fully developed. Therefore, he may be clumsy, impulsive, and relatively lacking in both control and judgment. Parents who use strong language to express themselves but expect a child to "control" himself are not realistic. Children imitate and also have less control than adults. It is invariably destructive when a parent says that when he was young he did not have foolish and devastating crushes, was always cooperative, was never too tired or lazy to help, did not do impulsive, foolish things, and so on. It would be helpful if parents could and did in fact recall their childhoods with veracity and reality. It is also helpful to remember that each new generation has its particular fads and value systems which deserve respect and understanding.

9. Do you help promote healthy sexual attitudes? Giving gratuitous information that a child neither asks for nor is capable of understanding is destructive. Refusing information that a child is ready for and is curious about is equally destructive. Sexual seductiveness by a parent produces confusion, guilt, and repressed rage and is very damaging. Conveying false information and fear about sexuality and sex is very damaging. Rejection of a child because she is a girl and not a boy or vice versa is disastrous. To whatever extent parents help a child to accept her sexual identification and sexual feelings, they are promoting general self-acceptance. Open, honest, unembarrassed conveyance of correct sexual information is invaluable.

10. Do you accept and cherish your child's individuality? I refer here to any and all individual characteristics and proclivities. It is inevitably destructive to stuff a child into a particular category for practical reasons if she doesn't fit. Ignoring particular talents, abilities, and desires cuts the child off from his vital center and source of self-esteem. Parents who fear uniqueness in their child because of their zeal to conform to what their immediate society seems to condone are contributing to self-hate in the child as well as a disastrous future parent-child relationship. A woman who feels her parents deprived her of a chance for a professional education only because she was born a girl may turn out to be unforgiving indeed!

Bring Back the Generation Gap

For a number of years now, there has been considerable propaganda extolling the virtues of family "togetherness." In the last five years additional social pressure has developed to eradicate differences between parents and children. Sameness has come to be equated with closeness, love, warmth, and healthy family relatedness. Differences between parents and children have come to be lumped together under the term "generation gap." Having a familial "generation gap" is unfortunately viewed by many people as suffering from a kind of social disgrace. I feel very strongly that what started out as a seemingly constructive social movement has deteriorated into a psychologically unsound and even destructive enterprise.

I must state immediately that I am certainly not against promoting good relating and communicating among family members, and of course this includes parents and children. But this is precisely my point! Under the guise of improving family relations, self-styled "closeness" experts have contributed to poor self-esteem, massive confusion, guilt, depression, communication impairment, and even communication breakdown.

Let me point out that there is simply no virtue at all in excessive "sameness" or stifling "closeness." We do not have to be like each other in order to respect each other. Compulsive pressure to be alike when in fact we are different causes self-hate and mutual contempt. Pressure to share all thoughts and feelings regardless of appropriateness creates emotional trauma and anxiety. Children are very often not ready to share all adult emotional information. By the same token, while it is good for children to feel free to share thoughts, feelings, and problems with parents, it is destructive if they feel compelled to share all. Keeping at least a certain amount to ourselves helps delineate us from our fellows. This delineation and feeling of separate boundaries are crucial to mental health. We are each of us separate individuals and it is important that we know this deep down in our innermost feelings. This is what makes for self—self-acceptance and self-adequacy. Pathological sameness and closeness destroys individuality. It also makes us feel guilty and depressed for daring to feel like separate selves, let alone different from our parents or children. I, too, believe that people need people. But I believe that people need themselves even more. In fact, each of us must develop and sustain respect for our own individual selves before we can relate effectively with others. This means that we each need our own ideas, feelings, tastes, desires, and values. By "values" I really mean the personal determination and deep inner feelings as to who and what are important to each of us. This contributes in large measure to the kind of people we turn out to be, the decisions we ultimately make, and the particular actions we eventually take. Self-respect is as contagious in a family as is self-contempt. Children who perceive their parents as self-accepting and self-respecting have an all-important advantage in establishing their own good and strong self-esteem. Children whose parents demonstrate self-derision and contempt must invariably suffer the consequences of following poor examples. Individuality and self-confidence have roots in the family. But much of the nourishment that makes for particular tastes and proclivities comes from the particular generation into which we are born and raised.

Each of us is invariably influenced by the time and place we live in. While we may be healthily individualistic, as communicating and relating creatures, we must as members of human society develop and contribute many cultural characteristics in common. Therefore, it always comes to pass that our very own individuality also contains much that is common to many people of our culture and generation. Another way of saying this is that each time and place has its own "language." Growing up with this "language" has an enormous influence on the way we feel, think, and see ourselves and the rest of the world. I use the word "language" here in the broadest sense. It is the language of each generation, and members of the generation know one another through this language, even though they may have great individual differences, too. This "language" cannot be learned by "outsiders," that is, by people of other generations. They can know about it. They can imitate it. They can also demean it, thus creating considerable damage to mutual respect and communicating. They can also demean themselves by giving up their own "language" in a futile attempt to take on another.

Well then, what is this "generation language"? I use it here to include mores and conventions; verbal expressions; music, art, and literature; fads and fancies; and so on. As one can readily see, this includes many, many feelings and ideas—ideas about God, religion, sex, clothes, economics, child rearing, fun, love, yo-yos, streaking, peace, war, beauty, politics, marriage, education, justice, sports, humor, parents, authority, assets, liabilities, mental health, and anything we may conceivably include in the term "style of life." How each generation's population is exposed to and feels about these and many other social items in large part identifies the members of that generation, and this is what constitutes their special language. This "generation identification" or "language" may be more or less subtle, but it is almost as important as nationality, religion, family, and all other possible social categories to which we belong and that describe who each of us is. To change these identifying characteristics is no small matter. To do so voluntarily through personal struggle and the adaptation of new ideas may well represent healthy growth. Certainly, one generation can learn from another. We hope each succeeding generation can make progress as it builds from the foundation of its predecessors.

Likewise, members of an older generation can learn and enjoy the stimulation provided by the new ideas of younger people. But to attempt to deny one's own language compulsively and slavishly in favor of another, without real belief and only because we have been told to do so, is inevitably destructive to all concerned. If we go against our inner beliefs only because we think it is stylish or endearing to our children or an attempt to stop the clock and to be eternally youthful, we are in effect deprecating and depleting ourselves. In the process we lose self-respect and our children's respect. Our children often view these attempts as contempt for them, too. The truth is they want to be different and view incursions of their territory as inappropriate, aggressive, diluting, and disrespectful of their rights in establishing their own language and their own selves. This serves to make parents, educators, and other people who have the experience, ability, and expertise to contribute to the succeeding generation ineffectual. Still worse, it makes them seem like wishy-washy nonentities and as such makes children feel terribly insecure and unsure of themselves.

Yet many people will in effect turn themselves inside out emotionally in order to be one of the kids. I have heard parents brag about the wisdom of kids and ignore their own expertise and wisdom born of huge living experience. Later on they can't understand their children's inability to learn from teachers and their children's contempt for older people, including teachers. I've heard others brag about how much like their children they are and how in their household there is no generation gap. How many adults—middle-aged and older adults—go to all kinds of inappropriate lengths to be "one of the gang," the current youthful gang. I see elderly people dressing like teenagers. Others engage in disastrous physical activities. Still others insert verbal expressions that are inappropriate to the main body of their speech and to the meaning they are trying to convey generally. Of course, meaning ceases to be important because their main concern is conformity to what they view as current trends and acceptance by the younger generation. But no amount of engagement in current dancing styles, clothes, language, or the like, will, in actuality, produce or sustain youth, nor will it close the generation gap. It will only cause irritation, mockery, and derision, and it will undermine the security that comes from wholesome family authority and appropriate leadership. It is always tragic to see people attempt to cease being themselves. If they are not themselves and if they are, in fact, not one of the kids either, then who are they? Very often they truly seem like lost souls, drowned in the very generation gap they so desperately want to eradicate.

Many of these people have no conscious idea of the extent to which they deprecate themselves. They certainly have no idea how much they cheat themselves and their children. Many parents in their zeal to "close the gap" have virtually given up all authority over their children. In an appropriate and really grotesque attempt to "be democratic and to make everyone the same" they have abandoned the role of parent. The children know this and hate them for it as well as for the attempted invasion of their youthful domain.

Family equality simply cannot work. The inevitable result is chaos and worse. In this kind of household no one knows who anyone is and there is neither a board nor a chairman of the board. An attempt at gap-eradication democracy is converted into family anarchy, insecurity, and eventually guilt for the destructive outcome that must follow.

The simple truth is that children require parents who are parents and not pals. This means parents who are active in taking responsibility for setting limits and commanding authority, albeit compassionate, benevolent, and reasonable authority. They need parents whom they can respect. These are parents who are adults, who are not afraid to be themselves, and who cherish themselves as representatives of the generation they come from. These are parents who want closeness but not oneness and who recognize the importance of separateness and individuality. These parents respect their children and attempt neither to wrest private "language" from them nor to impose private "language" on them. Children of these parents will not suffer from wide fluctuations between overpermissiveness and overprotection—the latter being a stifling reaction to the former. These children will not have to act out destructively against society in order to find limits and the pseudo-security of punitive outside authority forces. These children and parents will live well and naturally together on appropriate and different sides of the generation gap.

Q: I read your recent article on bringing back the generation gap and I know that you believe that parents should be parents and children should be children. But how about the adage about children "should be seen but not heard"? My eight-year-old son loves to participate in adult conversations. My husband encourages him. I discourage him. How do you feel about it?

A: Of course, there are all kinds of adult conversations and some that are appropriately private. I think it is inappropriate and burdensome for a child to partake in conversations where gratuitous and confusing information is pressed upon him. I also feel that it is downright cruel when conversations are converted into theatrical productions in which the child becomes a kind of midget performer. It is also plain foolishness when adults turn to a child and ask him to render his expert judgment to settle adult controversy.

However, I also believe that a child must be heard as well as seen. This is, after all, how we communicate. A child must not be confined to speaking only when spoken to; to speaking only when he has complaints and demands; to speaking only in defense of himself when he has possibly broken some household rule.

Sharing in appropriate conversations with adults is wonderful and important practice in articulating feelings and thoughts: in having a sense of belonging and acceptance, in developing self-esteem, and in adding to a growing storehouse of understanding and information. Appropriate conversations teach him to become both a listener and a speaker. But it is of great importance that if a child is welcomed into a conversation he must not be patronized or in any way tyrannized. Once admitted, he must indeed be given his turn to talk, and when he talks he must be listened to, seriously. If the people he loves listen to him with respect, then he, too, will learn to value his own feelings, ideas, and thoughts. This is the stuff of active self-esteem and over a lifetime has immeasurable value.

Chapter Three

FAMILY RELATING

Husbands/Wives • *Mothers/Children* •
Sisters • *Older Parents/Older Children*

RELATIONSHIPS ARE COMPLICATED; they can bring
us anything from love and fulfillment to pain and devasta-
tion. Learning to relate has its roots in early family history:
long before learning to speak, a child will pick up the attitudes his parents have toward each other, men, women, authority, or society. As the child's world becomes larger
there are other experiences that influence his ability to relate
and his manner of relating.

The one-to-one relationship is the basic unit of society,
and the microcosm within which we can best see that unit at
work is the family. Therefore, it behooves us to examine
this mechanism seriously. The deeper our understanding of
healthy relating is, the better our chances will be for global
cooperation and world survival.

Husbands/Wives

Q: My husband and I decided to ask you if there was any
one thing couples could do to improve relationships. What
do you think?

A: State preferences! Of course, the problems that exist in
human relationships are multitudinous, as are the potential
therapeutic steps to remedy them. One of the greatest prob-

lems is that couples do not tell each other what they really want in so many words. They expect their partners to know and even to anticipate their desires without being told. When this doesn't happen, disappointment, anger, and a further breakdown in communication takes place, compounding the problems enormously. Saying what you want is an unusually powerful remedy even though desires and preferences can't always be fulfilled. This applies to just about all relationships—including social ones, sexual ones, and those between adults and children.

Q: Like any other married couple, my husband and I argue sometimes, usually over silly things. Anyway, most of the time we work things out in bed, either before or after we make love. In fact, we do most of our important talking about the things that matter to both of us at those times. Recently I read that it's unhealthy for a couple to solve their problems with sex. Is that what we are doing?

A: There's nothing at all wrong with talking things over in bed. It is the ideal time and place for privacy, warmth, and closeness, greatly enhancing the exchange of real feelings and thoughts. Lovemaking after a quarrel is very common. Most people feel better about themselves and each other after they have "cleared the air." In fact, some people cannot make love *unless* they have a fight, and often must contrive fights in order to function sexually at all. The compulsive need for this kind of presexual stimulation is usually evidence of underlying emotional problems. Others compulsively have sex even when they are very angry at each other, going by the dictum that they "must not go to sleep until they have made up." This, too, is a contrivance and can be destructive. People must permit themselves to be angry for more than a day at a time. Sex itself seldom solves communicating and relating problems. Using sexual activity to avoid real solutions complicates the problem and eventually is destructive to sexual activity as well. Open, plain talk is the best way to resolve differences, and this can be done in or out of bed.

Q: Though my husband and I are reasonably open with our feelings, I'm most comfortable sharing my deepest emotions with another woman. Does this mean something is lacking in our marriage?

A: You are missing out on the satisfaction of intimacy derived from sharing your feelings with each other. Since you can experience this exchange with a woman, is the problem due to a special attitude or belief about men? Perhaps you lack trust in how a man—your husband—may receive open expression of your feelings and deepest emotions. Let me point out that sensitivity to other people's feelings is a *human*—rather than a feminine or masculine—characteristic.

Has your husband in some way indicated callousness or ruthlessness about what and how you feel? If this is the case, frank discussion is in order. But, if this *isn't* so, then some self-exploration is indicated. Are you afraid that—if you share your deepest feelings with him—an idealization of yourself in his eyes will be destroyed? That he will see you as less than perfect? Most people, men and women alike, appreciate the revelation of feelings, especially tender, warm, and deeply meaningful ones. They often reciprocate, and mutual trust and closeness grows. You may have some difficulty at first, but starting a little at a time may not be as difficult as you think. Try it—you may like it—both of you.

But a word of caution in this regard: contrived feelings are no good. It must be the real thing. For example, if you care about him, really care, you might start out by telling him just that. Initially, there may be some small embarrassment. This will pass, and mutual expressions of "I love you" may be forthcoming; they may generate more good feelings for both of you.

Q: My husband insists on taking naps in the living room with all of us around watching T.V. and talking. Periodically we disturb him and he gets angry, but he won't nap in the bedroom. You once wrote about why it feels better to fall asleep on a couch. I wonder if you can account for my husband's strange behavior.

A: Sounds as if he's trying to combine two activities at the same time: to nap and to socialize with his family. This is, unfortunately, an imposition on his family, but it's a great time-saver. This may also be an attempt to be in charge of whatever is going on. Some men cannot give up their feeling of being at the center of things and in charge, even while they are asleep. Others can't stand to be alone at any time. Has he tried napping in the bedroom with the T.V. on? This or the radio, giving the illusion of the presence of people, may be helpful.

Q: What about a man who would go out every single night of the week rather than stay at home? Movies, bowling, friends—it just doesn't matter—he wants to go out. Please don't get the wrong impression; he wants me to go with him. Some of my friends think I'm lucky because their husbands never want to go out. But I wish we could stay in more. We have a very nice home.

A: This kind of compulsive behavior is often a means of avoidance—avoidance of closeness with one's mate, one's children, oneself, and one's problems on just about any level. Compulsive going out is also often a means of seeking stimulation in order to combat emotional depression that threatens to surface.

Q: My husband and I fight a great deal even though we also have a lot in common and have a good deal of fun, too. Does this mean that deep down we really hate each other?

A: No! "Fighting"—especially if it's relatively gentle, unhurtful fighting—is often a way to cope with differences and underlying conflicts. It's a way of relieving pressures, frustrations, and anxieties. It may also be a way of making contact, a kind of touching and communicating, a ritual dance or exercise which is used as a prelude to making love. In general, it is much better to clear the air than to harbor differences and to sustain sullen silences.

Q: I am twenty-three years old and have been married for two and a half years. I love my husband and I love being with him and doing things together. Sometimes, though, I just like to be alone—by myself. He can't understand this and feels that I must be angry with him or something. I can't seem to convince him that this has nothing to do with anger or not loving him. I like to spend a little time by myself shopping or reading or doing nothing at all. Is this unusual? Could you please comment?

A: I think it is perfectly normal and reasonable to want to be alone now and then. The ability to be alone indicates good self-esteem and respect for one's resources. It is evidence that one regards oneself as a separate, real, and whole person. To be alone once in a while helps us to tap our own resources and to re-establish friendship with ourselves and a sense of personal identification. Your husband may have difficulty being alone with himself— feeling that when he is only with himself he is with nobody at all. This indicates low self-esteem. He may be projecting his inability to be alone to you in attempting to believe that it is you, rather than he, who has a problem. He is also confused about love. However in love two people may be, they are still two separate people. Always being together is not a function of love but is often evidence of mutual morbid dependency.

Q: My husband insists that women are more subject to nervousness and emotional disorders than men. I insist that this is an old, prejudiced point of view. What do you think? He says more women see psychiatrists.

A: I think you are absolutely right. Neither sex has a priority in this area. More women see psychiatrists because they are less afraid to get help when they feel they need it. Men avoid help even when they desperately need it. This is mainly because, in addition to other problems, men have the enormous problem of believing that getting help is evidence of lack of masculinity.

Q: I love to garden. I suppose I do spend a great deal of time at it. My husband complains that I ought to spend more time reading and "improving my mind." I'm a college graduate and I've read plenty all my life. I still read a bit; but, frankly, gardening is my passion. Any comment?

A: Perhaps your husband's pride does not permit him to voice his real complaint and so he uses reading and improvement of your mind as a smoke screen. Does he really want you to transfer your passion from gardening to him? Could he be resentful of the attention and time given to gardening? Sometimes, people become obsessed with a particular activity as a means of avoiding involvement with other activities or persons.

Aside from problems caused by overzealousness, I think that nonintellectual activity is extremely valuable in producing emotional tranquillity and a sense of well-being. Gardening is especially therapeutic because it provides activity, fresh air, beauty, and even artistry, and the good feelings that come in helping things grow.

Q: What do you think of a woman who likes to do woodwork? I've made some beautiful pieces of furniture, but my husband feels funny about telling friends. He feels it isn't feminine, even though we've had any number of discussions about it. I've told him time and again that activities are neither feminine nor masculine. I know you agree with me because you've written about this subject in the past.

A: I agree with you completely and find your kind of skill admirable and in no way deprecating to femininity. I think your husband may feel threatened because he has confused notions and doubts about his masculinity rather than doubts about your femininity. Your interest and skill in what he considers a masculine area threaten to upset his mental picture of the masculine/feminine status quo in your household.

Mothers/Children

Q: Is it advisable to let grown-up sons know that you are ashamed of them when they come home drunk? They are both currently in college. Recently they have embarrassed us when we had friends over for an evening.

A: I think it is important that you convey your feelings to them and that you share your feelings with each other. They may well be trying to embarrass you because they have conscious—or unconscious—hostile feelings. You in turn may feel more anger than shame where they are concerned. It would be a good idea to clear the air for improved and more honest communications between you. Your home *does* belong to you; you should certainly convey to them your standards for acceptable behavior when they are in your house, especially when they act irresponsibly and immature.

Q: Why would a mother dislike her own young son? I don't mean completely, but at least a good deal of the time.

A: I would have to know much more about the facts and history of the people involved. But here are some theoretical possibilities.

1. We all dislike our children at times. They represent responsibility and loss of freedom.

2. Children are no different from adults, and this includes our very own children, who—like anyone else—can be abrasive, irritating, and even downright nasty and insulting.

3. Some mothers have a compulsive need to be ever-loving, ever-forgiving, wonderful, warm—the ideal of self-sacrificing motherhood. The strain of keeping up this image results in a buildup of rage which eventually overflows.

4. Expecting children to be perfect leads to disappointment and anger at them.

5. In a great many cases of a seemingly inappropriate dislike for a son, a mother may be displacing hostile feelings for her father, brother, husband, or men generally, to her son.

6. Continuous dislike for a child is often a projection of dislike for oneself. In this case, a parent will be particularly unhappy with the child who is felt (usually unconsciously) to be most like her. She has particular difficulties with traits they share in common, but that she may consciously deny in herself.

7. Love of a child may sometimes inadvertently stimulate sexual feelings in a mother. This can be most threatening and anxiety-producing. She may attempt to cover up or to get rid of these feelings by rejecting him and, if necessary, attempting to convince herself of disliking him.

Q: When I was growing up, my mother never said two words to me about sex—except to assure me it was "dirty." So I had to find out on my own, and I made a few mistakes. I swore I wouldn't repeat the pattern with my own daughter. I've tried to explain the facts of life to her, encourage her to be open with me, but she doesn't want to listen. I think maybe she's already sexually involved with a boy she's been dating—she's fifteen—but I'm afraid to ask her directly. What should I do?

A: Despite yourself, you may be more prudish than you think—this is a result of residuals of experience with your own mother. This may be conveyed to your daughter, who may see you as somewhat judgmental and is therefore afraid to talk, even though you reassure her that there won't be any recriminations. Also, mothers often idealize daughters, who then feel constrained and embarrassed to talk about sex, lest they destroy their mothers' image of them. This is especially true of daughters who have somehow received the message that they must compensate for the kind of "mistakes" you describe yourself as having made.

It is much easier to talk about sex and intimate feelings
and matters as part of a household that is open, warm, and
nonjudgmental in expressing and exchanging all kinds of
feelings and thoughts. We sometimes expect to be able to
talk about sex to children without awareness that this is
inappropriate and almost impossible if we have avoided
discussing feelings in general (love, anger, desires, frustrations, whatever) all of their young lives. We should try to be
open—in this emotional climate talk about sex is much
easier. It is also important to root out any prudery in ourselves before we attempt constructive talk with young people. It is sometimes helpful to enlist the aid of a go-between
with whom both parents and child are comfortable. Asking
your daughter about where she is and where she is going
sexually is important. But it is absolutely vital that she
knows that you are a real *friend*—warm, supportive, and
loyal and interested in her feelings and aspirations in all
areas of life and relating. You can do this effectively only if
you see both yourself and her as nonideal, real people with
real feelings and needs on a nonjudgmental, nonrecrim-
inating level.

Q: Since I've been divorced I've been having problems
with my sixteen-year-old daughter. She's sulky, uncoopera-
tive, doesn't want to talk. Of course, I understand that she
misses her father—I haven't been in such good shape
myself—but it's been a year, and I think she should have ad-
justed by now. Surely she must know I love her—what more
can I do?
A: Do not take her knowing you love her for granted. Tell
her!

Your daughter blames herself for her father's leaving. She
unconsciously believes that she did something wrong: she
thinks that if she had been more adequate or lovable he
would not have left. The anger she feels at herself is unbearable, especially when linked to the rage she feels at your
husband for leaving—a rage she has also internalized. She
seeks relief by projecting this anger to you. This is the easi-

est route for several reasons. You are readily available. He is not. Also, since she believes he left because of her, she also believes that anger directed at him would produce further damage. Additionally, she identifies with you and has confidence in your loyalty to her. Deep down she knows that you will not leave her even if she is nasty to you. The fact is: *you* are still there—*you* did not leave!

A year is a short time for adjustments to take place in major dislocations. Divorce between one's parents is a major dislocation at any age. It is especially traumatic at an age when a girl begins to be most strongly aware of her own sexual development. At age fifteen she questions her sexual adequacy. Her father's leaving her (and it is *her*, as far as she's concerned, whom he has left) threatens self-confidence. Continuing camaraderie with her father is very important—provided, of course, that he really cares. She will perceive contrived interest as phony, and it will be destructive. Talking things over with her openly and gently, with a view toward clarifying the dynamics I described, can be helpful. Sometimes the intervention of a wise and compassionate third party can also help in these discussions.

Q: My mother and I used to get along. She's a successful professional and she always encouraged me to be an achiever, too. When I was just starting out in my own career, in my early twenties, everything was fine. Then I got my first promotion and everything changed. We seem to argue all the time. According to her, I can't do anything right. What's happened to us?

A: Your mother has not made an adequate adjustment to seeing you as a separate individual, whole and apart from herself. She has unwittingly and unconsciously established you as an extension of herself. The fact is, you are seen and felt as the ideal part of herself and as such have become a kind of conscience who reminds her of real or imagined inadequacies on her part. She must therefore comply with unattainable standards (symbolized by you); compete with those standards (again symbolized by you); and fight against you in order to feel adequate. This difficulty with you becomes magnified as you achieve more because this moves her goals to a still higher, unachievable level. The cure is difficult but possible.

1. She must come to see you as a whole human being, separate from herself.

2. She must come to realize that competition is destructive and tragic.

3. She must learn that achievement is not the road to either self-acceptance or happiness.

Psychoanalytic psychotherapy may be necessary for her to attain these insights on a deep-down, feeling level.

Sisters

Q: My sister always gives inappropriately generous gifts no matter what the occasion and occasionally when there is no occasion at all. What can this be about? Is she not-so-secretly buying love and approval?

A: She *may* be buying "love and approval." Some people do this because they are generally unsure of themselves and so in terror of being embarrassed by not "doing the right thing" that they grossly exaggerate their notion of "right." Others do it to cover up repressed anger. Some do it (unconsciously) to embarrass the recipient and sometimes to manipulate the recipient as part of a vindictive maneuver. Some people "overgive" to others to compensate for an inability to give to themselves. Some people can't give to themselves without attacks of guilt until they have given to everyone else. And then, of course, there are some people who are just plain generous, who greatly enjoy giving and sharing their good fortune and goods with other people.

Q: Why do I get so upset when a week goes by and my older sister doesn't call to see how I am? I spend hours wondering why she doesn't call. I ask myself, Doesn't she care?

What kind of person is she? I'm *sure* she cares, but that phone call is so important to me. We are both middle-aged.
A: You are *not* sure she cares, otherwise the phone call would not be that important to you. Also, even though you are both "middle-aged," you perceive your sister as your combined parents. You view her not calling as disapproval and rejection, and this in turn promotes your own self-rejection and adds to the general feeling of low self-esteem. You spend hours worrying about what she thinks and feels because you have placed your well-being or lack of it in her hands. You must struggle to take it back and to own it yourself. Raising your own self-esteem and feelings of adequacy will return your life to you so that your sister's attention or lack of it will be of relatively minor importance. In short, your problem is not with your sister but with yourself and how you feel about you.

Older Parents/Older Children

Q: How do I handle a critical mother-in-law? She treats every visit as an opportunity to find fault with my house-keeping, child rearing, and relationship with my husband. I resent her intrusion but don't want to cause a family rift. What should I say to her?
A: First, let me say that, despite the plethora of mother-in-law jokes that have circulated for years, I believe that yours is the exception rather than the rule. A great many, and maybe even most, mothers-in-law are quite appreciative of the people their children marry and treat them accordingly—with love and respect. I feel that mothers-in-law have been given a bad name often because of strong feelings of vulnerability on the part of the new daughter- or son-in-law entering the family and the powerful need for instant acceptance. It must be remembered that each marriage disturbs the status quo. It takes time for family adjustments to take place and for a new family center of gravity and equilibrium to be established. When people are emotionally

healthy and relatively open and trusting, less time and struggle are necessary than if the reverse is true.

Your own mother-in-law sounds like an extremely insecure person and was probably an overprotective, possessive, worried mother. She probably sees you as competition for her son's love and devotion and fears losing him to you and being excluded from his (and your) affection and attention. She must be reassured by both of you and especially by him that she will not be either neglected or forgotten. She must also be treated in all regards both compassionately and *firmly*. Therefore, however much it may initially upset the applecart, she must be told, gently but in so many words, how you feel and the importance of recognition of your competence and need for privacy. She must be told that privacy is not to be confused with exclusivity. While you need and must have privacy, this does not mean that she will be shut out. However, if her intrusiveness continues, you must set limits as you would with an obstreperous child and be prepared to uphold them. All of this will be effective only if you get the complete backing of your husband, which you deserve and, if necessary, must demand.

Q: My parents live out of town and visit us infrequently. On past occasions my wife and my mother have become unpleasantly irritated with each other by the time my parents returned home. In a few months my parents will spend about a week with us again. Is there anything I can do to make it pleasanter for all concerned?

A: There are limits to what you can do, since much depends on the maturity and past experiences of the people involved. There's a good chance that both women are competing for your attention and approval, and firm resistance to playing this game can be helpful. During the visit, absolutely refuse to hear criticism and countercriticism by either party. Do not permit yourself to be placed in the position of judge in any arguments. Should they argue, try to stop them with reason. If this is impossible, take a long walk (for several hours) alone or with your father.

Here are a few other practical suggestions that may be of some value in this all-too-common problem:

1. Prepare your wife in advance by talking over the problem and pointing out to her that she is and will continue to be the prime woman in your life long after the visit is over. Tell her that her cooking, housekeeping, and mothering are not being judged on any level whatsoever. Let her sound off—now, in advance of the visit—any gripes she may have about your mother, and try your best to refrain from a defense of your parents.

2. When your parents arrive, indicate to them and to your wife, graciously and diplomatically, that while their visit is important, your regular family and social life will not be totally suspended.

3. Arrange at least a few evenings for your parents to be with relatives and friends of their own age and interests while you and your wife spend time alone together.

4. You spend some time with your parents alone while your wife goes out alone or with friends.

5. During the visit, be particularly attentive to your wife and especially helpful with household chores.

6. However you can, keep your mother out of the kitchen, unless your wife indicates in your previsit talk that she prefers otherwise.

7. Toward the end of the visit, take everybody out to dinner once or twice and bring ready-cooked food in for weekend lunches, relieving your wife of the need for food preparation.

Q: My mother died four years ago, and my father has just become engaged again to a lovely woman. I should be happy for him, but I'm not. I'm very upset about his remarriage. How can I get over it?

A: You must come to realize that you have not taken, and will never take, your mother's place. Therefore, your father's remarriage does not and cannot alter your relationship with him. It remains a father/daughter relationship. Some daughters unconsciously see themselves as stepping into their dead mother's shoes. This position is threatened when a new wife arrives on the scene.

You must also come to realize that the new woman on the scene will not usurp your father's love for you. Again, your status as daughter will continue. This issue is particularly difficult for people who have suffered from more than usual sibling rivalry as kids. Remember, she will be his *wife*. You will still be his *daughter*: he will neither abandon nor forget you. Should these feelings persist, however, a talk with him—openly—may be reassuring to all concerned.

You must also confront whatever feelings you may have that your father is abandoning his feelings for your dead mother (and thus, for his children as well). Even as he continues to cherish memories of her—and to love you as a representative of that relationship—he can relate to another woman. One does not dilute the other or sully it in any way. People who have a capacity to love have enough love to go around.

Q: Although I act perfectly capable at work and with my husband and children, whenever I go to see my parents, I start to feel like an adolescent again. I bristle at my mother's advice, fight with my father even if I agree with his opinion, and burst into tears at a careless comment from my older sister. Why?

A: Your reaction is common in people who drag much "unfinished business" into adulthood. They have not quite grown up vis-à-vis their parents and older siblings and are usually unconsciously in conflict about growing up. On the one hand they desperately want to be adults and indeed have made the grade in most areas of life. But in the presence of their primary family they also desire to be dependent children again, and the conflict produces anxiety and anger, which is projected to parents as well as other authority figures. This kind of reaction is more common in people who have been overprotected and who have a compulsive need to be well thought of by their parents. In an effort not to fall back into line on home visits they react rebelliously and abrasively. Once they feel really adequate, grown up, and respectful of themselves, this kind of reaction disappears.

Q: My widowed mother is only in her late forties, but she complains constantly about her health, worries about money (though she's hardly penniless), and never seems to have any fun. Now she wants to move in with me, my husband, and our three kids. I just can't see it—our house isn't all that big, and we need our privacy. I want to be a good daughter—I've tried to encourage Mother to find other interests, maybe a part-time or volunteer job—but I simply can't sacrifice my life to her. Am I being too selfish?

A: No! And self-sacrifice in this case would be very destructive to all concerned.

Your mother sounds like a very dependent person suffering from a chronic emotional depression. Many people suffering from this disorder use their symptoms to manipulate those around them. Succumbing to these manipulations makes the symptoms worse. This is largely so because the symptoms (excessive worry, sadness, and so forth) are viewed as necessary in order to justify getting what one wants (or thinks one wants). Your mother was probably very (emotionally) dependent on your father and now wants to transfer that dependency to you and your husband. In effect, coming into your house would establish her as one of the children, and you and your husband as her parents. Unfortunately, this kind of metamorphosis is often necessary as parents become very old and infirm. Obviously, this is not the case with your mother. But it is important to realize that she is probably *sick*, quite sick, and *needs help*. Otherwise, she will become utterly resigned and old and helpless long before her time. Therefore, I urge you to urge her to seek psychiatric consultation, preferably with a psychiatrist trained in psychoanalysis.

Q: My husband and his father really love each other but never fail to get into an argument after they are together for as little as ten minutes. This doesn't seem to have any effect on them, but it is certainly disconcerting to me. Why do they do this?

A: Arguing can be a way of feeling and sharing love, particularly between men who love each other but who feel that more obvious means of showing love are less masculine. Friendly and even not-so-friendly arguments are often used as a means of making and sustaining contact. This is a continuation of the bantering and horsing around characteristic of friendly adolescent boys.

Arguing may also be an indication of confused and unresolved feelings about mutual roles. Your husband may not feel completely grown up in his father's presence. Your father-in-law may feel threatened in his need to surrender parental authority and to give his son equal adult status. Arguments may represent an unconscious attempt to affirm and sustain old positions on the part of the older man and to establish a new position on the part of the younger man.

The fact that they do not come away with bitter feelings may be evidence that their encounters are attempts to work things out; this ought to be reassuring to you.

Q: I am married and in my late twenties. I have two small sons. My mother is a very attractive lady in her mid-fifties. We lost my father a few years ago and she was quite depressed for many months. They had a wonderful relationship and had married very early. About a year ago we finally convinced her to go out with men. Now she does and is very popular and seems to be quite happy. But she is almost like a frenetic teenager. We talk about her boyfriends, and I almost feel as if I am the mother and she is the daughter. I feel peculiar. Is this strange?

A: No. Since she married very early, chances are that the last time she dated she was a teenager. It is not unusual that she continues her dating experiences from that point rather than from a subsequent stage. Remember, too, that going out is almost a new experience for her at this time. Additionally, it probably serves to mask residual grieving over the loss of your father. As such it may seem a bit "frenetic" and exaggerated for the moment. That you seem like the mother and she the daughter is understandable, since your social roles have in fact been reversed for the moment. Here she is dating while you are busy mothering. It is not unusual for daughters in your position to feel peculiar and also to feel resentful and jealous. In any case, she will probably settle down as the underlying grieving for your father subsides. You say she "seems to be quite happy." This is very important. If she is happy, chances are she is making a satisfactory adjustment to her loss and to her new position in life. Most "teenage" grandmothers make satisfactory adjustments. If, however, underlying depression is what motivates them toward periods of unusual elation, destructive relationships, and generally poor judgments (in money matters and the like), psychoanalytic treatment is sometimes indicated.

Q: No, this is not a mother-in-law problem! It is a mother/daughter problem.

We've been married three years and we have a beautiful year-old little daughter. My husband is a wonderful man and we are really very happy. But my mother, who has always been overprotective, is now more so than ever. Most of this is directed at my baby. She is always giving me directions about her on the phone. When she babysits, which she is very good about, she never fails to go into long lectures, acting as if I know nothing at all about child care. I'm really a very good mother. What is this about and what can I do?

A: As you indicate, your mother has a long history of coping with her own insecurity and anxiety by overprotecting you. In effect, she sees you as an extension of herself, perhaps the most important and vulnerable part of herself. She now sees the baby as an extension of you and therefore a further extension of her vulnerable self. You cannot change her! But you can resist your becoming overprotective of your child. It is also entirely possible that you are unwittingly giving your mother double messages that you do not want her to interfere but really do want her direction. The fact is that you do invite her interference in asking her to babysit. In view of the problem that exists, asking her to babysit is interpreted by her as also asking her for all kinds of guidance. I suspect that you must pay the price of dispensing with her services if you do not wish to be coerced by her. Also, you must steer clear of asking her advice or looking for reassurance from her as these, too, are seen by her as a need for her leadership. It is very difficult for some mothers to let go and to allow their children to be grown up. Children can help by being warm and supportive, by being firm and clear about their determination to lead their own lives, and by indicating that they are in fact grown up themselves.

Q: Is it strange that my relationship with my grandchildren is so much better than it's ever been or even currently is with my children? I understand that this is not terribly unusual, but why should it be this way?
A: You understand correctly because this is true of so many grandparents.

You are older, wiser, and more relaxed, too. Grandparents don't have to prove how good they are as mothers and fathers. They can relax more with the small children, knowing that major responsibility lies with the childrens' parents. They needn't concern themselves with worry about being overprotective or overpermissive. This makes for easier and more spontaneous relating. Of course, unlike parents, grandparents can pick up and go home when they've had enough. Living apart is never the same as living together. Intense rivalries, differences, status regarding authority, manipulations, and the like are much diluted by a little distance. This distance is maintained by living separately and also by having one's children as a buffer between oneself and one's grandchildren. Grandparents are therefore often in that exceedingly rare position of having their cake and eating it too.

Q: My mother is eighty-one years old and of late has been showing increasing signs of confusion and loss of memory. Is there anything that can be done or, more specifically, that I can do to help her?

A: Of course she must have a thorough medical examination and any medical problems that exist must be managed, for example, elevated blood pressure and improper diet.

It is very helpful to have elderly people participate—with respect and dignity—in regular family activities so that they do not lose self-esteem, lose interest in living, and become chronically depressed. Demonstrating continuing interest in their looks, clothes, and activities is very important. It is also of value to help them to remember people, facts, and events they have forgotten—without pressure, of course, and with compassion and patience. Any re-education is of value even in things that may seem commonplace and inconsequential to younger people who suffer no disorientation. A familiar place to live and a routine without precipitous changes are helpful in sustaining a sense of orientation and relative clarity.

Chapter Four

MOTHERS' CONTRIBUTIONS TO A HEALTHIER SOCIETY

IT IS NOT accidental that I am a member of the Horney school of psychoanalysis, and it is not accidental that Karen Horney, a woman, had the impact that she had on me and many other workers in the fields of psychiatry, psychology, and psychoanalysis. I feel that the great contribution that Karen Horney made to the understanding of human behavior and to the treatment of problems in human behavior—emotional difficulties of all kinds—was largely possible because she was a woman in our particular culture. Karen Horney was a courageous woman to have gone into medicine at all some seventy years ago; hers was a male-oriented world and one that was deeply prejudiced against women. But Karen Horney did more than just go into medicine: she went into psychiatry and indeed went way beyond that. She dared to challenge the essentially male-oriented specialty and its basic philosophy and from my point of view came out victorious. Her contribution was enormous both in terms of freeing psychoanalysis from the constricted, stultified position that it had been in and in terms of changing its impact on society as regards women. She wanted to elevate women to a status she thought they ought to enjoy, and today most professionals, at least, are beginning to realize that they deserve that high status.

There is no question of Sigmund Freud's enormous contribution to the understanding of human behavior and to the alleviation of emotional suffering in human beings. Perhaps without Freud there would be no Horney or Harry Stack Sullivan or other workers who have followed Freud. Someone once said that it is easy to be taller than a giant when you sit on his shoulder. Freud's understanding and his provision of an instrument with which to understand the human mind are in themselves works of great genius. His clinical contributions and his understanding and description of how human beings behave under stress and conflict and in response to anxiety are major contributions. Freud gave us a method with which to probe the mind. He told us of the importance of dreams and their interpretation. He taught us the use of free association, the interpretation of symbols, and the importance of sexuality in human life. He told us about relationships and the crucial importance of the relationship between the patient and the doctor in trying to understand the patient's other relationships.

According to Freud, the relationship between patient and doctor is a recapitulation of relationships from the past. The elucidation of that relationship clarifies relationships in the past and tells us how the patient relates to others in the present. Freud's contribution, as I have said, was a gigantic one, but Freud was a product of his time (and these were Victorian times) and a product of his environment (Vienna). From his particular male-oriented position, his influence had a constricting effect on our understanding of human behavior. This constricting effect, from my point of view, went in essentially two directions. First, his male-oriented outlook relegated women to positions of great inferiority in society. On the one hand, he recognized the enormous importance of women and their impact on children and how the relationship between mother and child to a large extent determines the outcome of what a child's personality and personality difficulties and problems will be like in adult life; but on the other hand, nearly everything he said in terms of feminine psychology—that is, development of understanding the feminine psychology—actually deprecated women.

Secondly, Freud had a relatively mechanistic outlook regarding human behavior. He saw people as complicated bundles of instincts responding to these instincts with little or no choice. He saw neurosis as the outcome of bottled-up instincts. One could readily understand how he became involved in a sexual theory of neurosis: he felt that when the sexual instinct was bottled up or frustrated neurotic development would follow. One could understand this in light of a culture that dictated great repression of sexual feelings and of sexual needs, especially in women. Interestingly, sickness and problems change with time and they change with place, too. In Freud's time, when many women had to, because of cultural pressures, bottle up their sexual yearnings and were terribly frustrated and could not admit their sexual feelings, there were many conversion hysterias. For example, paralysis from the waist down, for which no cure could be found, was relatively common. Freud became interested in human behavior in the first place largely through conversion hysterias, through hypnosis, and what hypnosis revealed of the sexual etiology of these kinds of symptoms. Today, there is very little of these particular syndromes because women can as a matter of fact express their sexuality and are even able to make sexual requests and demands of their husbands. We live in what has been called the age of anxiety and depression. We see very little hysterical paralysis or multiple personality (as described in *The Three Faces of Eve*), but emotional depression is now probably the most common symptom that exists. Yes, there is a fashion to emotional illness. There is a style to human behavior that transcends instinct and biology and reflects the culture and the social environment in which we live. Karen Horney recognized this phenomenon in her very early days as a theorist.

Karen Horney wrote a book entitled *New Ways in Psychoanalysis*, in which she describes Freudian theory and her own ideas and why she veered away from the Freudian

movement. She developed her own theoretical pursuit after
having been in a Freudian analysis herself and after having
achieved an important position in the Freudian movement in
the United States. She was at one time associate director of
the Institute for Psychoanalysis in Chicago, which had great
influence on psychoanalytic thinking in those times. That
she did this was a wonderful thing, and it was not accidental
that it took a woman to do this. Karen Horney took a much
broader look at human beings and broadened the general
outlook regarding human behavior. She essentially applied
the necessary feminine touch to broaden the outlook. She
got away from the wholly mechanistic. She got away from
the purely biological. She realized that people were much
more than bundles of instincts, that they could and do transcend instinctual drives, could and do make choices, and
can and do change and grow in a healthier direction regardless of age and condition. She realized the enormous impact
of culture on people.

Her first book was *The Neurotic Personality of Our Time*.
That title is important and revealing. It indicates that neurotic personalities change with time. She realized that character structure, which is really the great determinant of
human behavior, is largely a function of what goes on in a
family, that the family is largely a function of what goes on
in a given environment or culture, and that the cultural value
system is of paramount importance. She also realized that
anatomy is not destiny. She believed that women were not
naturally and instinctively passive, dependent, and masochistic, but that these traits were the results of cultural pressures and upbringing. She refuted the Freudian concept that
feminine psychology was largely a matter of penis envy (a
little girl finding out that she had no penis and going through
life feeling castrated and envying boys' possession of pe-
nises). She felt that penis envy, if anything in little girls and
their dreams (and girls and women sometimes do have
dreams of having a penis or obtaining one), was not a function of wanting a penis, but of wanting a position in society
that men have largely arrogated to themselves, in short,

wanting equal rights and the same privileges that men have. She believed that second-class citizenship ought not to be conferred on one sex or another. She went further than that. She began to take a more realistic outlook as far as feminine psychology was concerned; and she was one of the first serious professional liberators, as it were, of women. She also realized that there was far less difference between the sexes than one would suppose. Subsequent papers that were written both by Horney and her followers, largely based on clinical information obtained over the years, indicated that differences between men and women and, particularly, differences in the intellectual capacity of men and women were negligible if not nonexistent. If differences appeared to exist they were not biological, but were rather the result of cultural pressures, prejudices, and constricted upbringings. Men and women have everything in common and very little apart. Differences are actually contrivances that sustain a battle of the sexes, if you will, on which society has been based for a long time, and which society continues to foster in a peculiar way.

Karen Horney long ago recognized that the feminine role insofar as contributions to society were concerned, was potentially an enormous one. The influence of that feminine role is to a certain extent being felt now (witness the women's peace movement in Ireland), but not nearly as much as it might be felt someday. The truth is that the waste of feminine impact cannot be measured. For example, in one small area—medicine—women can make an enormous contribution. I feel that they make better doctors because they are not as cut off as men are from the many feelings they have. They can bring more of themselves, especially the ''softer'' feelings of nurturing and affection, to the application of helping the sick and the desperate. Unfortunately, much male chauvinism still exists and often it exists among women themselves. So many women I see in consultations refuse to be referred to women doctors. This I feel is an expression of their own self-hate and lack of self-appreciation. If I were a woman, I think I would be in a constant rage having to live in a world largely governed by adolescent men. Women have been made to foster their role of dependence on men, and they have been made to look dependent, when actually the reverse is often true. It is men who are dependent on women.

I would like to say that from the Horney position—from my position—women ought to have the right to leave home and do whatever it is they care to do—to be professionals, engineers, mathematicians, surgeons, or what have you. But it is of vital importance that we do not deprecate their role in the house. Our society, which takes violent swings until it straightens out and finds the middle road, has unfortunately relegated the raising of the family to a second-class position, so that many women in our society now actually feel ashamed of being homemakers. Yet, I can think of nothing as important as homemaking. The home is the germinating ground of the adult human being. The home is where that all-important development will take place and the home will determine ultimately what kind of human being will evolve. I am talking of what kind of *adult* human being will evolve. I can think of nothing more important than the raising of children. This is not to say that I would, like the early Freudians, relegate women to the house, the kitchen, and the children—I, for one, do not believe that women are specially endowed biologically to do one job or another. Human beings—men and women—are marvelously adaptive, but this adaptivity or ability to learn is largely influenced by their exposure to the values of the particular society in which they are brought up. Our society has cast women in the role of child-rearers, however, and by taking care of children, women have a unique opportunity to influence them—especially their sons, who need this influence much more than daughters. In a way women have the same opportunity to make a contribution to society as Horney did to psychoanalysis.

Women have to teach men that it is all right to be dependent, vulnerable, and helpless, because there is not a human being alive who isn't—at one or another time in his or her life—despite preachings and teachings by the culture to the contrary, despite the heroics we see on television and in the movies. The average human being, regardless of sex or sexual identification, is helpless at times, and to teach young boys and future men that it is all right to be helpless and all right to weep and all right to have limitations or be confused and all right to fail as well as to succeed—this is what makes human relating a possibility on a realistic, fruitful level.

This kind of acceptance really means accepting people as they are with all their human proclivities—that means with all their human limitations, failures, and negative aspects as well as positive ones. One must remember that human beings are not saints. I feel that women know this to a much larger extent than men and therefore it falls upon them to teach it to their men, and especially the men that their sons will one day be. Men who have been taught—largely by example—that gentle, compassionate feelings are human and to be highly regarded and cherished by both sexes grow up to be good lovers and fathers. They are capable of openness, tenderness, and intimacy—three characteristics that combine to spell love. I don't mean a movie-picture, idealized version of love. I mean love that is real and possible. Men who come from compassionate households are capable of openness, tenderness, and intimacy, all of which make it possible for people to build common interests, to build a common language, to continue to grow individually even as they grow together, and to care about each other and other people so as to enable them to get great satisfaction out of helping each other and other human beings.

Part Two

PERSONAL ISSUES

I'VE BEEN ASKED what I think is the most important time in a person's life.

NOW! Regardless of age or condition, the present is the only time we actually live in. The past is gone and the future is not yet here. Spending excessive time in ruminations about the past or anticipation of the future deprives us of energy and involvement in the present. This destroys the very substance of our lives.

We can control the ''now'' of our lives. The now is all the personal issues that make up the everyday stuff of living. The routines and mechanics of daily living from the time we rise one day to the time we rise the next. Those twenty-four hours and how we live them or live through them is largely it: how we look or think we should look; how we feel about ourselves, about fun, relationships, and money, just to mention a few of our daily involvements. Our awareness of the manner in which we handle these personal issues and the acceptance of the responsibility of our actions can lead to a fulfilling and satisfying ''now.''

Chapter Five

COMMUNICATING AND RELATING

Do We Say What We Mean? •
Relating • *Commitment* • *Friendship*
Doctors and Patients

Do We Say What We Mean?

THE FACT THAT man so competently uses symbols to represent feelings, desires, goals, objects, the most abstract concepts (mathematical symbols), and everything else in and even out of the world probably distinguishes him more than anything else from all other species. But using symbols gets him into trouble, too, with both himself and his fellows. Symbols themselves— and these include words, expressions, body language, sign language—take on all kinds of subtleties, meanings, and combinations of meanings, so that language doesn't always mean the same thing even to the same person, let alone to different people. Things become even more complicated when people of different cultural backgrounds attempt to communicate with each other. This is especially true of people who lack a common ground of mutual experiences and who have different value systems. How we feel about morality, sex, innumerable customs, and even objects around us is bound to affect what we say, how we say it, and what we really mean when we say it. An Eskimo has some half a dozen or more ways of saying snow, and snow in its various forms is very important in his world. When a market trader in the Algerian marketplace in Marseilles asks for a thousand francs for a rug, he really means two hundred francs and is fairly certain his customer knows this, too. In some cultures screaming and much waving of hands are evidence of enthusiastic warmth and happy exuberance, while in others these are almost always evidence of rage and potential aggression. But breakdown in communication occurs most often and most destructively on an everyday basis between an individual and himself and between people of the same background and environment.

The fact is that many of us don't say what we mean or what we feel because we often don't know ourselves enough to know what we feel and because we are often afraid to let other people know how we feel. To a large extent we cut ourselves off from feelings and deeper meaning in ourselves and also put up blocks to expression of real meanings to make sure that no one else gets to know us either. Anesthetizing our feelings and covering them up so that neither we nor our friends know what they are, so that what we say is often a million miles away from, or is even the exact opposite of, what we feel usually happens unconsciously and automatically. In other words, we have learned to put what we say in a kind of code so as to fool ourselves and others and have learned the code so well that we use it as a matter of course without any thought or awareness at all. Indeed, some people have been doing this for so long and have so cut themselves off from what they mean that they cannot break the code themselves. Many need psychoanalysts to help them get to the real meaning of what they say so that they can get back to knowing and feeling who they really are. This kind of talking without talking, or talking and not conveying real feelings, meanings, and desires is especially common with feelings we have unfortunately come to see as less than ideal but that are, of course, human. These include anger, envy, jealousy, possessiveness, greed, and, for some people, love, warmth, and even any ordinary human desire. Yes, many of us feel so undeserving that we feel too threatened to express any positive desire at all, even to ourselves, let alone anyone else. Therefore (assuming people are not in the process of some wily business or diplomatic negotiation with each other), our tendency to mean what we say and, more important, to say what we mean to ourselves and to anyone else are directly proportional to the degree of our self-acceptance. Duplicity and hypocrisy are less often due to selfish manipulation and immorality than they are to fear—fear of aspects of ourselves leaking into conscious awareness and being seen by other people. Those of us who like ourselves, who are not ashamed of being human and having human limitations and liabilities as well as assets, who see ourselves favorably although far less than godlike, have little to fear in self-revelation either to ourselves or others. Those who desperately attempt to meet impossible, perfectionistic standards, hate what they've come to consider shortcomings in themselves, and therefore fear their real selves and fear the world, too, tend to use language that hides real meaning. Yes, emotional health produces both spontaneity and a greater degree of straightforward communication.

None of us is so healthy that we don't use at least some small degree of *protective camouflage*. But *protective camouflage* can often be pierced by keen observation, and this is made easier by the fact that many of us living in the same culture use the same camouflaging or obfuscating or coding techniques. Let me at this point list just a few examples. But we must remember that even these very common ones don't always have the same meaning for the same person, let alone for all people. Knowing the person in question well and for a long time is the best aid in confirming what he really means when he says this or does that.

1. The man who never admits he's tired or has drunk too much and insists on driving the car home from the party.

2. The woman whose speech becomes increasingly rapid when she feels threatened.

3. The woman who becomes gossipy when her need to be liked or admired is stimulated.

4. The woman who smiles, giggles, and laughs as she becomes increasingly angry. (I know one woman who can

hardly control hysterical laughter, which is almost invariably a substitute for a rage reaction.)

5. The man who yawns and stretches when he is anxious and tense.

6. The woman who says no whenever she means yes and no, no when she means ask me again.

7. The man who never lets you get to know what he really feels and keeps you at a distance with constant, chronic, compulsive joking.

8. The man who has angry temper tantrums to cover up a sudden emergence of feelings of warmth and love.

9. The woman who becomes increasingly compliant, agreeable, and sweet as she boils with inner rebellion, resentment, and total disagreement.

10. The man who laughs at funerals and whenever he's frightened or feeling sad.

11. People who go on eating binges and others who stop eating when they are enraged, particularly with themselves.

12. The woman who tells you exactly what she wants when she wants something else but can't be good to herself.

13. The man whose bearing and language become increasingly arrogant in proportion to his feeling threatened and fearful.

14. The child who brags whenever he feels frightened.

15. Men and women who tease one another, often with considerable sadism, in order to cover up feelings of mutual affection.

16. The man who says he is not hungry when he is hungriest.

17. The man who uses intellectual discussion as a substitute for sexual seduction.

18. The man whose words become sweeter and whose manner becomes calmer as his feelings become murderous. Often, he is as surprised as his victim when his real feelings burst forth.

19. The woman who always agrees with whoever seems to be the strongest person in her vicinity and who actually

believes in her opinion and has no idea of her attempt to identify with strength.

20. The woman who voices passionate arguments in favor of any position contrary to that of her husband without awareness that her *anti-argument* has no basis in real belief.

21. The "yes, but" man. This man always says, "I agree with you, but" and believes none of what he says prior to the word "but," which always signals his real belief.

22. The man whose questions, "Are you tired?" "Are you hungry?" "Are you angry?" meaning, "I'm tired, hungry, and angry."

23. The bigot who proclaims his "love of everybody."

24. The paranoid who states that he "trusts and believes everyone."

25. The man who will tell anyone who listens how much he loves his wife, his friends, his work, and who is really attempting to push down his self-hate and all aspects of his life.

26. The man who says, "Nothing to it" when he's most worried.

27. The woman who says, "I look terrible, don't I?" when she's fishing for compliments.

28. The adolescent who "hates" the girl he feels most attracted to.

29. The woman who talks about how wonderful her children are when she's most distressed with them.

30. The husband and wife who can express closeness and warmth only through mutual sadistic jibes.

Of course, there are clues in the camouflage, and if we listen to the "music" rather than just to "words" we pick up much that is not immediately conveyed. The music is often most loudly heard in humor, in temper tantrums, in drunken bouts, and in slips of the tongue. People will often convey their angriest feelings in jest. Sigmund Freud knew the extent to which humor is used to convey hostility, especially the kind that puts someone down. He also told us how slips of the tongue often convey real truths. Rages and episodes of overdrinking can have a loosening effect so that our usual censoring devices are paralyzed and expressions of what we really feel come forth. But these messages can be exaggerated, too, and in this way may convey distorted visions of true feelings. There is no substitute for knowing the person in question and knowing him or her well. More important, there is no substitute for health. With emotional health our messages to ourselves and to others tend to be direct and clear regardless of particular cultural symbols used.

Q: I don't believe in numerology or anything like that, but I do have funny feelings about numbers. For example, I like the number six, but I don't like the number four. I'd rather sit on an airplane seat that has the number six than four. Truth is I won't sit in seat four or forty-four. Does this mean that I'm surely a disturbed person on some deeper level that I'm not in touch with?

A: If you are, so are countless other people who share your feelings about symbols of all kinds. With some it's numbers, with others it's colors, still others have all kinds of feelings about certain words and names, and on and on it goes.

The reason we feel differently about different symbols exists on a deeper level, hidden from consciousness. They are usually related to various associations to the symbol, of which we are no longer aware. To know how either an attraction or repulsion to a particular symbol started we must know what one's associations to the symbol are. Indeed, associations to symbols are highly revealing and are a major instrument of psychoanalysis. Let me give myself as an example.

I never liked the number two but liked the number three. This never made sense to me, but the feeling about these numbers was strong. What came out when I was being psychoanalyzed was that in grade school when I was a child, each class was labeled a two or a three. Poor students were put in the two class (called the dumb class by the kids) and good students were put in the three class (called the smart class). We moved around a great deal in those days and each time a student entered a new school he was automatically put in the two class until he demonstrated that he was smart. When this came out in my own associations of these numbers, much of my feelings about these numbers disappeared. Some feelings about them still persist. It is not easy to get rid of old habits.

Q: Could you explain why a person when upset or hurried would say the exact opposite of an intended word?
A: One may say what looks like the exact opposite and what may indeed be the exact opposite of what we intend to say, but is actually exactly what we really feel. Often when our guard is down, these so-called Freudian slips reveal our true feelings about particular issues, people, and ourselves, too. These self-revelations are often very close to the surface of awareness and only need that unguarded moment to come out.

Q: I find it so much easier to take criticism from some people than from others. Could you tell me why? It really has nothing to do with what they are saying. Some people seem to turn me off no matter what they say, while I'm completely open to the words of others.
A: There are people who are particularly abrasive, judgmental, arrogant, and patronizing. However valuable their words may be, it is difficult to be open and to use what they have to say. Other people say what they have to say with charm, respect, sensitivity to others' feelings, and with obvious good intention. Listening to them is much easier as it in no way produces a feeling of being put down.

In general, the greatest difference lies in the kind of relationship that exists. Criticism is easier to take in a relationship that has for the most part been deep, long, and constructive. It is harder to take from people with whom we have either had no relationship or one that has been marked by negative feelings. Psychoanalysts know this. They know that interpretations that are difficult for a patient to digest will be taken much better after enough time has passed so that a good patient-doctor relationship has developed. Most people simply do not develop instant trust. We need time and experience with each other before we are ready to hear things, especially important things about ourselves, without feeling threatened or hurt.

Q: I am a high school English teacher and this will be my first year teaching. I am terrified that I'll make a fool of myself in front of those teenage adults. (They are a critical lot!) I have had some experience teaching as a student and substitute teaching, and I felt no apprehension at that time. However, as the time approaches for me to start the term and to become a real teacher, I'm afraid that I will not be able to perform. My anxiety about this is increasing each day. I am fearful of becoming incapacitated by the time school opens. Can you give me a clue as to why I feel this way? Can you give a thumbnail insight?

A: May I suggest that you don't perform? Teach! It is interesting that you chose the word "perform" to describe your function in the classroom. To help yourself, try to keep in mind that you are the expert in this situation and the students are there to learn. This is not a show or T.V. drama about the classroom. You are not there to entertain; you don't have an audience. You are there to impart knowledge, and both you and your students are participants in this process.

Q: I am seventeen years old and I go out with a boy who is six months older than I am. We like each other very much. He is not talkative and when he does talk does not express himself very well. He gets good grades in school and seems bright to me. Sometimes he tells me how he feels and I like what he says. Can a person be intelligent and even very intelligent even though he is not good with words or in expressing himself and his feelings? Some people don't seem to see him in the best light.

A: Yes. Many people are very bright but are not terribly articulate. There are those who are shy, reserved, and self-conscious. Some have not had ample experience expressing themselves. Others lack confidence. Some are emotionally blocked. Some simply lack a talent with words characteristic of more articulate conferees. Interestingly, there are some people who are superb writers, professionals included, who are relatively inarticulate when they are called upon to speak. There are also people who are particularly glib and adept at turning a phrase who are not particularly bright or deep in either thought or feelings. But it is important not to generalize. There are bright and dull people among both the talkers and the listeners or nontalkers.

The fact that you believe that he is bright and that you like what you hear when he tells you how he feels is very important. It is extremely important not to get caught up in conventional and popular attitudes and opinions as to what constitutes being bright. Your opinions and your feelings are much more important in this regard than what other people think.

Relating

There are all kinds of people in this world and all kinds of feelings we develop about ourselves and others so that there are countless varieties of relationships. I suppose that for me, relating is just that—a question of how I feel about someone and the kind of feelings that develop between us. This includes how much we care or how much emotion we invest in each other. It also includes the kind of communicating or give-and-take that goes on between us—how closed or relatively open we are with each other. In this way, relating includes both what and how we feel and how we tell and show (with words, motion, touching) each other what we feel. Obviously, some relating is relatively shallow, stunted, blunted, and limited. Some is duplicitous, manipulative, opportunistic, and designed for exploitation and self-gain. Some relating is relatively open, warm, sincere, honest, and designed to promote greater closeness without impingement on personal individuality and freedom. Most relating is, I suppose, a mixture of all the possible give-and-take emotional and intellectual and physical activity that takes place between people. The ratio of constructive effects to destructive effects (and both are always present, since the individuals involved are human and therefore always imperfect) determines if the relationship is a relatively healthy or sick one. No relationship is simple because people are never simple. Therefore each relationship is unique and complex, however subtle and hidden the differences may seem.

Sometimes I like to think that each of our relationships constitutes a special language that any two people in question start to invent and to build and add to from the moment they meet. That language will consist of all they have in common, all they give to and get from each other, and the mutual respect and understanding they build. That language or common frame of reference will be either poor or rich depending on the kind of mutual contribution they make.

Commitment

"I Just Can't Make It"

"I just can't make it." "Can't hack it." "Won't work." "Feel like I'm drowning." "I've just got to do my thing." "Sorry, but I'm not cut out for it." "I guess I'm just not for the long haul." "I love you but what can I do?" "You understand, don't you, baby?"

Women are not babies and for the most part they don't understand. The fact is that the above expressions and their many equivalents are heard throughout the land repeatedly. They are uttered by men of all ages and particularly by men who in the not so distant past would have been considered excellent candidates for long-standing relationships and even marriage. They are directed at women of all ages and particularly at those who are eligible and desirous of long-standing, exclusive, committed relationships, especially legalized ones such as marriage.

The message is relatively clear: no commitment, no serious emotional investment, no responsibility, no deeper sharing of problems and their solutions, no real caring, no risk, and therefore no potential for pain. Keep it all shallow and keep it all fun.

But for many people—particularly women—it is no fun, and is not just painful, but often devastating. Lack of deeper relating, commitment to and from a partner and all that constitutes serious "living together" causes a deep, unrequited yearning, painful loneliness, feelings of hopelessness, and often serious emotional depression. Sometimes the very men who are most terrified of deeper involvement suffer the most in the craving for closeness. Many of these men spend their lives in destructive unconscious conflict seeking emotional attachment and freedom from attachment at the same time. These are the men who seemingly can never make up their minds; who come and go and come and go again and who hit and run emotionally. Some keep women "on the hook" for years and years seemingly ready to take the plunge and then at the last moment pulling away still again. Many of these men seem as if they are constantly having a great time and are sometimes the secret envy of their more committed friends. But more often than not the men go home lonely and feeling empty and are just as miserable as the women they repeatedly disappoint. One of the most common statements I've heard them make is, "I just have to find the right woman." Pathetically, most of them actually believe the statement even though they have gone with hundreds of women and are fast approaching an advanced chronological age. Then what is the nature of the problem of fear of commitment and is it much more prevalent in men?

As with all human psychological problems, there are many factors involved. For the most part these factors exert influence on an unconscious level out of awareness of the person involved. One factor does not preclude another. Indeed, they often exist in combination and there are different combinations of factors present in various individuals who seem to have identical *symptoms*. The symptoms I speak of here range from mild anxiety and running away to severe and incapacitating depression and isolation resulting from conflict over serious emotional involvement and commitment or even contemplation of attachment.

Let me now list a dozen of the principal factors involved in commitment jitters. Some of them represent societal changes. Most of them involve individual psychologies. Remember, they exist in various combinations in different people and often overlap.

1. Our society has made sex much more available without commitment and with much less fear of impregnation.

2. There is increased anxiety in the male population, resulting from economic changes, stresses, and problems, making potential economic responsibility very threatening, especially to men with poor self-esteem.

3. Some men see women as economically independent and they therefore feel less needed as well as less in control of a potential relationship. Some men are threatened by the possibility of competition and view a relationship as a competitive one rather than as a cooperative one. Since women increasingly overtly show how competitive they are in all areas of life, these men are particularly panicked.

4. In our society most women still view marriage as an accomplishment and see the family as the basic unit of a strong and healthy society. But many men have come to believe that marriage is a "sucker's trap" and represents the end of youthful fun and the beginning of long-standing economic enslavement, serious problems, old age, and even a feminine institution. They view commitment as defeat and surrender and a blow to masculine pride rather than as adult accomplishment and a sign of maturation. "Did you hear—Johnny finally bit the dust." Too often the so-called stag party is actually a symbolic wake.

5. Some men unconsciously harbor great hostility toward women, often displaced from rage at their mothers. They express this hostility by teasing and frustrating women

of their choice. Others are terrified of their own anger and fear getting too close lest it be ignited. Still others project their anger toward women in their lives and then become afraid of being hurt by the women they secretly hate.

6. A great many men (in my opinion, to a much greater extent than women) have been infantilized by their mothers. Some of them hold down important jobs, but they feel like little boys and are terrified of emotional responsibility. How can they take care of a wife and children when in their heart of hearts they know they are children themselves, despite gestures to the contrary?

7. Some men have never cut the emotional umbilical cord and sustain the unconscious feeling and commitment of fidelity to the only woman in their lives—Mama.

8. A great many men try to avoid and dull emotional pain by attempting not to care too much about anything or anybody. They unconsciously feel that detachment from serious involvement and coolness give them personal independence, strength, and protection from emotional entanglement and pain. When they do marry, their wives often say, "He's here, but he's not here."

9. There are secret mama's boys who are unconsciously terrified of their proclivity for dependency. They feel that closeness will result in complete surrender of their selves to the self of the partner and loss of identity.

10. Men who see themselves as princes of the realm (usually as a reaction to unconscious feelings of inadequacy) and who seek nonexistent perfection: a woman who never ages, is assertive but submissive, glamorous, competent, endlessly inventive sexually, responsive but never intrusive, a perfect nurse, etc., etc., etc.

11. Men who have both conscious and unconscious sexual problems, including unresolved conflicts about homosexuality.

12. Avaricious men who fear depletion and feel they have too little to share economically, sexually, emotionally.

The problem is prevalent and it is complicated. As in all emotional problems, complexity and degree are very important. Some men who are only mildly tainted have jitters initially, but eventually do make it. Some can't without professional help. Over the years I have seen a significant number of men in severe anxiety states precipitated by terror of an impending emotional commitment, usually marriage. Those who seek help often make it. Others run away.

Q: Why can't a man be more like a woman? I hate to sound like a female chauvinist but I can't help it—maybe being a woman I am in fact partial to us. What I'm talking about is a woman's ability and willingness to get involved and a man's fright about it. So many of the men I meet seem scared to make up their minds about anything. This includes getting involved with a woman, especially marriage, having a child, or for that matter taking any important step, especially one that there may be no easy turning back from. Women, on the other hand, are willing to take a step and to assume responsibility for the consequences, at least that's how it seems to me. If a man and a woman were on a shore and there was someone drowning out in the water, the woman would probably jump in and pull out the victim, while the man would still be giving it heavy masculine thought.

A: I have found both men and women who have a lesser or greater ability to make decisions and to act on them. I don't think there is a real sexual division on that score. People with relatively high self-esteem can take chances and responsibility more easily than other people because they know that whatever the outcome they will be loyal to themselves. This means they will stand up and fight off any recriminations from either themselves or anyone else. If men are in fact more inhibited about involvement than women, this may be a function of a culture that demands higher standards of performance (and even perfection) from them and therefore greater fear of self-hate as well as outside chastisement will be there.

One pet theory I have about a major difference between men and women concerns a woman's ability to bear children. Once a woman is well along in a pregnancy, she knows that she must eventually give birth. This is a kind of deep, basic, no-turning-back encounter with one of life's most important functions that men never experience. Living with inner knowledge of this "encounter" may make all other decisions and moves easier to encompass.

Q: I am twenty-eight years old and my girl friend is twenty-six. She suggested I write to you. We've been together for two and a half years and now she wants to get married. I just can't understand why this is so important to her. Neither of us wants children right now and we are very happy with each other. But she brings this up more and more. Why?

A: Marriage to most people signifies commitment. She probably desires marriage to signify mutual commitment to your relationship to each other. She may further want it to announce to yourselves and to the rest of the world that your relationship is of utmost seriousness and involves maximum emotional investment or what we ordinarily call caring, really caring about each other. This kind of caring involves much more than mutual attraction and interest. It involves caring about each other's welfare in all areas of living, including healthy growth and evolvement. It may be of value to ask yourself what marriage signifies to you and what any reluctance you may have regarding marriage may be about. Are you afraid of commitment? Exclusivity? Responsibility? Symbolic new status of being grown up? This explanation of your reluctance may be of much more constructive value than the question of your friend's desire to marry.

Q: Why do I sometimes feel that I just can't be with other people and have to get away from them—all of them, anyone I'm with—and be alone with myself for a while?

A: Of course, being alone with yourself is not being alone at all, since you yourself are a person, and when you are with yourself you are with somebody. We often need to be with ourselves—alone—in order to re-establish and sometimes to rekindle the sense of self that comes only from separation from others, at least for a while. Sometimes being only with ourselves is helpful in re-evaluation, self-exploration, and reflection, which we may require from time to time. This is true even for those of us who are ordinarily most gregarious and also those of us who have a genuine affection for people.

Some of us need to be alone because we expect ourselves to perform constantly, to be entertaining, to be properly responsive, to be constantly conversational when we are with other people. This is, of course, exhausting and requires periodic respite and rest. However, we can remedy this situation if we realize that being with other people does not require constantly "being on." We must let ourselves be quiet with other people and even silent if we feel like it, just as we must allow ourselves to be alone if we so desire.

Q: I am unmarried. I think I would like to marry. However, some dreams I've had about it bother me. Once I dreamed I was married and being followed by my husband, whom I was trying to escape down flights and flights of stairs. He was right behind me and fussing all the way. Another time I dreamed I was married on a ship. I was trapped on the ship and wanted desperately to get away. What do you think?

A: Many people under a veneer of seeming independence feel enormously compliant and unable to assert themselves. They maintain a sense of individuality and freedom of action only by avoiding deep emotional involvement. The idea of sustained close contact becomes frightening because they feel that they will be absorbed and inundated by the other person and lose all sense of personal identity. As a result they come to value freedom from involvement inordinately and become anxious and depressed if they contemplate emotional ties, which take on the semblance of entrapment.

Remedy often involves psychotherapy, through which the person increases self-esteem and his/her ability to appreciate and tap his/her own resources. This treatment encourages self-assertion, so that fear of engulfment through relationships becomes diminished. As this happens, the value of independence and freedom from involvement with others comes down to normal proportions.

Q: I am twenty-four years old and have been seeing my boyfriend for two and a half years. We have a wonderful time together but still don't feel ready to marry and have a family. My mother is after me constantly to get married. What makes her feel so strongly about this?

A: Several reasons may be involved. Many people are influenced by convention, feeling that a sustained relationship of a sexual nature ought to be legitimatized socially, legally, and religiously by marriage. To many parents, marriage, especially of a daughter, indicates entering adulthood and responsibility. Thus, marriage to them means a job well done and completed as well as liberation from parental cares. Marriage also means family and children and thus represents self-continuation and perpetuation of one's origins. These are powerful influences, even though they may not be realized on a fully conscious level.

Friendship

Making and keeping friends can be the most satisfying, frustrating, happy, and sad of human experiences. More often than not, friendship involves a combination of just about all our feelings, reactions, and experiences. This is so because a friendship is actually the basic structure of human relating activity and through this activity we experience all facets of the personalities of the people involved. The one-to-one relationship—the feelings that go on between two people— invariably brings out the best and worst of ourselves. Through our friendships, through this, the basic human relating experience, often unbeknown to ourselves, we demonstrate our greatest emotional health and our greatest emotional sickness. Those of us who have a history of having sustained long and fruitful friendships usually are blessed with considerable mental health. Indeed, this is often one of the key questions in a psychiatric mental health examination. "Have you had any sustained relationships?" It is immediately reassuring to the examiner if the answer is yes (unless the relationships turn out to be very destructive). It is especially significant if people have a history of long-term, fruitful, mutually giving, and happy friendships. This is immediate indication of self-worth, and the feeling and the ability to give without fear of becoming depleted. Many people have not had any history of long friendships. Indeed, those of us who are severely disturbed emotionally often have a history of having kept no friends at all, and of being almost completely withdrawn and seclusive.

Of course, there are all kinds of friendships, and depth and duration vary a great deal in our relating lives. There are fleeting social contacts of an extremely superficial nature, in which a few pleasantries are exchanged now and then and little else. There are complex, profound relationships, in which two people give deeply of themselves, exchange deep emotional information, and are genuinely involved and concerned about each other. And, of course, there are all kinds of in-between relationships, which are neither shallow nor very deep. Some friendships involve having a great deal of mutual fun; others are built on mutual need for emotional support; involve sharing hatred for mutual enemies; are of a sadomasochistic or competitive variety; involve great warmth and love; are based on similarity of interests, including interests in sports, money, sexual conquests, intellectual pursuits, politics, or whatever. The great majority involve facets of all these characteristics and still more, and these are true of business, social, marital, sibling, parental, and professional friendships. Yes, we bring all aspects of ourselves into a friendship, and because as human beings we are so infinitely complex, friendships, especially those of the deepest variety, are usually very complicated and taxing.

What do we bring into a friendship? We bring our view of ourselves and of other people and of the world generally.

We bring our view of friendship itself. If our views are realistic, then chances for a mutually gratifying and sustained friendship are good. Unfortunately, many of us, without awareness, have views of ourselves and others that are quite distorted. Many of us, again without full conscious awareness, also have very distorted views concerning friendship, too, and this makes fruitful, long-term relating impossible.

Let me now make a list of what I think are important questions and statements we may consider in exploring our ability to make, keep, and enjoy friendships.

1. Are you aware that as hard as it may seem to be to make friends, it is usually much harder to keep them? So many people I see in consultations tell me that they make friends, but then can't seem to hold on to them. In many cases they've "hung on" too hard and have driven them away with overwhelming needs.

2. Making friends on any level always involves some degree of self-trust, trust in others, and eventually mutual trust. If we have no trust for ourselves, we are inevitably untrusting and expect the worst of others, even though we may be making impossible demands on them for the best.

3. "Daring people" to break down impossible barriers of self-hatred, feelings of severe vulnerability and great distrust, and challenging them to love you despite inordinate displays of arrogance, jealousy, envy, cynicism, bitterness, and general unpleasantness is not usually fertile soil for friendship.

4. Are you aware that friendship needs at least some degree of optimistic openness and willingness to take a chance with closeness even though periodic hurts are inevitable?

5. Are you aware that friendship can survive only if there is mutual exchange? We are not selfish if we want attention, warmth, caring, and the like from a friend, providing we are willing to give, too, and providing we know that there are limitations to giving. Some of us have the mistaken notion that in pure friendship it is wrong to want or to take anything from a friend. We are always wanting and taking. This taking, whether in the form of material or emotional satisfac-

tion, is an entirely human aspect of friendship, but, as in all other areas of life, there is the issue of appropriate degree and mutuality.

6. Are your expectations of friendship exorbitant? This invariably leads to disaster! Do you expect friends always to remember, always to be in a giving mood, never to hurt you, never to make mistakes, always to prefer your company, always to understand, always to be sympathetic? This is to expect the impossible and strains friendships beyond endurance and out of existence.

7. Mutual respect for each other's unique characteristics, interests, idiosyncrasies, need for privacy, and individuality is vital to friendship. Even the closest and best of friends must not seek to meld into a grotesque single unit. There are times we prefer other people's company and there are times we prefer to be alone. Good friends respect each other's individual needs and do not insist on exclusivity of attention. They may share a great deal, but insistence on sharing all feelings and things creates disastrous pressure.

8. Deep friendship involves much more than physical proximity. Many very close friends live thousands of miles apart and see each other only infrequently. But they retain interest and involvement in each other and mutual emotional investment so that help when needed is at once forthcoming.

9. Are you aware that many people cannot make or keep friends because they are entirely too critical and perfectionistic about themselves and other people? Some of the most glaring and irritating faults we find in others are really projections of what we dislike in ourselves.

10. Nothing is more destructive to friendship—in marriage, socially, in business, with one's children—as sullen, suppressed rage and withdrawal. This causes coldness, in which friendship cannot survive. Between real friends, gripes, complaints, expressions of hurts, disappointments, and anger are freely and openly expressed so that reparations and clearing the air can take place. No friendship is perfect, and misunderstandings are inevitable. Really good friends—this includes wives and husbands—can freely ex-

press differences, dissatisfactions, and hurt feelings, too. Even more important, they can let go and express their *anger*, loudly and warmly, without fear of vindictive, sadistic reprisals, without fear of emotional or sexual reprisals or deprivation, withour fear of rupturing their relationship.

11. People who always seem to get easily bored with friends—no matter who they are—nearly always turn out to be expecting too much and giving too little. Boredom in relationships, as in all other areas of our lives, always involves neglecting areas of ourselves that need expression and development. Waiting for and claiming stimulation from others not only drives people away because we ourselves become bores, but also causes stagnation. When we feel bored with friends, we must ask ourselves how much we have given to our friendship of late and what we can contribute and do to increase areas of mutual interest and involvement.

12. Some of us have many casual friends with whom we make superficial contact. Very few of us have more than a few very close friends with whom we exchange deep feelings. Those of us who have neither usually make demands on friendship that are much too great. Human beings are not perfect and cannot be selfless and all-giving. We can live only as people and with human limitations.

There are, of course, a number of people who have been terribly hurt in childhood and who are too frightened and threatened to have friends and who need professional help. Understanding that a friendship has limitations and that we have the freedom to terminate it makes for the healthiest and best friendships—be they social, romantic, or professional. This realization helps us to stop making impossible demands on ourselves and on our friends. Friends, however close, must retain their individual identities and freedom in order to be proper friends to themselves and to each other.

Q: I am forty-two years old, married, and have three children. I also have a full-time job as a secretary, which I enjoy. On the job I make friends very easily and am comfortable in office surroundings.

My problem is this: I avoid inviting people or friends into my home. This condition has existed ever since I've been married (twenty years). If people should drop in for a visit, I get very uncomfortable—so uncomfortable that I'm anxious for them to leave. What can this be about?

A: One or more of several possibilities may account for your primarily unconscious feelings:

1. Resentment at having to be both full-time worker and hostess.

2. Fear of revealing some private secret or secrets that may be symbolized by your home.

3. Fear of not measuring up to perfectionistic standards of homemaking and being a hostess.

4. Shame and embarrassment over imagined shortcomings in your husband, children, self.

5. Embarrassment about sexual feelings as symbolized by home, husband, and children.

6. The desire to promote and sustain the image of a career woman and to hide embarrassing feelings of domesticity—which you view with disdain and self-contempt.

7. Desire for a more lavish home and envy of others who may have more material possessions.

Q: How come people go on a cruise (or other kinds of vacations), meet nice people, have a good time, exchange addresses and phone numbers, and then never see each other again?

A: Sustained relationships are not initiated or solidly established easily. They require a good deal of work as well as a considerable amount of common interest and involvement. Geographical proximity and availability help, too. On vacations, and especially within the confines of a cruise, we are often lonely and particularly open and motivated to form instant friendships. These instant relationships do on rare occasion blossom into the real thing. But once the cruise is over and we are once again among our long-standing friends, it is difficult to invest the time and energy necessary for instant friendships to be converted to sustained relationships. This does take place on occasion, but only if the parties involved have a good deal more in common than being lonely and finding themselves on a cruise together.

Q: We sat around the other night discussing what was most important in making and keeping friendships going. One of us felt that loyalty in a friend is most important. Another thought that having things in common makes for worthwhile friendship. I said that openness and honesty are the key things. My wife said that interesting people make good friends. We've decided to write and ask you what you think.

A: Constructive friendships invariably enhance our self-esteem. They make us feel good about ourselves. I do not mean the momentary delight of superficial flattery. I mean the good feeling that comes from a relationship that is mutually respectful, appreciative, and rewarding. Relationships, however interesting, that somehow invariably lead to lowered morale, self-hate, self-doubt, and poor self-esteem are destructive and need to be terminated.

Q: I have a friend who suffered a terrible loss of a child through suicide. Two other children she has are away at school. She is divorced and lives alone. I keep meaning to call and to see her but something keeps me back even though I feel guilty. What can it be?

A: You may feel too vulnerable yourself at this time to confront so much tragedy. Also, you may mistakenly feel that it is incumbent upon you to effect great change and good in your friend's life. You may also feel guilty for your own good status in life relative to your friend's and the gratitude you feel in being in better shape than she. But why don't you just take the chance and call her? You'll both be comforted by it.

Q: I have a friend who recently separated from her husband. During the separation she made me her confidante and I gave her much support. After a few months she and her husband reconciled. Since that time I hardly see her. We are less in touch than before her separation and in several telephone talks with her she sounded a bit cool. Could you explain?

A: She may now see you as a supporter of her separated status. She identifies you with that period and maintains distance from you as a form of confused loyalty to her current "together-again" status. She may also feel chagrin and embarrassment in having divulged too much to you, especially in terms of her husband, now her new-found friend again. If you value your friendship, open but gentle confrontation of these issues may be helpful.

Q: We have a friend whom we both like but who has one big fault: he always puts his feet on the couch, shoes and all, and manages to get ashes on the rug. If I don't watch closely he usually manages to brush something off a table or a shelf when he takes his coat off or puts it on. He doesn't do this on purpose. He's a very nice guy but I don't know what to do. My husband and I just moved to a new apartment and we've taken great pains to fix it up real nice. We haven't invited our friend over yet, and I dread the hour he arrives. What do you suggest?

A: This kind of destruction by "nice guys" is often a form of unconscious hostility and/or envy. It may also be evidence of poor manners and/or just plain ignorance. In any case, the only "cure" in cases like this in terms of self-protection—your self—is direct confrontation. You must tell him how he behaves and demand proper changes, otherwise it is only safe to visit with him in the outside hall.

Q: I put a great deal of thought into choosing presents for people and feel let down when friends give me tokens in return—gift certificates, for instance—which don't show much attention at all. Am I wrong to expect as much care in gift-giving as I'm willing to devote to others?

A: Yes. Let me explain. That you enjoy carefully choosing gifts for people is just fine. It is your prerogative, choice, and wonderful source of satisfaction. To enjoy and even to desire reciprocal action in your direction is only natural. But when your desire becomes a claim on others to feel and do the same as you, then you are indeed wrong. Other people may have feelings as strong as yours, but may not choose to express them through giving gifts. The fact that you do does not obligate them to do the same. Your hurt feelings indicate that you feel there is an unexpressed, hidden contract with which they do not comply. But this contract exists only on your part and claims based on it are spurious and bound to be thwarted. Thwarted neurotic claims lead to frustration and rage and are usually very destructive to fruitful relating.

Real gifts, I feel, are given for the joy of giving rather than as any kind of manipulation for reciprocal action.

Q: What do you think of a chronic telephone talker? I have a girl friend who is constantly on the phone and can talk for hours at a time. Interesting thing is that she is not particularly talkative or outgoing otherwise, but get her on the phone and your day is wasted. If she has nothing special to talk about she fills in by relating just about every detail of her day or week, if necessary. She is not ordinarily a bore at all. Why does she do this? Incidentally, several of her close friends, including myself, have told her about this habit, but it hasn't helped. She was not overly offended and said she just couldn't help it, and just to hang up if need be, and she would understand.

A: This is not at all an uncommon problem. Some very lonely, shy, insecure people visit and relate to people by telephone because there is no other way open to them. The physical pressure of other people, particularly in unfamiliar places, is felt to be too involving and even threatening and produces withdrawal. In their own homes, at a distance, they feel safe and can use the phone as a means of visiting, relating, and communicating. This relating of every detail of one's life is a way of ensuring contact and exchange by telling what is felt to be intimate.

It is also a way of sustaining and prolonging contact once it's been established. As much as too much contact is feared, being left to oneself after the phone is hung up is feared even more. Many chronic telephone talkers act without conscious awareness, caught in the awful predicament of feeling a desperate need for people and at the same time fearing being overwhelmed and absorbed by what other people feel as ordinary contact with them. Thus they can't stand being with people or being without them. The telephone offers some relief. They can be alone and at the same time can maintain contact. Once contact is established, dread of loneliness pushes them to continue conversations, however meaningless the subject matter of their talk may be.

Q: Lately I have become aware of a strange phenomenon among some longtime acquaintances of mine. As I look back over the years of our friendship, I realize that their behavior has not changed, but my awareness of it has become acute. It seems to me that some of my friends are hostile, aggressive, careless of other people's property, and a general nuisance to entertain in my home. However, when these same people meet me in a public place or entertain me in their own homes, they are wonderful company and gracious hosts. What is this Dr. Jekyll and Mr. Hyde behavior all about? Incidentally, my husband concurs with me on this observation.

A: It is not uncommon for some people who find themselves not in charge of a situation to become uneasy and anxious. Some compensate or overcompensate for this unpleasant feeling by being bombastic, aggressive, and even downright hostile. They don't enjoy this neurotic solution, but they know no other way out. They are, in fact, suffering from a temporary identity crisis. In the familiar surroundings of home they are the masters; in the anonymity of a public place, at least you are all on the same footing; but in someone else's home, these people are at a loss to know where they fit in. If you plan to continue your friendships, I would suggest you assign this kind of guest a task. Serving some drinks, passing the canapés, or placing the other guests around the table may give him/her a feeling of being at home and perhaps you will have a more pleasant evening.

Doctors and Patients

Q: I find it very difficult to talk to my medical doctor. I understand from other people who see him that he is a very good doctor, but he doesn't like to answer questions. I don't think I'm a nuisance or particularly interested in diseases of any kind. I'm not a hypochondriac. I think I'm fairly intelligent and can understand simple explanations. But he won't explain anything at all! He tells me what to do, but won't tell me why or what—not an extra word—just clams up, seems irritated, and sends me on my way. Do you think I am wrong to want to understand something of my condition and my treatment?

A: No. I feel that you are entitled to an explanation and surely would understand if it were properly explained. I believe some doctors won't explain because of arrogance and pomposity that hide fear of inadequacy. I, for one, feel it is of vital importance for doctor and patient to have free and open communication and mutual understanding. If a patient feels intimidated by the doctor and afraid to ask questions it may well be time seriously to consider changing to another doctor.

Q: I am in my second month of pregnancy and I have been referred by my family doctor to an obstetrician whom I saw and don't like. My family doctor thinks I am being silly about this and tells me that he is an excellent obstetrician even though he is a kind of cold person. I get along well with people and I'm not hard to please. I just don't like that man. Do you think I'm being silly? My husband and I are twenty-two years old and this is our first baby.

A: First, much luck and congratulations on an important and wonderful coming event. Congratulations also on using your own good sense and fine instincts. There are surely any number of excellent obstetricians, *one* of whom you can be comfortable with. You are not being silly at all! The patient-doctor relationship is crucial to the well-being of the patient, and this is especially so in obstetrics, where there are really two patients. Good emotional climate reduces anxiety, especially in a new experience, and this has good physiological reverberations in both mother and child. This, I believe, can make both pregnancy and delivery more relaxed and easier all around. None of us honestly relates well to all people and this certainly includes doctors. We are definitely entitled to a good and pleasant relationship with a doctor, however expert he is. Seeking a doctor who is an expert in his specialty is very important, but it is at least equally important and therapeutic to be doctored by someone we feel comfortable being with and with whom we can talk.

Q: I have a skin condition for which I go to a dermatologist who was referred to us with very high recommendations. He has helped me but the condition still persists and I go on being treated by him. I don't question his treatment as far as my condition is concerned. But he is always brusque and patronizing to me and I always feel demeaned after I leave his office. I'd like to see another doctor but my husband says I don't have to like this man, I just have to be treated by him. You once wrote about the importance of the relationships between pregnant women and their obstetricians. Do you think I am wrong about my situation?

A: As with obstetricians and some other doctors, relationships with skin doctors are often long ones, sometimes even lifelong. I feel that how you and the doctor relate is very important. This is especially true of people suffering from skin disorders. Their emotional difficulties often complicate the skin conditions they already have. This is especially true of repressed anger and repressed tears. It may be a good idea if you can have it out with your doctor and clear the air, but if you can't, I feel it would be wise to change doctors. No specialist is indispensable and there is no reason to be demeaned. There are almost always a number of qualified doctors in each specialty in a given geographical area. Too many patients become much too dependent on particular doctors and mistakenly feel that change will bring disaster. A patient-doctor relationship is very important and like other relationships can be complicated and either destructive or constructive. It is most important to terminate relationships that are destructive in order to initiate constructive ones that help the healing process.

Chapter Six

LOOKING AT OURSELVES

Looks • Obesity and Diet • Vacations, Holidays, and Relaxation • Money • Retirement

Looks

LOOKING GOOD CERTAINLY has importance—for men and for women. Because society puts such a premium on women's looks, though, women are more concerned about it than men. Doing what she can to look good is good for a woman. Enjoying admiration is good, too. But isn't it possible that society has pushed the value of looks much too far for the well-being of women? Is it also possible that being *admired* does not sustain inner peace or happiness for very long?

Most women have the capacity to look good. Few are innately beautiful, but just about all of them have the potential to be attractive. But activating this potential has only a little to do with looks. Looks help. But obsessiveness and total concentration on looks, however brilliant the result, detract from attractiveness. Narcissism is not attractive! Total concentration on self can even be repelling, especially when that concentration serves the function of enhancing shallow superficiality and little else. But it does more than that. This kind of overdoing or preoccupation with looks reduces women to trinkets. At best it makes them collector's items. At worst it makes them objects that no collector wants for very long; the collector tires of them as soon as a new collectible is on the scene who might enhance his prestige by having still better looks. And people—male or female—inevitably become bored with superficiality. The person who concentrates on looks and on getting narcissistic delights—admiration through looks—has little time, energy, or motivation left over for anything more than skin-deep. She—or he—has no real involvement with values, issues, causes, people, or activities that don't enhance personal looks.

Values determine who we are. What and whom we believe in are the cornerstones of our identities. Total absorption in the shallowest aspect of physical self simply does not permit the time and struggle necessary to develop ideas, feelings, decisions, and priorities characteristic of a value system. If how we look absorbs all of the self, then that self is drawn inward, producing no possibility of outward, healthy expansion in which other people, ideas, and events indeed have value.

Interestingly, many people have the mistaken belief that people who are totally preoccupied with looks "think much of themselves." This is absolutely a false notion. Highly narcissistic, looks-oriented women inevitably have very low self-esteem. They know how shallow they are and they are terrified by the inner emptiness and deadness they feel. They are reassured only by admiration and adoration. But they remain highly vulnerable and terribly fragile because all reassurances are short-lived and become addictive substances, of which greater amounts are needed with increasing frequency. People who become dependent on this kind of narcissistic gratification are highly susceptible to serious depression and collapse when admiration is denied.

From my point of view, a culture or society that fosters more than moderate importance and attention to looks is obviously a highly destructive one to women. This kind of culture dehumanizes them, destroys their dignity, and robs them of the opportunity of being full human beings. It makes them concrete, simplistic objects compulsively dependent on admiration by men. It makes them highly vulnerable to emotional disturbance and misery.

I do not suggest we throw the baby out with the dirty bathwater. To look good is good. To spend some time, energy, and creative ingenuity in this pursuit is good. But to work at being *attractive*—for the long run, one's whole life—to self and to others is much better.

This means time and energy spent in cultivating all aspects of the self. This means never cheating ourselves (and especially our daughters) of any opportunities because we—or they—are female. This means exploring books, music, museums, discussions, lectures, and education. This means that women should and must be heard from; they must from the earliest age be encouraged to participate in expressing and exercising their feelings, thoughts, ideas, opinions, likes, dislikes, preferences, and decisions. Our young daughters must be encouraged to know that it is nice to be good-looking and even nicer to be beautiful, but that it is most important to be a whole and independent person who has the training and ability to take care of herself with or without admiration. This is the stuff of full humanity. This is what provides a self with whom a good relationship can take place. This is being a real and attractive person regardless of gender or looks.

In teaching young girls to be less dependent on looks and more dependent on themselves as whole human beings we are also teaching them the lesson of independence. In so doing we are, without direct intervention, promoting the cause of more constructive relationships in their lives. This is so because they will not seek out people who admire them and give little else. They will also be averse to seeking out purely dependency relating for lack of a sense of identity and self-esteem. However beautiful or plain they may be, development of the self—the whole self—aids in the belief and trust in the self. This is inevitably attractive to those who find people interesting because they have real self-interest, which is not to be confused with fleeting, shallow self-preoccupation.

Q: I have a friend who is constantly looking at herself in the mirror. She can't pass a window without stopping to look at her reflection. She is always fussing with her hair, her nails, something. She is very attractive and seems to want people to tell her this. In conversations we always seem to come around to talking about her and I've come to realize that she's the one to manage to be the center of attention. Is all this a form of self-love?

A: It is more likely a form of self-doubt. Some people must pay much attention to themselves and get other people to do likewise as forms of reassurance. This is a way of convincing themselves that they are really there—really exist and are of at least some consequence. These people often lack self-esteem, and despite very good looks or other obvious assets such as humor, charm, intelligence, and the like they do not feel attractive. This results in a chronic concentration on self, often to the exclusion of other people's needs. This kind of narcissism is the antithesis of self-love. Real self-love is born of self-esteem and involves self-care without undue concentration on attaining reassurance through concentration on the self. Real self-love does not exclude other people and interest and involvement with them.

Q: My girl friend likes to dress sexy. Sometimes I think she overdoes it a bit and shows off too much. We've talked about it because there are times people stare at us and it can be embarrassing. But she says she likes the way she dresses and it's just a question of taste. I must say I know that she is not all that sensual. If anything, she is kind of on the cool side. By the way, it takes very little for her to look that certain way because she is very shapely to begin with. Is it just a question of taste or what? She likes to talk sexy too—things with sort of double meanings and all.

A: I doubt that it's just a question of taste. Some people dress and some also "talk sexy" in order to guarantee attention because they believe that nothing else about them is attractive. Some suffer from low self-esteem and attempt to overcome feelings of inferiority by manipulating people through exhibitionistic dressing. Interestingly, many highly exhibitionistic people are not very sensual in either their feelings or responses and dissipate the sexual feelings they have through their exhibitionism. The attention they get sometimes is all they want—*nothing more*. This, of course, can lead to grievous misunderstandings. There are women who use exhibitionism to tease and frustrate as a function of hidden feelings of hostility to men.

"If you've got it, flaunt it" is not an expression that applies in this context. Most people who've got it and really know and feel they've got it do not flaunt it. They're quite subtle about it. This pertains to nearly all things—physical attributes as well as almost anything else.

There are people who dress and talk suggestively as a form of extended rebellion against parents they feel were too constraining or repressive and perhaps punitive. This is often true of people who are rebelling against their own inner constraints. In this case these people actually dress, talk, and act in reverse of the inner tyranny (often an extension of childhood training) they really feel. Some who eventually free themselves of inner constraining bonds and *really* grow up become truly sexual and no longer have the need to show off at all.

Q: I have a friend who dresses poorly. I don't mean "poor" in the literal sense. She actually spends quite a lot on clothes. She's a rather nice-looking person but her taste is awful. I am not talking about strange or exotic or kooky clothes or anything like that. I'm just talking about no taste for color, line, or anything else that might flatter her. I know that taste is highly individual, but all of our mutual friends agree that she is the poorest dresser that we know. We've tried to help her. She seems appreciative and then reverts back to her "no-taste taste." Do you have any explanation for this kind of thing? Is it inborn?

A: Let me list a number of possibilities and related thoughts.

1. How people dress reflects how they feel about dressing, how they feel about themselves—or, most frequently, how they feel about both.

2. Your friend may not care much about how she looks or dresses, but this lack of interest in one's looks is very rare.

3. She may be chronically depressed and may unconsciously reflect her depression and self-hate by neglect and even sabotage of her looks.

4. Some people just have no experience in choosing clothes and require enormous education in this area to compensate.

5. Some people express early rebellious feelings toward parents and continuing rebellious feelings toward authority and society generally by dressing in a contrived, "uncaring" way.

6. Some people project hostility by confronting "friends" with a distasteful appearance in order to irritate and confound them and to deprive them of the possibility of a pleasant sight.

7. There are people who use "poor dress" the way some people use "good dress," to attract attention. Some dress poorly in order to evoke pity and to manipulate for help by conveying an impression of martyrdom and helplessness. Putting themselves in a dependent position is in a way an attempt at some kind of distinction.

8. Taste is sometimes missing as part of a lack of touch with one's feelings generally as well as a detachment from people and life.

9. Many people dress poorly even though their taste in clothes for other people is good. This may be due to an unrealistic, inappropriate image they have of their looks, which usually exists on a relatively unconscious level. Their distortion may include age, height, weight, coloring, and so on. Thus, they can see themselves as much heavier, younger, older, or whatever, than they actually are.

10. There are a number of people who unwittingly dress poorly in an attempt to efface themselves, to blend, to fade, and to be as unnoticed as possible. This, too, is a form of self-hate and poor self-esteem.

11. There are undoubtedly a handful of people who are

born with a particularly good and creative sense of color and form. There may be some few who are born with a lack of talent in this area. But I believe that this "lack" is much more often (and maybe even completely) due to environmental and personality difficulties.

Q: Do you think women dress for women or for the effect they have on men?

A: Both—and neither. Dressing is a form of self-expression and as such reveals how people feel about themselves and about themselves relative to the rest of the world. I think there are relatively secure women who dress to please themselves both in terms of personal comfort and for esthetic pleasure. Women also dress to compete with other women, to be envied by them and in some cases to feel a sense of vindictive triumph over other women. Being attractive to men also, of course, accounts for a large motivation in this regard. Combined motives are most common here as in all areas of human behavior.

Q: My husband keeps worrying about the size of his penis. I've reassured him that it's perfectly normal and that I like it just as it is, but he still worries about it. What can be done? He is twenty-six and a great guy.

A: The underlying difficulty is probably related to poor self-esteem generally, which is symbolized by the fear of having a small penis. This may be coupled with sexual misinformation about the size of the male genitalia as well as the requirements necessary to please women.

A psychoanalytic consultation would probably be of benefit. In any case, the fact that you believe he is a "great guy" helps considerably. If his difficulty contributed to disturbances in your sex life, consultation with a psychiatrist or psychologist who specializes in sex therapy (not to be confused with a sex surrogate) may be very helpful. These experts usually do psychotherapy with both husband and wife.

Q: My wife worries about the size of her breasts and feels that I am somehow cheated because she is too small. I don't feel that way at all and love her just as she is. But I can't seem to get her to forget this foolishness. What is this about?

A: Many women equate breast size with femininity and some even equate it with capacity for sexual response. This equation is patently false, but to those who believe it this is a terribly real problem, which does not go away by calling it foolish. Many women who feel this way actually suffer from long-standing feelings of lack of attractiveness. This usually has no real basis but stems from childhood feelings of inadequacy and sometimes from parental rejection.

If these problems persist, men and women who feel physically inadequate find that psychotherapy is often of considerable value.

Q: I am very seriously considering getting cosmetic surgery done to my breasts (to enlarge them, of course). And I would not consider this if I didn't need it. So the significance of this letter is to try to find out if there are any natural ways to develop my breasts. I have heard that massaging a certain way will help and exercising and hormone treatments. Do you know of anything that develops the breasts? Because if there aren't any methods that really work, then I have no choice but to get cosmetic surgery. I really don't want to go through with that, but will if I have to. Also, could you tell me about cosmetic surgery and your opinion of same?

A: You say "to enlarge them, of course." May I point out that many women want their breasts to be smaller and some undergo surgery for that purpose. As far as I know exercise does not develop the breasts, but can enlarge the muscles that support them, thus giving the appearance of increase in breast size. Hormonal treatment of any kind must be approached with great caution even if it did work, which is questionable, especially on a sustained basis. Hormone balance is extremely delicate and an upset of that balance can bring on serious adverse effects.

A great many women have undergone breast plastic surgery with good results. Of course it is imperative to have this done only by a qualified plastic surgeon, one recognized as a fellow of the American College of Plastic Surgeons and referred by a reliable family physician.

I must point out that a large number of people do not find their looks or some physical characteristic acceptable as an extension of poor self-esteem and self-hate. No amount of constructive surgery changes their poor self-image, for which competent psychotherapy is indicated. Indeed, many of these people often feel disappointed and depressed following surgery, however good the results may be. I for one feel that it is a good idea for anyone who is contemplating a radical change in looks to have at least one good psychoanalytic consultation before a surgical procedure is undertaken.

Obesity and Diet

Psychological Factors and Suggestions in Weight Control

I've been interested in problems of obesity for the last thirty years. I've come to the inescapable conclusion that real overweight—except in the case of a small percentage of people who suffer from hormonal disorders—is due to emotional factors.* I've written three books about these factors and I've acquired some insights connected to the problem; let me list some very important points here as well as some suggestions that may be helpful.

1. If you want to lose weight, nearly any diet will do. Fat people usually know more about diets than anyone else. Skipping from diet to diet, however, is almost always a rationalization to eat and invariably results in weight gain.

---

* For a long time I've also realized that sticking to a diet and sustaining weight loss depends almost entirely on one's frame of mind. Of course, overweight is due to overeating, but overeating is due to emotional factors.

2. The best diet is one that is nourishing, includes a variety of all foods necessary for good health, and is closest to the diet one will adopt for a lifelong sustaining of the weight loss. Whatever diet is used should contain at least several foods that can be eaten in any quantity without hurting our purpose—celery, mushrooms, salad, and the like. It is important that the fat person does not allow him- or herself to become too hungry, especially in the initial stages of weight loss.

3. Losing weight over a long period of time makes adaptation to a new image easier and greatly increases the odds of sustaining the weight loss.

4. Fast, radical diets may result in quick weight loss, but almost always destroy the possibility of sustaining the loss. Long-term continuation of radical diets is often dangerous. Switching from these diets to regular, normal diets is very difficult.

5. Exorbitant goals invariably lead to failure and disappointment. It is extremely important to start out on a realistic basis and to avoid the goal or even the hope of being very thin. It is extremely valuable to avoid the all-or-nothing approach. This means that any move toward an appropriate weight must be viewed as successful and constructive even if one never becomes as thin as a fashion model.

6. Do not expect life to change radically after weight has been lost. This can and often does produce unconscious fear of thinness and avoidance of weight loss. This is so because fat people are afraid that too many changes (social, sexual, professional) will be expected of them once they become thin. They are also justifiably afraid of the disappointment and feeling of hoplessness that follow exorbitant expectation of a solution to all personal problems with weight loss.

7. Be wary of friends and relatives who are used to seeing and having you fat. People unconsciously hate to see a change in the familiar. Friendly saboteurs will make statements, such as, ''You've really lost enough weight,'' ''Don't want to get too thin,'' ''Come on, a little taste of this cheesecake won't hurt you.'' Some friendly saboteurs

will "somehow" bring you presents of food—all kinds of sweets—something they never did before your serious dieting began.

8. Be aware that most seriously overweight people are food addicts. It is therefore imperative that tempting diet-breaking foods be kept out of the house. It is also helpful to stay away from restaurants, especially during the early phases of dieting. If you are going to someone else's house, eat (your diet) before you leave home, arrange for your friend to cooperate and prepare appropriate food for you or bring what you can eat along. Remember, as I said in #2, you must not make yourself more vulnerable by permitting hunger, especially in the presence of food and people who are eating it freely.

9 Try to avoid tempting food odors. The smell of good food is a diet killer. It produces a conditioned reflex in most fat people that makes eating almost irresistible.

10. Avoid as much as possible stress, anxiety, anger, and fatigue. Nearly every food binge is connected to one or more of these factors, usually on an unconscious level. Of course, having these feelings is often unavoidable. But to the extent that we can make ourselves consciously aware of how we feel we will be better able to avoid binges. This is especially true of anger. I feel that repressed anger is the single largest cause of binges. If we can allow our anger to come through when we feel it we will avoid food binges, which are the equivalents of temper tantrums. Fat people often use food as a stimulant and as a way of coping with fatigue. Knowing this in advance can be helpful in being especially careful when we know we feel tired. Avoiding stressful situations is especially important in early dieting and just after the arrival at the desired weight goal. It is important to try to trace each binge back to what we felt and held back before the binge. This makes our feelings more available to us and helps to avoid the next binge.

Remember we (I, too, have always had a weight problem) are especially vulnerable when the maintenance period is beginning. This is because the excitement of seeing some-

thing happen—weight loss—is over and there is a letdown.
Also, this is the beginning of the period of great expectation
and potential disappointment.

11. Fat people love to eat with abandon. Transference of
involvement and interest into other areas of living is very
helpful. These may include love, sex, work, and play. It is
important to be good to yourself, however you can. This is
especially true after a binge. Remember self-hate leads to
still more binges. Compassion for self leads to continued
constructive trying.

Some final advice: please avoid quacks, gimmick diets,
fad diets, and doctors who dislike fat people. Yes, there are
qualified physicians who are prejudiced and actively show
dislike of fat people. Stay away from them. Do see a qualified, unprejudiced physician before seriously undertaking a
diet. Do not take pills unless so directed by a really competent internist. Pills can be harmful and dependence on them
makes taking responsibility for yourself and sustaining
weight loss virtually impossible.

Q: I know that you wrote two books on the subject and are
an expert on the psychology of obese people. I often feel
that I could manage okay if I didn't take that initial bite. Is
there any one thing to prevent that big surge of appetite that
hits me?

A: Overeating is generally a compulsive way of responding to anxiety and tension. Too often we are unaware
that we are anxious and tense. It can be helpful to try to become aware of the link between eating attacks and anxious
feelings that may be pressing. Attempted resolution of emotional problems in ways other than eating can sometimes,
but not always, be successful without psychoanalytic help.

It is of immediate help to stay out of the geographical
range of food. The sight and smell of food can be overwhelming to the compulsive eater who is affected even by
conversation about food. The moment you feel a craving for
food, try doing something very absorbing with your hands
(such as laundry, carpentry, painting, making beds, wash-

ing windows, gardening)—or, if necessary, go out for a walk.

Q: You once said that overeating or eating binges are sometimes really hidden temper tantrums. Then what causes *lack* of appetite? I have a seventeen-year-old daughter who is down to skin and bones and just never cares to eat.

A: Lack of appetite can also be the result of repressed anger as well as emotional depression. Many young women lose their appetites in an attempt to be stylishly and dangerously thin. Your daughter should be thoroughly checked physically by a competent internist. If no organic difficulty is discovered it may be wise to have a psychiatric consultation. Anorexia nervosa is a serious condition in which eating is shunned and a dangerous loss of weight takes place. This illness is often connected to early disturbances in family relations. Where it exists it is urgent to seek proper professional help long before critical weight loss takes place. Not every thin girl is anorexic, but the illness mainly occurs in young women and expert consultation can be lifesaving.

Q: There is something crazy I've noticed of late. Every time I get off the phone with a certain girl friend I have, I can't seem to resist going to the refrigerator and eating up a storm. Since I have a weight problem I was wondering whether there can be some kind of connection or is this just plain crazy on my part?

A: Your observation is not crazy at all. May I say that it is very valuable in food addiction to try to make connections between stimulating events and eating binges.

Does this girl friend put you down? Is she competitive with you? Does she bring up and remind you of demeaning events in your life? Does she remind you of other critical people in your life, especially parents? Does she directly or indirectly demean you and make you feel less substantial about yourself? Does she make you angry and, if she does, do you know it and do you ever tell her off? Lastly, is she a real friend, and is your overall relationship worthwhile?

Food addicts often have a desperate need to be nice, to be liked, and not to get angry. Therefore, they repress anger—automatically hide it from themselves. But it usually comes out in the form of an eating binge, which is a common form of temper tantrum. Food addicts also attempt to add substance to themselves when they feel demeaned. All this occurs on an unconscious level. They are aware only of the overwhelming need to eat. Making the connections can make it much easier to overcome the problem.

Your discovery is very valuable. Now go on and explore what it is your friend really tells you and how you really feel. When you tell her how you feel relative to what she tells you, your eating urges relative to her will probably stop. You may then go on to do the same with other people in your life.

Q: Do all people suffering from overweight resulting from compulsive overeating get overwhelming urges for sweets? **A:** No, many do, but many don't. Some compulsive overeaters don't care for sweets particularly, and some are almost totally indiscriminate in their appetites for food—any food. Still others form obsessive appetites for particular foods having symbolic value only for the person in question. In my opinion, craving sweets involves an almost physiological addiction some people have for sweets, probably related to particular kinds of blood-sugar-level metabolism and a psychological craving that is due to a desire for more sweetness and love in life and personal relationships. Greater acceptance and love of self may be helpful.

Q: I have read several books you wrote on the psychology of obesity and weight reduction, so perhaps you can answer this question. Why do I sometimes get such an overwhelming desire to eat something sweet? Many of my friends in our weight-reduction group get the same urge. I can't believe that it's only due to sudden sugar depletion in the blood. **A:** I think you are right. Food has enormous symbolic significance for all people and especially those of us who are overeaters. Each food and kind of food has special symbolic significance. "Sweets" are often related to childhood habits of being rewarded and a yearning to experience once again those sweet times of childhood. A yearning for sweets sometimes occurs when we especially need mothering or some form of emotional sweetness in our lives.

Q: I have read your books on the psychology of obesity and losing weight. I know that you said that losing weight slowly helps to sustain the weight loss. Do you still believe this? I have a terrible time losing it slowly. It seems like an endless task and gets very discouraging.

A: Yes, I do believe it. Losing weight slowly gives us a chance to become acclimated to a changed body image as well as to a different kind of eating. It is also less traumatic both physiologically and psychologically. Some people cannot do this, however. For them I suggest that they lose several pounds (not too much—10 percent to 15 percent of the total weight to be lost) relatively quickly and then to transfer to a slow-loss diet.

Q: I know that you've written about obesity and believe that its roots are almost always psychological in origin. But do you believe that the condition is curable?

A: If the patient is an adult, no. I believe that overweight is controllable with insight about oneself, especially as regards connections between anxiety and overeating. But like alcoholism, the emotional condition or obese frame of mind, once established into adulthood, is here to stay. This means that the truly obese person (unlike a temporarily overweight person) who has struggled with the illness for years must continue to exercise vigilance however thin she becomes.

Q: My friend is a health-food freak. She spends a fortune in health-food stores for foods and vitamins that I'm sure she can buy for a fraction of the price in other places. It particularly burns me up how she listens to the store clerk. I can tell that the woman knows less than I do, yet she can sell my friend anything and does! She confided in me that at this point (several years) she's really afraid to eat anything that doesn't come from these places. What can this be about?

A: Fads sometimes turn into obsessions, especially in people with deep underlying problems who are in search of magical solutions. Health foods are sometimes unconsciously seen as a fast way to take in health and to feel better. People who are highly suggestible are particularly susceptible to the use of "magical symbols" and will swear that they feel better, think better, look better, and so on, despite medical evidence to the contrary. Many health-food enthusiasts are seeking everlasting youth, beauty, and life itself. They feel that health foods are magic potions that will lead them to Nirvana and no argument otherwise is to any avail, even when great and glaring sickness may be in evidence. Some people become extremely fanatic. It sounds as if your friend has come to regard the store she deals with as a temple of worship, and the sales person in the store as a high priest. In such cases logic has no effect, as the entire belief and dedication take on a kind of religious aura and devotion. This may be coupled with fear that any deviation from continued practice will lead to some kind of catastrophic breakdown in health. In short, the victim is hooked by her own problems and unrealistic outlook; she can become the easy mark of unscrupulous operators.

Q: Is it common to gain weight when you first give up smoking?

A: It is very common indeed. Smoking is an addiction, and giving up an addiction produces a great deal of anxiety. Smokers, overeaters, and overtalkers are mouth-oriented people. When mouth-oriented people become anxious they tend to switch from one mouth-oriented activity to another. Many smokers, on giving up smoking, switch to overeating and, of course, may gain a good deal of weight. The solution lies in reducing nervousness and anxiety and in developing better tolerance in handling both inner and outer stress. To stay free of both nicotine and overweight often requires treatment by a professional therapist.

Q: I just read your book *The Thin Book by a Formerly Fat Psychiatrist*. Are you still thin after all these years? And can fatness or obesity really be cured so that weight can be dropped off permanently? What diet did you eat?

A: I last reported on my weight about five years ago, so I guess it is time for a progress note.

I am still six feet two and one-half inches tall and have a large frame, and yes, my weight is okay. This morning I weighed 187 pounds. Some twenty years ago I weighed 255 pounds. I don't think the condition is "curable" but it is controllable. However, it takes constant watching not to slip those extra pounds back on again. I try to eat small portions of a regular mixed diet. I try not to exceed 190. If I do I diet down more stringently immediately so as not to slip back into a serious weight gain. So far, so good.

Q: I haven't had a period in four months. I am not pregnant. I have been on a 1200-calorie diet and have lost about twenty pounds. Could dieting or an emotional problem cause menstruation to stop?

A: Yes. Dieting sometimes can do it and anxiety stemming from dieting or any other source can produce irregular periods, cessation of periods, or other irregularities. But it is extremely important to have a thorough examination by a well-trained gynecologist and also a competent internist. If they feel it is indicated, it may be necessary to see an endocrinologist for hormonal tests.

Women sometimes have disturbed menstrual periods when they have emotional conflicts of which they are unaware and which largely exist on an unconscious level. Sometimes psychoanalytic help is indicated to remedy the problem, but thorough physical investigation by competent and appropriate physicians must be done first to rule out physiological disturbances.

Q: My wife is always on a diet. She does have a chronic weight problem. But I do not! She accuses me of bringing food into the house that she should not eat in order to sabotage her. I do bring an occasional pie and ice cream home, but don't do it to keep her fat. I like her any way she is, but if she wants to lose weight I'm all for it. I bring these things home simply because I like them—and I'm thin. I really have no questions to ask, but I promised her I'd write you and see if you have any comments.

A: Spouses do unwittingly and unconsciously (without conscious awareness) help their dieting mates to sabotage their diets and to stay fat. This is largely because people often get very anxious with any change in the status quo and familiar images, patterns, and relationships.

People with "chronic weight problems," like all addicts, have a hard enough time dieting without also having to cope with the temptation of having the substance of their addiction thrust under their noses. Your bringing pies and ice cream into the house has a further demoralizing effect. To your wife, it means that you don't take her efforts seriously, that you feel hopeless about the outcome, and—worse yet—that you probably don't even care.

You must ask yourself if you do care and also if you are secretly fearful of a change in her weight. Some spouses fear that increased attractiveness may result in dilution of dependency on them and the possibility of attraction to and from another person.

If you clarify these issues and really want to help her, why don't you eat tempting foods that she must refrain from when you are not at home?

Q: I have a friend who believes that eating different kinds of food affects your mood, feelings, and mental health. For example, she believes that eating a lot of beef makes you more aggressive and eating vegetables makes you more peaceful and content. What do you think?

A: To date I know of no studies that validate your friend's beliefs, and my own experiences also do not give these beliefs credence. I do believe, however, that good nourishment and eating foods that are compatible with one's needs and taste are important to general well-being, and this includes emotional health. Poor nourishment and foods that a person may be allergic to or may not be able to digest can have emotional repercussions.

There are a number of people who become food faddists as an attempt to resolve unconscious conflicts and to deal with anxiety and emotional pain on this simplistic level. Sometimes this works for a while, largely, I believe, because of the power of suggestion. The onset of sudden bizarre appetites and preoccupation with strange foods often signals the beginning of a severe emotional disturbance.

Q: I'm forever dieting and I do all right if I fast completely for a day or two at a time. But regular diets just don't work for me, however sensible they may be. Can you remark on this?

A: Many overweight people are addicted to feeling and tasting food in their mouths. They are not hungry in the ordinary sense until they taste food. This taste of food, as with all addicting substances, creates a desire for more and more and still more. Of course, food cannot be avoided indefinitely, as in the case of other addictions. Thus, the mouth-oriented food addict—or, more accurately, the food-*tasting* addict—has an especially difficult time coping with the addiction. I believe that fasting simply does not work in long-term maintenance and can be dangerous to some people even when done for short periods of time. Sensible low-calorie diets, which can be prolonged into lifelong healthy eating regiments, are still best even if they are not dramatic. Serious addicts usually need outside help, either through psychotherapy or organizations such as Overeaters Anonymous.

Vacations, Holidays, and Relaxation

Vacation Blues

"Why are vacations such bummers?" "I always look forward to them and then I'm always disappointed." "I come back early each and every time, and to tell you the truth I never fail to be glad it's over." "I don't know why we even bother. I guess we still hope to find the perfect vacation."

These and a great many other statements just like them give ample evidence that "vacation blues" are an extremely common phenomenon. Well, what is this problem all about? Are there any remedial steps short of a complicated psychoanalysis of each blues sufferer?

May I point out that we are largely a nation of workaholics. This means that a great many of us are not only "work oriented," we are addicted to work and achievement. This work-addiction is the antithesis of pleasure-orientation; its victims find it very difficult to enjoy leisure time in a leisurely way. Simple leisure and lazing around often engender tension, anxiety, guilt, and even depression in work addicts. Some addicts can dilute these withdrawal symptoms to some degree by a variety of stratagems. These include combining work and play; being in touch with the office while at play; attempting to fulfill goals of all kinds while at play (for example, studying, taking self-improvement courses, exercising, getting to know the children better, improving a marriage, and the like); rationalizing the need for a vacation by waiting until one is physically and emotionally exhausted or gravely ill; getting drunk or/and gambling excessively; getting sick or having an accident or a fight with one's spouse on vacation, and so on. All these are attempts to assuage guilt by either justifying or rationalizing the need for a vacation or spoiling it in advance or during the process of vacationing.

A large part of the solution to the problem is recognizing that the problem exists. There are a great many people who—even as they describe the kind of difficulty with vacations we've been discussing—do not recognize their inability to enjoy leisure time. Why are these people so reluctant to become fully conscious and aware of the problem? There are two principal reasons. First, even though we are largely work-oriented, we are also brainwashed into believing that the only reward for hard work is leisure time and some kind of vacation activity. We then go on to develop pride in our ability to use leisure time effectively—that is, pleasurably. Finding out otherwise creates anxiety because we must then ask ourselves, What are we working for, anyway? Without leisure time and vacation as goals, we remove a large part of our motivation to work, and, since we still go on being work addicts, this makes us very anxious. The best way to avoid this anxiety is to avoid or to deny that the problem exists. The second reason for our lack of awareness is that awareness may lead to a change in behavior, and most of us are afraid of the unfamiliar even though the familiar may be not too good—or even bad—for us. What, if anything, can be done?

1. Examine and reassess past vacations and their aftermaths and honestly determine if vacation blues exist.

2. If you are a victim, it is necessary to develop a compassionate rather than a harsh view of yourself. This means that you must do your best not to vilify yourself no matter how your vacations turn out. Do what you can. Take a chance. Be grateful for small changes in the form of pleasurable moments.

3. Do not unwittingly set up disastrous traps. This means do not wait to be sick, tired, about to be divorced, or whatever before taking off. Do not go on vacation with "friends" who will use you poorly (to solve their problems, to exploit you for various services, or to use you in any way).

4. Have reasonable expectations rather than impossible ones that will invariably lead to disappointment.

5. Take short vacations if long ones make you homesick, especially when you start out to solve the problem. But do not expect to unwind fully unless you take off enough time

to get over the hump. This means at least three or four days to get used to a change of pace and activity. Orientation to leisure time is not often instant.

6. Do not fight calling the office or home if it makes you more comfortable to do so.

7. If you have a feeling of loss of identity, either take a vacation at home, close to home, or similar to home to start with. Do not impose a foreign country on yourself if you are already in the middle of an identity crisis.

8. Leave the kids home if you can. If this gives you too much anxiety, take them along—don't fight it. But separation from them is usually good for you and for them. You need the relief and renewal. They need separation to grow up. Also, they will learn from example and will be better able to vacation on their own when they grow up.

9. Choose the place and activity based on past experience, appetites, and feelings. You are entitled to be among people and at a place that pleases you. This can be learned from past history, though I do not discourage attempting new experiences.

10. Remember that sayings such as "hard work deserves a rest" are really in your head. A vacation has nothing at all to do with just deserts and has everything to do with how you feel. If you want it, this is reason enough to be nice to yourself and to do it. With practice, this compassionate kind of behavior toward oneself gets easier.

Q: I look forward to vacations and each time really think I'm going to have a great time, and then can't wait until I get home. In fact, I almost never do wait and almost always cut my vacation short and come home a few days early. Truth is, I get somewhat blue when I'm away. What possibly gives?

A: One or more of several factors may be involved in vacation blues. Let me list what I consider the most common.

1. Feeling coerced about going on a vacation at all.

Going because it's the thing to do rather than because you really want to.

2. Exorbitant expectations—of sublime joy, meeting the love of one's life, or whatever—rather than the anticipation of a relaxing change of place and pace. This can lead to depressing disappointment.

3. Feeling put down by not being able to afford another kind of vacation.

4. Loneliness. For some people who are single, going away only heightens loneliness: it accentuates the non-self-accepting state of being single.

5. Leaving one's friends, relatives (especially children), job, and all other familiar landmarks. This can make some of us feel a kind of identity crisis and this heightens vulnerability to moodiness.

6. Guilt owing to an inability to accept pleasure or "neglect" work.

7. Guilt about spending money on self.

8. Somehow getting caught in chronically and consistently taking the wrong kind of vacation—one that's too long or too short, too sedentary or too active, too far away or too close, too isolated, or too populated. Obviously, a vacation ought to meet each person's individual needs. Insecure people find it particularly difficult to tackle unfamiliar territory. They are usually better off taking vacations that provide more familiar settings until they can gradually experience more exotic diversions.

I should note that unwinding does take time. If sitting out an initial period of anxiety is not too painful, the vacation after that may be enjoyable.

Unwinding with Television

Television soap operas are a diversion. They're entertainment. They're time fillers for those of us who are sick enough to be hospitalized or immobilized. On occasion—too rarely, unfortunately—they add to our education and even contribute a small bit to our general sophistication about life and living. They are usually better than game giveaway shows, which are exploitive, sadistic, and very often make fools of nice people under the false guise of good clean fun. They are almost always better than the foolish night talk shows that subject us to the same celebrities discussing with "expertise" things they know nothing about again and again and again and still again, ad nauseum. They are better than the pseudo-intellectual late-night "serious" talk shows because at least they don't pretend to be what they are not. Surely nothing is perfect, and we certainly don't expect perfection of light entertainment that is meant to be nothing *more* than light entertainment. That college professors should permit and even encourage themes and dissertations about "soaps" on the grounds that they are a current art form reflecting life in our times is sad indeed. Light entertainment must not be confused with real art and literature, and God help us if the awful mediocrity of general television invades and dictates our tastes and values on all levels!

Unfortunately, we have become insidiously addicted to passive trash, and there are even a great many of us to whom the television soaps have become more real than our own lives. To me it is not funny but sad when I hear people on a grocery line discussing T.V. soap-opera characters with enormous concern for their problems and crises—almost as if these were real. Soap-opera plots develop day by day, from one crisis to another, from one excitement to another: in comparison, their own lives may seem humdrum, boring, and drab.

This kind of "entertainment" removes us from the centers of our real lives. It dulls our sensibilities, deadens and empties the mind, and kills the imagination. Shallow and superficial ready-made fantasies make no demands on their audience's understanding or feelings; fed to us like pap, they kill our own ability to fantasize, to create, and to use our own minds. They destroy sociability and the ability to converse. In some cases—particularly in the case of kids—we become so mesmerized by watching television that we lie back on couches or eat while glued to the set, refusing to participate *actively* in family life. The family life of the T.V. program has become more important than our own.

Great drama, music, literature, and painting are not always easy to understand and to enjoy, especially when one first encounters them. Considerable effort is required. That great art is enriching goes without saying, but what is even more enriching is our *active participation* in the struggle to understand and to relate to it. This activity and the total experience lead to personal growth, creativity, and increased self-esteem. I don't expect this of television, alas. If we could only have less but better T.V.! We are a vigorous people, after all, and need to apply ourselves actively—if television would only give us the chance.

Q: My life seems to be going well . . . I have a caring husband, a bright school-age child, am studying part-time to finish my degree. Yet I don't seem to have *fun* anymore. The pastimes that used to bring me pleasure—movies, out-of-town trips, dinner with friends—nearly always disappoint me these days. What's the matter with me?

A: Your inability to have fun may be the result of one or more of a number of factors of which you may not be fully conscious.

1. Though your life seems to be going well you may, in fact, be largely involved in doing things you really don't want to do. Some of us feel we should be happy with what we are doing because we have been told that these things bring happiness. But these things may be inappropriate in terms of our individual needs and desires. Your inability to have pleasure may be a hidden form of rebellion against your style of life, however productive it may seem, rather than evidence of any fault with your pleasurable pursuits.

2. Some of us don't have fun because we can't relax. When we are too concerned with accomplishment-producing activity to the exclusion of all else, any activity *sto-*

len from duty and goals produces secret guilt, which inhibits pleasure.

3. Expectations regarding pleasure and fun sometimes become unconsciously exorbitant, so that ordinary "fun" activities nearly always bring disappointment.

4. Some of us, without any awareness at all, have become excitement and stimulation addicts. Ordinary pursuits of pleasure fail to produce enough stimulation for a "fun" response to take place. As with all addictions, more and more of the addictive substance is necessary to satisfy an increasingly insatiable need.

5. An inability to have pleasure often signals the onset of a hidden emotional depression. A consultation with a qualified psychoanalyst is necessary to determine if this is the case and its underlying causes.

Q: Help! I'm married to a golf nut. I really don't object to being a golf widow. My husband is a great guy, and being obsessed with golf would be fine if he enjoyed it. The trouble is, he takes it so seriously that it makes him miserable. Lately his mood seems to be more and more dependent on how his game is going. I think the whole thing has gotten way out of hand. I told him I was going to write to you and he promised to read whatever you have to say. Though he won't admit the obvious, I think he secretly knows very well that for him golf is no longer fun.

A: You describe a fairly common phenomenon. It's the case of the perfectionist who turns a fun activity into a painful burden. Unfortunately, impossible goals and standards are easily shifted from one area to another, and recreational areas are not exempt. To make matters worse, any athletic activity also often unconsciously becomes a test of masculinity and self-esteem generally. Some men, however old they get, continue to retain childhood fantasies about physical prowess and skill. They continue to believe that competition, especially athletic competition, brings out the best in them and is a measure of self-worth. In actuality, it often brings out the worst and is a measure more of unresolved childhood emotional problems than anything else. It is said you can tell much about a man from the way he plays poker and especially from the way he reacts to losing. This is true of how we react to any situation, but for many men it is particularly true about how they approach and react to games. These will often indicate how a man tolerates frustration; how much anger he bears; how much he needs to conquer and win.

The only advice I can give you is to try to have a talk with your husband. Tell him he is spoiling the game by inappropriate, perfectionist demands on himself. This kind of conversation is not unlike the kind one would have with a hurt little boy, but so many men continue to harbor hurt little boys, who require solace and support, in themselves. Entering into the game with him may be helpful, but since a man's reaction to a game is based on deep personality traits, it is doubtful that vast changes will be forthcoming. In many cases, and I'm absolutely serious, giving up the game is lifesaving, inasmuch as playing can in certain people raise tempers and blood pressures to dangerous and deadly levels.

Family Holiday Get-Togethers

There was a time, not so long ago, when many of us enjoyed the security and pleasures of membership in extended families. Children, especially, benefited from the warmth and interest of grandparents, cousins, aunts, uncles, and other relatives as well as from their immediate families. Camaraderie, mutual interest, the sharing of common problems, celebrations, and joys brought feelings of emotional support and satisfaction. This kind of closeness gave family members much in common; "get-togethers," which were frequent, took place among people who were *friends,* even though they were also related through blood or marriage. These get-togethers seldom required excuses such as holidays or special events, either joyous or tragic.

But times change, or at least we change with time. For

many of us, the simple joys of family socializing have disappeared. Cultural changes and pressures have contributed to a sense of personal isolation and alienation from other people—even from those with whom we might share many common bonds. Some of us have enough difficulty sustaining interest and healthy involvement with nuclear families (parents and siblings), let alone with extended families. So many of us seem to be caught in a time press and feel uneasy, or even guilty, if any time at all is taken away from pure drives for success. In short, we simply cannot find time for getting together with "loved ones"; too often we have little time to experience feelings of love for anyone at all.

In these circumstances, holidays are often used as attempts to make up for lack of closeness to others. Because on a deep, often unconscious level, we suffer from lack of involvement with members of our own families. This suffering is often experienced as a vague mysterious yearning. We need practice in relating, to sustain our emotional lives on a healthy, fully alive level in order to feel the security that comes from being full members of the larger family of mankind. Without this kind of active participation with others, in which we really care about them and they care about us, an inner deadness and emotional shrinkage ensues, which makes happiness impossible.

And so we attempt to build bridges from positions of relative isolation. We do this on holidays because it seems we need holidays as excuses to "take time off" from all kinds of compulsively busy lives. Small wonder, then, that so many holiday family dinners and parties lead to disappointment and even to depression. The yearning we have to be family members cannot be satisfied by yearly or twice-yearly get-togethers. We often have exorbitant expectations of these events, which simply do not pay off with the kinds of feelings we require of them. Additionally, the events are often marred by attempted communication among people who do not really know one another, don't really care about one another, and sometimes do not really want to be there at all. If ancient rivalries or old distortions of each other's character are also added to the mix, some holiday get-togethers even become disastrously explosive events. Of course, it we expect to be happy because " 'tis the season to be jolly," we burden ourselves still more with contrived notions and consequent disappointment.

I am all for Thanksgiving and Christmas family get-togethers, but I am also for all kinds of family relatedness in addition to these special holiday events. We must not expect too much of these events—but it *will* be too much unless we spend much time between events getting to know one another, sharing time and feelings, and caring. We must attempt to make get-togethers a nurturing experience for all, in which the competition and striving so many of us are addicted to are shed in favor of real sharing of interests and concerns. It's very helpful to approach family get-togethers with minimal expectations and maximum compassion for ourselves, our relatives, and our friends.

Q: I go to parties and almost always have a good time. But when the party is over I almost never fail to feel dejected. I ought to feel satisfied but the letdown is nearly always there. Why does this happen? Am I deep down some kind of wretched ingrate?

A: Many people are addicted to parties, good times, and "highs" without being aware of it. Without conscious awareness they experience high degrees of stimulation and even exhilaration at parties and other entertaining events. Some people feel this way on vacations. Of course, inevitable "downs" always follow highs, and these represent a type of withdrawal symptom. To many people parties are extensions of secret fantasy lives and as such are like fairy tales come true. To step from fairyland into the real everyday working world is not easy and precipitates at least a little depression.

Money

Money plays a most significant role in our lives. Aside from its practical importance in purchasing food, shelter, and clothing, for many people money is a measure of self-worth. In using wealth as a criterion of self-worth, these people have negated the human values of intelligence, integrity, and compassion. For others money is a tool for manipulation and the attainment of power.

To me money represents a person's labor. It also represents time—time spent and time that can be purchased. In a sense, money saved represents freedom from further labor.

Money, what you do with it, the relative importance it has in your life, how you use it relative to other people are often reflections of a person's character structure. It is, therefore, one more personal issue to investigate in our efforts toward self-enlightenment.

Q: Why are most people—especially men—so secretive about what they earn? I can understand not wanting to brag or shout it from the rooftops. But some people seem to guard the secret of how much they earn with unusual zeal. Are they afraid of Internal Revenue or afraid of someone asking them for a loan or just what?

A: These may be motives, but I think it's something much deeper. Many people, men in particular, regard the amount of money they earn as a measure of where they stand relative to others. Amount earned unfortunately becomes confused with self-worth in areas other than money, too. Thus, telling about money earned is equated with giving away one's status relative to others and to society at large. The degree of secrecy is directly proportional to the extent that a man measures himself by the amount of money he earns, and is inversely proportional to his self-esteem generally. His secrecy will be greater if his self-esteem is lower.

Q: Six months ago, I lent a friend $50, which she promised to pay back by the end of the month. Since then, I've mentioned the loan several times, but whenever I bring up the subject, she becomes upset and accuses me of not trusting her . . . says she'll get the money to me as soon as she can. Her friendship is important to me, but I'm afraid to raise the issue again. How should I handle this situation?

A: You are being blackmailed by her irrational response. Important friendships must be strong enough to bear confrontations when they are appropriate.

The responsibility being shirked is hers, not yours. Your asking for what is yours is not a function of trust at all. It is a function of your rightful prerogative to do what you wish with what is yours. Besides, you may conceivably need the money, too.

Remember and remind her, too, that you did her a favor when you lent her the money. She is not doing you a favor when she returns it. She is only fulfilling an appropriate adult obligation. Her concern with trust may well be a projection of her own lack of trust in herself and other people and perhaps she indeed does not, in fact, warrant much trust.

You are being blackmailed by your need to be liked all of the time. Your friend is counting on this need. You must struggle against it if you are to like yourself and if you are to treat yourself accordingly. This will bring self-respect as well as respect from others, including your friend. Incidentally, chances are you will not be liked an iota more, even by this "friend," for succumbing to blackmail.

Q: I have a girl friend who borrows money from me and then doesn't pay me back until I ask for it. Can you tell me why some people are this way and also why I should feel so shaky about asking for what is rightly mine after all?

A: One or more of several possibilities may be involved for both of you:

1. Some people actually do go by the dictum that possession is nine-tenths of the law. Immediately upon possessing

anything, even though it may have been borrowed, they feel it belongs to them. Giving it back represents parting with something they feel they really own. These are usually people with selective "faulty memories."

2. There are people who have an unconscious need to be in someone's debt. This is one of the few ways they have of feeling a close tie on a social basis.

3. Some people do not pay back as an unconscious form of rebellion against authority generally.

4. Making someone ask for money or an article that rightly belongs to them is often a manipulation for superiority and power. It places the creditor in the position of supplicant. In these cases the negligent debtor often acts annoyed, as if the demand is rather crass and in bad taste, even though it is both moral and legitimate.

Now, about the problem of asking:

1. Many people who can't ask for what is rightly theirs feel basically inferior and inadequate. They are terrified of not being universally liked; they want to be seen as saint-like.

2. Some very grandiose people who also basically feel inadequate won't ask because they see asking as being too petty and demeaning for their exalted status.

3. There are people who generate and repress enormous rage in these kinds of circumstances and are afraid to ask, lest they unleash an unwanted and uncontrolled temper tantrum. Rather than ask for what is owed, these people sometimes surreptitiously carry on vindictive moves against the debtor. This may take the form of direct snide remarks, malicious gossip, and any other maneuvers to create pain in the offender.

Q: My husband and I are always fighting about the management of our money. Is there any set formula that works for most newly married couples?

A: No—because the way money is managed is usually a reflection and extension of a couple's relationship generally.

With equals, money is usually managed cooperatively and democratically. In a sadomasochistic relationship, money is used to manipulate: through deprivation as punishment and through liberal giving as reward. In dependency relationships, the person playing the part of the child is given an "allowance." Fighting over money is usually an extension of an underlying power play that extends into all areas of life. If constructive financial cooperation seems impossible, one must look to a psychotherapist rather than to an accountant or an economist. No one will provide a simple working formula. Therapy may remove underlying emotional problems and manipulations. If this doesn't succeed, sometimes an outside manager—a third party—will ameliorate the financial hassle even though the emotional problem will usually continue.

Helping Ourselves Emotionally During Economic Recession

Facing up to reality is almost always helpful and constructive, even though it may at times be painful. And this applies on an individual, local, and national level. The reality of financial hard times may not be pleasant, but it should be confronted as squarely as we confront the realities of our personal lives.

The economic climate of the past ten years—in which we have seen diminishing energy resources, recession (some might call it depression), unemployment, high interest rates, and lowered expectations for the quality of life—has not been pleasant. But do these harsh realities need to be depressing? Can we avoid sinking into an emotional depression as so many of our illusions are shattered, almost simultaneously? The tough reality of no jobs, dwindling bank savings, and high prices is indeed depressing, but so much less so if we realize that we are tough. Even if we don't like it, we can sustain frustrations and deprivation. It is, of course, extremely helpful to be able to separate need from desire. Our needs are always so much smaller than our desires, and when we can separate them this relieves pressure and boosts morale enormously.

For me personally, facing the truth, knowing the worst, knowing what is ahead of me are far less threatening than circumventing reality by reconstructing illusions that in the pit of my stomach I know are false. This repression of reality creates anxiety and true depression. Knowing the naked truth is like being in the eye of a storm. I feel calm and clear-headed.

I don't mean to suggest that people who are without work should keep a stiff upper lip. The situation calls for hostile, angry, and depressed feelings. However, once these emotions have been tasted we can go beyond them and help ourselves out of an emotional slump by taking some self-protective action.

I would like to start with the premise that all of life is a growing experience. This means that in our present economic slump there are certain steps we can take to keep ourselves from slipping into an emotional slump and to help us become more fully developed individuals—more human to ourselves and others.

1. We must not hate ourselves for not preparing ourselves for hard times. Time spent recriminating over what we should have done, what we have invested in, etc., is time and energy spent in the service of developing more self-hate, wallowing in it, and leaving ourselves paralyzed and helpless. We must not blame ourselves or those close to us who share our burdens. Mutual recrimination and attempts to lay blame on each other destroy morale and the benefits that mutual support makes possible.

2. We must refuse to equate economic loss with loss of self-esteem. When we make a personal assessment of ourselves, we find that we are still the same human beings we were yesterday, before the economy changed. We have the same assets today that we had yesterday: good health, loving parents/children/mates, people who care, whom we care

about, personal possessions that make us feel good to look at and own, imagination, sensations, sexuality, whatever.

3. We must make a realistic assessment of our personal financial situation with an actual list of credits and debits. From this list we can decide where to place our priorities for a healthy and sensible way of life. There have been many generations of families who lived happily and successfully without air conditioning, automobiles, steak three times a week, new clothes of the latest designer to suit our whim, vacations abroad, and so on. If we take time to recall happy childhood memories, I think we will find that they consisted of family picnics and church or other community seasonal celebrations; for myself, I treasure memories of my family crowding onto the fire escape on a hot summer's night, everyone drinking ice-cold water with raspberry jelly, talking, laughing, and crying, too, but all of it human and alive. We children were allowed to stay up past midnight, when our apartment finally cooled off, before we were put to bed.

4. We must make every effort to keep in touch with the actual facts concerning the economy, rather than avoiding the truth and living with imaginary monsters. The truth is invariably less frightening than imaginary monstrous problems. We must refuse to become demoralized by excessive anticipation of disaster. We must learn to distinguish between rumors and factual news; between dramatization of news stories, which are presented as Greek tragedies, and news editorials presented by reliable sources. In this way we can stand up to panic-mongers and prevent the onset of hysteria.

5. Whenever possible, it is good to be with people who are cheerful and optimistic. Do not sustain relationships with people who put down our country, are generally "down" on everything, are patronizing to you, are eager to spread and exaggerate the worst kinds of news, and, when this creates the desired effect (panic), feel buoyed themselves and leave you depressed.

6. Be kind to yourself in every way possible. If you have adult children and their company leaves you feeling

good and hopeful about yourself, by all means call them and tell them *you* need *them*. Don't allow your "sick" pride in your being the "parent" and they the "children" stop you from helping yourself in this manner. Of course, the reverse also applies: if you are an adult with parents or a parent who can nurture you for a bit, and thereby renew your hope and self-esteem, you must absolutely allow yourself this nurturing experience.

7. Just as we can put down "sick" pride in seeking emotional sustenance from loved ones, we can do the same in aiding personal economy. There is no disgrace whatsoever in asking anyone and everyone about the possibility of work. If there is an offering that is not quite what one is qualified for, or that is not quite what we are accustomed to, we must allow ourselves to tackle something new, to stretch our minds and to allow ourselves to be open to creative possibilities. Being out of work sometimes proves to be a golden opportunity to try for that change of occupation some of us have secretly desired for years.

8. Take healthy pride in "cutting corners" in personal expenses. Look upon this not as a put-down but as a challenge, and as part of a constructive re-evaluation of your standard of living. Our sense of humility is often strengthened in crises and this can create real strength. Finding out that we can withstand hardships invariably increases self-esteem and adds to emotional strength.

9. Do not deprive yourself or your family of good medical care because of financial reversals. Search out the best free or low-cost medical and dental facilities. You must remain healthy, strong, in top physical condition to enable you to meet the vicissitudes of life. And indeed, if you do find that life is tough going and you need psychiatric help, look for low-cost treatment in hospitals and clinics and through mental-health associations.

10. Do enter into community activities. This will enable you to enlarge your circle of friends. A community group, whether it is religious, political, social, or cultural, is a valu-

able vehicle for getting recognition of community needs from local government and local business associations, too.

11. Don't let sick pride and false loyalties keep you shopping in the same old places and using the same services if you can find similar items and services elsewhere at a cheaper price. Remember, your first loyalty is to yourself.

12. Do have friends over and entertain often by letting each guest bring a contribution for the evening's meal. Perhaps you haven't done this for a very long time, but it can be good fun. Don't lose your sense of having fun. Keep in mind that long walks in the sun, or even in the rain, can be enjoyable and invigorating; playing board games with the kids may also make you laugh. Pick up that old musical instrument of yours and see if that can't renew old pleasures. Try a new hobby or learn a new skill or make love. These are all inexpensive pleasures.

13. Above all, retain your sense of humor. Many comedians came into their own during the Depression because the ability to create laughter was a precious commodity.

14. *Remember*, what other people think is not important. If they are willing to help, that can be important. Financial difficulty is not a sin or a stigma of any kind if you refuse to see it that way.

15. Above all, realize that economics, like every other aspect of the human condition, is subject to cyclic change. This makes hope possible and hope is a good morale booster. However, avoid letting hope turn into inappropriate expectations that lead to disappointment and depression.

Sometimes when the going is rough it is good to look back at the development of our families and that of our land. When I do this, I can't help having admiration for our ancestors who did endure all kinds of terrible hardships. We all have heard family stories told with great pride about how these hardships were weathered by our families. Yes, we here in the United States are the products of a very strong people. This country was founded by people who did not give up, who found ways to cope and survive. We, their children, shall do the same, and whenever necessary our children will do the same, too. Our problems are tough, but so are we.

Retirement

Retirement presents the possibility of a joyful retreat into a timelessness somewhat akin to summer vacations when we were in grade school. This applies to fortunate people who have the health, energy, money, and above all the desire to learn and become involved in new interests. It is enormously helpful to prepare for this time in our lives just as we prepared for secondary school and college. As with all new situations in life, some pitfalls are inevitable and flexibility in terms of new possibilities is invaluable. It is wise and may even be lifesaving to realize that retirement is not for everyone.

Q: My husband retired five years ago, at age fifty-four. With the loss of his position went his self-respect and the companionship of his peers. He is often ill as well as impotent. I understand and try to have patience, but it is wearing thin. He reads the paper then watches T.V. He doesn't leave the house or want to see friends. He has a hobby but does not pursue it. I am the same age and also have a restricting illness, but I refuse to give up living altogether. He will not even discuss it with me, much less see a counselor. What can I do?

A: This kind of reaction is sometimes a rage at oneself, one's spouse, the world, and the inevitable process of aging.

Very few people, especially men, take retirement well at any age, and it is particularly difficult for a man who is only fifty-four. People who are work-oriented suffer a severe blow to self-esteem when they are no longer gainfully employed, and an enormous number of them suffer from the symptoms you describe in your husband. To make matters worse, many men have convinced themselves that the main goal of their working life was to retire one day. They have therefore developed a vested interest in retirement, and great expectations of it; they suffer all the more when retirement turns out to be more pain than pleasure. Admitting this disappointment is very difficult because they come to see it as a great personal failure. They feel that they *should* enjoy retirement, no matter what. Caught in this trap, they often project much bitterness, inappropriately blaming their wives, children, the country, the world. In an attempt to extricate themselves, some—like your husband—develop somatic symptoms and unconsciously attempt to feel much older and more infirm than they are. They can then use this argument as an attempt to put down yearnings to return to work and to old activities and relationships. For the most part this doesn't work. Some retirees can put down sick pride and go for counseling or psychiatric help if they are depressed. Some can tap inner resources and develop old and new hobbies and interests. Most cannot, and as a result many do get sick and even die before their time, having lost motivation to go on. For these people it would be best if retirement never took place at all. Some can barely tolerate a lighter work load. For those who are retired and who are developing more and more depression and resignation from life, the best treatment is usually a return to gainful employment regardless of need or lack of need for money.

Q: My dad retired about six months ago. Both my parents are healthy people in their late sixties. Since he has retired, they are always together and have both become so cantankerous that it has become exceedingly unpleasant to be with them. They constantly complain to me about each other. It seems to me that they did get along splendidly before my dad's retirement. Is there anything I can do to help them? Also, is there anything I can do to help myself? I find myself not wanting to visit them and then I feel so guilty about this feeling that I cannot live with myself. Your advice would be greatly appreciated.

A: Retirement, like any other period of change in one's life, is an upheaval and requires great effort, patience, and time to evolve a satisfactory adjustment. Your parents are probably unaccustomed to spending so much time together. Your mother has probably been used to having the house to herself much of the time and to following her own needs and demands. Now with your dad home, every day is like Sunday. If your father is like so many other retired men to whom I've talked, he probably tries to find things to do around the house, or does the marketing and in some ways is usurping your mother's position in the household. Though this may keep him occupied, it is not really satisfying his own needs for leading a fulfilling life and is undoubtedly a great nuisance to your mother.

I find that retirement is a dreadful mistake for most people. It often leads to emotional, physical, and social deterioration. It might be wise to investigate opportunities for retirees with them. Some church, hospitals, youth, and golden age groups have important community programs in which your parents might involve themselves. There also may be some group-therapy programs available at local outpatient clinics for people in your parents' position. Some "retired couples" have the mistaken notion that *now* that they are through working they must spend all of their time together. Permitting themselves some daily separation and the freedom to go off alone for a while can provide relief and add to mutual attraction.

It may be helpful for all of you to have a frank discussion about their problem and how they make you feel. It may help them to recognize where their differences lie and to work out a program, a new way of life for themselves. You all have to realize that adjustment takes time. Some experimentation involving both failure and success is necessary in adjusting to radical changes in life-styles.

For yourself, it would be helpful to realize that you may not be able to play a large, active role in helping them through this period in their lives. They may have to work it out themselves. You can protect yourself by requesting that they don't argue when you come to visit.

Q: Some friends of mine are in their early seventies. They have always had an excellent relationship and had been married for over forty years. Now both of them are rather ill with various sicknesses. Their children are grown up and have gone off to tend to their own lives. My friends did the strangest thing: they've separated! They told me that they've had no disagreement at all and as a matter of fact still care for each other very much. This must be so because they took apartments only a block away from each other and are always helping each other, especially when one or the other is sick. Now why in the world did they do this?

A: I can only theorize. Sometimes older couples have legal, estate, or other financial considerations that might make living apart easier, but whether or not this applies to your friends I don't know. I have known couples who could not stand being in the presence of mutual illness. Witnessing a mate's physical decline or suffering produced intolerable pain. In some cases anticipating death was too much to bear. These people were not immediately aware of their reasons for desiring some separation and usually rationalized their actions in different ways. But their real motivation for separation was inability to see a loved one in pain or in decline.

Q: My husband and I are in our fifties. For the past year, we have been dying to get in touch with some old friends we had when my husband was in the Air Corps during the war. We lived on the base and had such good times there, even though we were at war. I really would love to see them, but I just can't get myself to write or call. Why don't I get in touch with them? What is stopping me?

A: It is significant that you mention your age right at the beginning of your question. Many people have difficulty admitting that they are in their middle years. When we look back at old friendships and live with those memories, we can still maintain the illusion that those times were "just the other day." Our memories of those friends are of people in their twenties and of us in our twenties. Coming face to face with those people today breaks the spell and destroys the illusion. We protect ourselves in ways we are not conscious of. Your inability to effect the reunion may well be an unconscious, self-protective device. Apparently you are not quite ready to face the reality of time gone by and the fact of age. However, your ability to open your question with the acknowledgment of being in your fifties indicates that you are on your way toward acceptance of yourself, at any age. Perhaps the ability to have that reunion is almost within your grasp.

Chapter Seven

CHOICE AND CHANGE

Living with Change and Choice • How Much Can People Change? • Help Through Therapy

Living with Change and Choice

THAT WE CAN seriously address ourselves to the subject of change and choice in our lives is in itself enormously significant. In other eras and places this discussion probably would not have been possible. There are still many places in the world where the preoccupation of whole populations is survival—nothing more! For these people nothing has changed in centuries, and the possibility of choice isn't even a vague hope. Even in our society at the current time, despite considerable progress made, women are still denied a full opportunity to change and grow psychologically in a healthful way. But fortunately we are making progress in that area, too.

Now what do I mean when I speak of change and growth and choice? When we think of change we must consider the fact that people can move in either a healthy or a sick direction and sometimes in both directions at the same time. I have seen people who, even as they became increasingly depressed and disoriented, also became more compassionate toward other people and the human condition generally. In neurosis, however, constriction and repression and compulsive behavior make *healthy* choice very difficult. It is very hard to exercise the full range of choices inherent in being human when one must obey the dictates of inner neurotic tyrannical compulsions. Of course, what goes on individually and internally, intrapsychically—that is, in the minds of individuals—cannot be separated from the particular society in which the individual lives. Where and when—vantage point and cultural frame of reference—are of crucial importance. There have been, and there still are, societies in which a desire for healthy change was, and is, looked upon as sick. What is sick in one culture may be viewed as healthy and wholesome in another. We view hallucinations as evidence of major mental illness. Certain cultures have viewed these manifestations as evidence of special power and ability. As peculiar as it may seem, the idea of change and the possibility of choice—especially for women, or for those in the working class—would be looked upon as lunacy in other times and in other places.

Among enlightened people in our country, constriction, rigidity, and unthinking fidelity and resistance to change are no longer seen as virtues. Indeed, many professionals, including myself, view rigid adherence to the status quo as almost certain evidence of neurosis. From my point of view, the major goal of psychoanalysis is to bring the patient to a condition or position in which change in a healthier direction becomes possible and in which free and personal choice can replace compulsion. This goal was first—and perhaps best—articulated by the psychoanalyst Karen Horney.

Karen Horney was one of the first people to recognize the serious impact of culture on society and on the emotional lives of people. People continue to reinforce the very cultural forces—some of them malevolent—that affected them the most. Horney believed, however, that people have a natural proclivity and desire to move in the direction of *health*, even in a very sick society. But Karen Horney also realized that people cannot be separated from their culture, and that if the culture is sick and antithetical to human aspirations, then misery ensues, despite heroic struggle to the contrary. Her perception of and compassion for the human condition, added to her considerable brilliance and creative talent, enabled her to formulate a practical theory involving character structure and the ways people relate. Her insights did not fit into the Freudian frame of reference, or at least they were not utilized prior to the development of her own theories. She realized that people are not simply instinctual bundles of protoplasm that respond to inborn impulses, which when frustrated lead to anxiety. She knew that people are complicated creatures who transcend the dictates of instinct, who construct societies with which they are, and often are not, compatible. She believed that women, and women's psychologies, are very much more than a question of simple envy of the male sexual apparatus. She realized that people who live in certain cultures are deprived of the possibility of healthy change and of the possibility of choice and as a result develop severe anxiety and all kinds of neurotic stratagems. She realized that women had been historically deprived in most cultures, and that this deprivation made great difficulty for them.

This was a revolutionary concept, and it had reverberations in many areas of psychological thinking. But unfortunately, the psychoanalytic establishment was slow to recognize Horney as the great thinker she was, the great physician and healer, and the first great liberator of women. It still has not quite done so. Perhaps if a man had conceptualized her various theories, much more progress would have been made in their acceptance.

She also realized the degree to which resistance to change can be evidence of great emotional sickness. People who are disturbed suffer from all kinds of compulsive thinking and acting. Some people are terrified of any kind of internal emotional conflict; other people have not developed the independence they are capable of. Horney alluded to a sickness that prevails among all of us to a lesser or greater degree, which she called morbid dependency. If we are morbidly dependent, we become fearful of the possibility of choice and change and seek security in the status quo. We are afraid of geographical change, political change, philosophical change, or changes in how we see the world. We are particularly afraid of changing the way we see ourselves and other people. We have this fear because, for the most part, we're uncomfortable and somewhat frightened by what is unfamiliar, and we tend to cling to the familiar as a kind of security blanket. It takes pioneers among us, very often, to indicate that freedom of choice is more important than any other freedom, because this is the freedom that most characterizes the human species.

For some people freedom of choice is too much: it gets them into conflict, which they cannot tolerate. As a result, many would rather live by the orders and dictates of other people. They prefer to be told what to do rather than to live their own lives according to their own proclivities. But the fact is that discomfort is often characteristic of progress, of good growth, and of healthy change. If we shun discomfort, and if we shun struggle, then we will chronically avoid change and choice and will, indeed, treat them as shabby commodities. Karen Horney recognized from her own work in treating patients that as people became less neurotic, healthier, and flexible, they desired greater change in their lives and desired the freedom to make choices. Free of both inner and outer tyrannies—the inner tyrannies of neurosis and outer tyrannies of sociopolitical systems connected to power brokers of all kinds—people desire the responsibility of personal and individual free choice.

It's interesting that early psychoanalysts felt that psychoanalysis was only for the very young. Horney believed otherwise. She felt that anybody could profit from therapy based on psychoanalytic dynamics. Because she felt that the struggle to change and grow, to make good choices, is a struggle that goes on all of our lives, and that this very fine struggle is the stuff of life itself—the best part of life. People confuse struggling with suffering, and perhaps this is one of the major reasons that they avoid the struggle. However, they are not the same at all. Suffering is very often a process that is engaged in for its own sake and is very often involved with neurosis and neurotic aspirations, especially those aspirations concerned with self-glorification and self-idealization, as opposed to the development of the real self. Struggle, on the other hand, is a function of self-expression, of self-realization, of finding out who one is and what one freely wants to do with one's life. And struggle is the inherent characteristic of choice—free choice. Free choice in turn leads to much more than survival. Free choice leads to greater growth, to great possibility of change.

The biggest change we've seen in our country in this century—one that is making waves throughout the world and will, I hope, continue to do so—is the greater choice that women will have in their lives—choices of all kinds. Now these choices initially create chaos and turbulence because, as I indicated earlier, any change of the status quo means a shift in the emotional center of gravity and the seeking of a new kind of equilibrium. Needless to say, these kinds of changes have their inherent dangers, too. Initially, there's more than the danger of pain. There's a great deal of anxiety. There's also the danger of overreaction—in the women's movement, otherwise constructive participants tend to dismiss some of the healthiest contributions women have made to our society. For example, I for one feel that working in the home, working with children, is one of the most important and complex occupations that exists. Mothering determines the well-being of all the people who live in a home, and especially the well-being of the children. This is not to put the burden for the well-being of children on mothers and women exclusively, because fathers certainly should play a role also. But to deprecate a woman's role in parenting in favor of other roles is simplistic and foolish.

The fact is, however, that women have and will have still greater choices in what they want to do with their lives and in how they want to affect the world. Many women will have to redirect much energy, in terms of all kinds of value systems they devise for themselves. They will be in greater personal conflict about what they want to do with their lives. Of course, the potential rewards are enormous: not only for the individual women involved, but also for society as a whole, because I am convinced that the resources that are available for women to tap are almost infinite. They're nothing less than fantastic. And this applies to almost every area of living. The untapped resources in terms of intellect, emotion, creative enterprise, the arts, and we can go on and on, is enormous.

Great changes will be necessary for men, too. Their view of their relationships with women must change; their view of the world must change; and their view of themselves must change. This may perhaps represent the biggest struggle of all for the next decade or more because men, with their enormous pride, with their enormous and constricting masculine image, find it very difficult to change. The big change I'm talking about is accepting with grateful equanimity what our culture has destructively chosen to call feminine characteristics. I say destructively because I think that many characteristics that we dub either masculine or feminine are neither—they're simply human characteristics. And as long as we label one masculine and one feminine, women will continue to cut off those human characteristics and assets that have been erroneously labeled masculine; for example, being self-assertive, objective, logical, or capable. These are not male attributes. Some men are afraid to be understanding, compassionate, or sensitive to various creative enterprises. Some men feel embarrassed because they are interested, for example, in the ballet and enjoy romantic poetry or sentimental music. Perhaps all this will come to a stop in the not too distant future.

How Much Can People Change?

If we think of *change* in terms of *healthy growth*, I feel that nearly all of us can change and can change a great deal. Not everyone believes this. Some psychologists, psychiatrists, and psychoanalysts feel that people repeat the patterns they learned in childhood over and over again and that change is represented only by minor variations of a lifelong theme. Others believe that surface changes can take place through various kinds of ''behavior modification,'' ''conditioning,'' and ''learning processes'' similar to those used to ''train'' both children and "animals." But I emphatically do not agree, and neither do those of my professional colleagues who agree with the late, great psychoanalyst Karen Horney, who felt that people can change *and* grow in a healthy, constructive direction all the days of their lives, regardless of age.

Let me first point out that we are not simple creatures singularly responsive to biologically determined instinctual drives and conditioned reflexes! We are not rigid machines permanently and unalterably programmed to perform in predictable patterns in the first months of existence! We are the most complicated, unpredictable, flexible, and adaptable creatures on this planet. One human brain contains psychoneurological structure and potential larger than all the computers and technology of the world. This enormous gift makes us creatures capable of perceiving the possibility of all kinds of variations in behavior, capable of making decisions and choices and capable of making all kinds of change in our lives. If this wasn't so, it would not be possible for us to invent and to adapt to the many variations in life-style that have existed through the years and throughout the world. This potential for growth and change makes us unique in our ability to invent almost endless kinds of environments in which to live. These include environments, or I suppose a better word would be *cultures,* of the most diverse values and life-styles. A species that is capable of producing ancient Rome, Shakespearian England, the United States of America, the music of Beethoven, Bach, and the Beatles, the art of da Vinci and de Kooning *must* be constituted of individuals who are each capable of considerable change.

I believe that change is not the sole province of the very young! On the contrary, life itself—living—produces endless perceptive experiences that inevitably must and do change all of us. Of course, there is considerable variation in the degree of change or changeability in various members of a given population. I feel that this mostly depends on a person's emotional health. Those of us who have been subject to traumatic experiences, to a great deal of threat to self-esteem, and to a choking off of natural talents and proclivities tend to be afraid of change. Emotional illness causes hopelessness, resignation from life, constriction, and rigidity. Emotional health is conducive to greater flexibility, hope, confidence in one's adaptability to new situations, people, and development and a willingness to risk the unfamiliar.

But change is possible in anyone—either healthy or sick—provided there is ample motivation and a willingness to struggle. Psychotherapists of all persuasions agree that motivation to change in the direction of healthy growth is very difficult to generate from the outside. Most people who come to a qualified therapist's office can be helped, but they must get there under their own steam. It takes much work and stick-to-itiveness for worthwhile growth to take place, and that's what real change is all about.

Let me now list several of the most important real changes I have seen take place in my years as a psychiatrist and for which I think nearly all people have considerable capacity.

1. A healthy and compassionate re-evaluation of oneself in relation to others and life generally. This is not to be confused with self-torturing ruminating and recrimination.

2. Developing more realistic expectations of self, others, and the world.

3. Developing interest in exploring and extending one's proclivities, talents, and interests. This includes any and all educational processes as well as creative possibilities.

4. Resolving long-standing emotional conflicts—about sex, money, relationships, parents, children, or whatever.

5. Deriving greater pleasure and satisfaction from what is available in life.

6. Reduction of self-hate and growth and enhancement of compassion and empathy for self.

7. Growth of self-acceptance, including both assets and limitations.

8. Developing dignity and humility (not humiliation).

9. Diminishment of false pride.

10. Giving up destructive addictions of all kinds.

11. Breaking destructive relationships and avoiding self-debasing and humiliating experiences.

12. Becoming capable of greater spontaneity as opposed to responding to rigid self-imposed constrictions.

13. Becoming increasingly aware of and interested in one's own feelings, ideas, and opinions.

14. Developing greater self-honesty.

15. Developing ever-increasing self-esteem (not to be confused with grandiose pomposity) based on an increasingly solid foundation of self-knowledge and knowledge of what constitutes being human. This involves surrender of illusions of having godlike omnipotence or/and suffering the glories of saintlike martyrdom.

Yes, people can *change*, really change. Most of us change in a thousand subtle ways all of our lives. Some of us are motivated—and have the ability for considerable struggle—to attain healthy growth *alone*. Many people need professionals to help them in their struggle. They need well-trained people to help uncover areas of stultification and paralysis and to restore hope and movement.

Q: I'm fifty-six years old and for the first time in my adult life I find myself relatively free. I've thought of spending my new-found time learning to enjoy art and music and even learning a foreign language. Is this possible for a woman my age? I have always enjoyed reading, but I have very little education and just about no experience with either music or paintings. Am I being foolish? Is it really too late for me and should I forget it?

A: It is certainly not too late and your desire to open doors to new possibilities and experiences is healthy, wonderful, and appropriate to any age, regardless of education or experience. Initial confrontation with unfamiliar material and experiences may be difficult and can, at first, require some time, struggle, patience. But this is a wonderful struggle, leading to self-growth and pleasure. I can think of little else that is more worthwhile. I wish you much enjoyment in your new explorations and in the self-realizing growth you will surely experience.

Q: I keep hearing that a man who is an incumbent, who is already in office, has an advantage in an election over adversaries seeking office. Why should this be, especially in the U.S.A., where we seem to like change so much?

A: We may like change, but a great many of us are afraid of it, and this applies to areas other than politics, too. Most of us prefer the familiar to the unfamiliar and find adaptation to new people, new situations, and new moods and feelings frightening and difficult. Over the years I have seen any number of people suffering from very long-standing depression who desperately wanted to be relieved of their pain but who at the same time clung to their depression and to situations that promoted it because it was familiar. In order to grow and to change—and this applies to all areas of life, of course—we must evaluate the relative value of change in each case, but we must do more than that. We must struggle against inertia and the false belief that clinging to the status quo is best. We must have faith in our ability to make new adaptations successfully when necessary. This is, after all, what our country is all about. So many of us are here because our ancestors resisted inertia, risked change, and refused to cling to static situations, however familiar, where they might have starved to death, been slaughtered, or enslaved.

Q: My daughter is thirty-one years old and is a lawyer. For a while she was involved in civil rights work and was particularly interested in the rights of women and in the women's movements generally. She is now married and has a young child and seems perfectly content to stay home and to take care of her family. Isn't this strange for a person who just a few years ago was all for women's liberation?

A: Personal liberation for both men and women involves having the choice to live a life that is personally fulfilling. This includes the right to change styles at different times in one's life. That your daughter freely delights in raising a family at this time in her life is no indication of loss of interest in the rights of women. That women have the free right *to choose* and are not coerced in any direction is what is crucial, not the particular choice made at a given time.

Q: Can you possibly tell me why some people have such incredible inertia? My husband won't change jobs, location, friends, or anything else.

A: People cling to the familiar and most often avoid and even dread anything unfamiliar. This is especially true of insecure people who tend to extend their feelings of identity beyond their own selves to the place they live, their job, and so on. A move to unfamiliar territory is felt as a loss of self and produces fear and anxiety. This results in avoidance of moves and clinging to the status quo. However, it is also possible that your husband is a happy man, content with his life as is, with no special motivation to change things for the sake of change.

Q: Is it possible for somebody who seems to be normal to hate to work? I've been working since I graduated from high school nine years ago, and I suppose I'm just naturally lazy because I'm sick and tired of it. If I had the money I'd just stay home and read books or take a few college courses or something. Sometimes I think being a housewife would be paradise.

A: Not everyone likes to work, but a great many people don't like the work they are doing. We are entitled as human beings to feel lazy at times, to want to quit and to take things easy. But working at what we like can give enormous satisfaction and the good feeling that comes with increased self-esteem. Interestingly, you mention reading books and taking college courses. Perhaps what you really desire is increased education, scope, and more interesting work than you are doing. While being a housewife can be highly satisfying, make no mistake about the fact that this is probably the hardest work of all, with hours no office worker would stand for. Life can be easier when we realize that there is in fact no paradise on earth that we are missing out on, but that each situation invariably has inherent advantages and disadvantages.

Q: I've always been stubborn—even when I know I'm being unreasonable—I never want to back down. People tell me I should be more flexible, but I grew up thinking stubbornness was necessary in a competitive society. What's your opinion?

A: I believe that being stubborn must not be confused with self-assertion or strength. People of real strength are seldom afraid of examination of issues and the possibility of constructive change. Chronic stubbornness and rigidity usually stem from poor self-esteem, underlying feelings of inadequacy, and neurotic pride. These cause feelings of vulnerability and a fear of being taken advantage of. This is all masked by stubbornness, rigidity, and often arrogance, too. People who suffer in this way usually have disturbed relationships and difficulties in performance of all kinds. As with many cases of emotional difficulty, neurotic elements are idealized, and in this case the belief is sustained that being stubborn represents strength of conviction. Unfortunately, people with this emotional problem feel that flexibility and productive changeability will make them feel weak and inadequate. This deprives them of the healthy and constructive possibilities and opportunities that flexibility makes available.

Q: Can a young woman change her ideas and belief and even her whole personality radically in a short time? Take the example of someone like Patty Hearst, who apparently never questioned her parents' way of life until she suddenly denounced it. I just can't believe it's a case of brainwashing. The people involved just don't seem expert enough to do that. What possible explanation can account for this kind of thing?

A: I can't tell you anything definitive about Patty Hearst since I don't know details of her personal history nor have I ever met her, let alone interviewed her. However, there are several explanations for the kinds of cases you describe; "this kind of thing," as you put it, might happen to:

1. A person with less-than-average intelligence who has for a lifetime taken orders from authority figures.

2. A normally bright person who has led a life of severe constriction and overprotection, and as a result has had a minimum of exposure to worldly goings-on. This kind of person has very little sophistication or self-reliance and always needs someone, anyone, to tell her what to do in order to "get along." She has simply never learned to cope with ordinary things on her own and suffers from moderate to severe emotional and intellectual dependency.

3. A person who suffers from what psychiatrists have sometimes called an "inadequate personality." This is someone who is essentially self-effacing, dependent, compliant and conforming. He takes on the coloration of his immediate social surroundings. Instead of having a good sense and feel of his own identity he reflects the personalities of people he is currently with. He is particularly drawn to people he considers strong and will take on their ideology as well as personality traits as long as he is in contact with them.

4. Someone who represses aspects of her personality and feelings. Such people do not know they are doing this. "Repression" takes place automatically and out of conscious awareness. This is especially true of strong emotions and most certainly includes .age against authority figures, particularly parents. Like a time bomb, the "right circumstances" may provide an opportunity that may result in a great emotional explosion, in which repressed aspects surface and take over. Thus, the formerly compliant, quiet person can suddenly become an incendiary revolutionary who displaces underlying rage at parents or to any authoritarian institution she identifies them with in her own mind.

5. A person who acts out rebelliously whenever he can in order to put down his enormous unconscious need to comply

and conform. This person rebels periodically in order to give himself a synthetic sense of self and self-esteem and to countermand what he feels has been "brainwashing" in his early life.

The kind of behavior you describe is not as uncommon as you may think. It occurs fairly often between prisoner and jailer, in which a prisoner comes to feel that his keeper is his big brother or father and acts accordingly. It sometimes also happens between hostages and their kidnappers, in which fear and uncertainty are converted to "instant neurotic love" and dependency. There have been many cases of this kind, in which victims have refused to prosecute their kidnappers and some who even felt a great sense of loss when they were finally freed. A few not only described greater loyalty to their tormentors than to their rescuers but also said they would happily marry them if they could. This kind of masochistic subservience is, of course, quite common in many marriages. In these cases a woman completely represses and subverts her own self as she adopts the ideals, thoughts, opinions, and even feelings of the person with whom she lives. This kind of severely neurotic self-hate and self-effacement is often confused with love, and its highly dubious virtues are too often extolled in books, movies, and songs. To a large extent it exists on a subtler, but nevertheless real level whenever we vote a particular way, like certain things, hate things and people only because our neighbors and friends do or because we think it is the current "in thing"—in short, whenever we conform without thinking or feeling *ourselves*.

In cases such as you describe the brainwashing that has taken place is never of recent origin. Current conditions may be optimal for the kind of behavior taking place, but the possibility of this kind of changeable behavior taking place at all is the result of conditions that have taken place years earlier. As with nearly all kinds of behavior, influence and conditioning during childhood are of prime importance. The key to most behavioral problems can be found in early family relationships, and the best preventative for destructive acting-out is therefore, of course, a healthy background and upbringing. This essentially means a family atmosphere characterized by warmth and real love. In this kind of healthy emotional atmosphere, children can freely and fully express and develop feelings and all aspects of their evolving personalities. They are neither overprotected nor neglected. They are encouraged to develop ideas, opinions, and talents, however they may be the same or different from other family members. This promotes a healthy self, strong self-esteem, and a capacity for having individual feelings and values that create a strong sense of personal identity. Furthermore, it prevents repression, the stunting of emotional and intellectual growth, general inadequacy, and severe suggestibility. Most important, it prevents confusion about one's own feelings and values.

Help Through Therapy

We are complicated creatures and we have created complex social structures. Any change in our lives can be fraught with anxiety and can create a great deal of turmoil. Some may be wise to seek professional help before making any major changes, although most people seek psychoanalytic help only when they are in pain. People with emotional difficulties often don't know where to go for help. Should it be therapy, group therapy, analysis, or what? The following are some of the most frequent questions I have been asked over the years by people seeking help.

Q: Can psychotherapy make you worse? I know that it can make you feel better—healthier and happier. But is the reverse ever true? I have a friend who has been in psychiatric treatment for several months and seems to be worse off for it. An honest answer to a simple question, please!

A: Your question is not simple. It is of primary importance that psychotherapy is practiced by a therapist who is well trained and qualified. Many people fall into the hands of quacks and do indeed get worse. They are, in fact, not in psychotherapy at all. Source of referral is all-important in this regard. So let the buyer beware!

Often what seems worse to one's friends and relatives is better for the patient. Many people like their friends to stay the same. In other words, they feel threatened by change. This is especially so if the patient is compliant and self-effacing and through psychotherapy begins to assert himself; in so doing the patient can become somewhat feisty and abrasive. His friends may not like it, but this change may be very good for the patient.

People in therapy often go through much trauma and anxiety at various times in their treatment. Revealing and facing difficult issues and problems about oneself and one's relationships can be very painful and disturbing. This often makes a patient seem worse for the moment but usually serves to make her or him better in the final analysis.

Q: What is the difference between "therapy" and "analysis"?

A: Therapy really includes all forms of treatment—chemotherapy, electroconvulsive therapy, hospitalization, music therapy, work therapy, psychotherapy. Psychotherapy includes behavioral modification treatment, supportive or reassurance therapy, group therapy, marriage counseling, as well as psychoanalytic psychotherapy and psychoanalysis.

I think your question relates mainly to the difference between psychoanalytic psychotherapy, often called therapy, and psychoanalysis, often called analysis. Both, of course, ought to be conducted only by psychiatrists, social workers, and psychologists trained in psychoanalysis. Both analysis and therapy are concerned with helping the patient to understand underlying problems of which he or she is not aware (because they exist on an unconscious level) and which produce a multitude of symptoms, including anxiety, depression, phobias, and compulsions as well as disturbed relating to self and to others. The main difference between psychotherapy and analysis from my point of view is intensity. In analysis the patient usually sees his doctor three or four times a week. In therapy the patient may have weekly sessions. Analysis usually lasts longer (at least three or four years) and goals involving large personality changes are usually more ambitious than those of therapy, which sometimes involves only solutions.

Q: I have decided to seek psychotherapy. As a woman, should I look for a woman analyst or a man? Does it matter?
A: Rarely, but on occasion, it can be helpful to see one or the other. This depends on the problem in question and on the history of the individual involved. This is best determined by consultation with a highly qualified psychoanalyst of either sex. Members of either the American Academy of Psychoanalysis or the American Psychoanalytic Association are graduates of qualified analytic training institutes and are usually well trained. It is particularly unfortunate when a woman is in treatment with someone who has prejudiced and stereotyped ideas about women. Male chauvinism occurs in both men and women therapists unless they themselves have been well analyzed and no longer suffer from constricting ideas promoted by a prejudiced society. Graduates of the American Institute for Psychoanalysis (recognized by the American Academy of Psychoanalysis) have been trained in Karen Horney's theory. She was one of the first psychoanalysts to make a considerable impact on prejudicial thinking and outlook with regard to women.

Q: My seven-year-old daughter seems to suffer from many inordinate fears. Someone suggested that I take her to a child psychoanalyst. Can a child be psychoanalyzed? How could she understand the doctor's interpretations?
A: The kind of formal psychoanalysis—lying on a couch and reporting all thoughts, feelings, and dreams—that is applied to adults is not for a seven-year-old. However, the trained child psychiatrist or child psychologist who has been trained in analysis makes use of his or her training and understanding in treating the child. The treatment of children

is highly specialized and may include play therapy, dramatic
acting out with models, conversations, and the like. The
methods are much different from those used in the treatment
of adults, but the goals may be the same. Both the adult and
child therapist tries to get at underlying difficulties and to
acquaint the patient with their real emotional problems and
their solutions.

Q: Can older people profit from psychoanalytic treatment,
or is this a form of therapy used only for the young?
A: Psychoanalysts used to believe, and some still do believe, that psychoanalytic treatment is applicable to relatively young people. Many of my colleagues and I believe
otherwise. Goals may be different for people in different
stages of life. But people of all ages can profit from insight
about themselves. I've had several people over seventy
years of age in analytic treatment who have done very well.

Q: I have a friend who has been in a hospital for the last
five years. She no longer seems to recognize me when I go
to see her. She has some kind of mental condition. I was
wondering if there is any purpose in continuing to go to see
her.
A: Absolutely!
    While she may not indicate that she recognizes you, she
may nevertheless know who you are. Even if she does not
know who you are, the fact of your visit probably registers
on her and has a therapeutic effect. It is extremely important
that a patient does not become a forgotten person. This is especially true of chronically ill people, be they young, old,
physically ill, or emotionally ill. Regular visits help hospitalized people to retain some sense of identity both personally and in terms of the larger world.
    Extremely important is the fact that hospital personnel
know who gets visits and who doesn't. Despite themselves,
some hospital workers lose interest in patients whose relatives and friends also demonstrate a loss of interest by sus-
pending visits. Along these lines, it is an excellent idea not

only to visit but also to ask hospital staff about how the patient is doing. Do not be intimidated! Ask and indicate interest and concern, especially if you feel that the patient is in any way being neglected. Remember that lack of interest in a patient both inside the hospital and outside contributes to a downhill course, especially with psychiatric cases.

Of course, there are times when we feel too fragile or vulnerable to go, and we must not hate ourselves for that. But we must fight the tendency we all have to separate very sick people from ourselves by forgetting and ignoring them. This comes from fear of sickness and, of course, nobody is exempt from the possibility. This makes it all the more important to contribute to any process that prevents the dehumanization of sick people. Visits and attention do that. They also do much more! They contribute to the visitor's personal feeling of humanity, which has a therapeutic effect.

Q: I'm fifteen years old. Do I feel better talking to someone when I have a problem because I get whatever it is out of my system?

A: That's part of it—feeling better through what therapists call ventilating. Regardless of age, it also makes us feel better to find out that other people have similar problems and that we are not "strange" but quite human. It often helps to talk in order to get reassurance or other people's wisdom, and experience and everything we may call *human* help. It also helps to relieve guilt feelings. Mainly it helps to reach out and to touch emotionally and to share human experiences with another human being.

Whom we talk to is all-important. It is important to talk to people who make us feel better and not worse. These are people who care about us and who care to share rather than to use us for their own purpose. These are people who do not somehow put people down in order to feel "up." They are not judgmental and moralistic. They are more interested in listening and sharing than in giving directions.

Q: Can you tell me if psychotherapy is effective for drug addiction?

A: I do know of some cases in which psychotherapy has been effective. But there are many factors involved, such as motivation of the patient; whether or not he continues to live with people who use drugs; how long he's been addicted; what drugs he uses; his emotional health in other areas; family cooperation. Actually, I suspect that very few addicts consult psychiatrists and even fewer stay in treatment for the time necessary to resolve major problems. Many people with serious addictions need hospitalization or at least much outside care additional to psychotherapy.

Q: I wonder if you feel that T.M. (transcendental meditation) can result in the great personal growth psychoanalysis can produce? I must say it has a calming effect on me. I really believe in it. Comment please?

A: To date I personally know of no treatment that replaces or equals psychoanalysis in helping a person realize her or his potential. The extent to which one is calmed by a particular activity is often directly proportional to the strength of one's belief in being calmed by the particular activity. The more one believes, the more effect it is likely to have.

Q: Is it true that psychiatrists are for the most part against religion?

A: No. Psychiatry and religion are not necessarily on opposite wavelengths at all. It depends on the individuals involved. There are a number of dedicated psychiatrists and psychologists who are also priests, ministers, rabbis, and nuns.

Q: Do you think that the ages of the patient and the psychotherapist matter? Is it better for the patient to see a doctor who is older?

A: This is a highly individual matter and depends on the people in question. Different therapists have different professional as well as life experiences and like all people have different levels of maturity. Some people do better with contemporaries, feeling that they have more in common and therefore a greater intimacy possibility of understanding each other. This is especially true of young people. Some older people are reassured by older therapists who they feel have acquired expertise born of years of living experience. But some feel better with young therapists, who to them impart a sense of vitality and optimism.

Q: Can you suggest a few psychoanalytic writers whose theories and books see women and their rights in a favorable and dignified light rather than just as statistics of men?
A: Karen Horney! Karen Horney! Karen Horney!

Q: If a person would like to go to a psychiatrist, why can't he without making it public? I'm referring to the fact that when you fill out job applications they ask this question. If a person were to say yes they would most likely not get the job. Doesn't this show that if a person does seek treatment that he or she is aware of a problem and is trying to straighten it out? Isn't this better than not going to a doctor at all? I think this procedure deters people from seeking help when needed. What do you think?
A: I agree with you completely and deeply regret any social pressure that inhibits people from seeking help when they feel they need it. There is, I believe, considerably less stigma associated with getting help for emotional problems than there used to be. Unfortunately, prejudice, ignorance, muddled thinking, and stigma still exist in this as in so many other areas of living. It is my belief that people seeking help are not only personally better off for seeking it and getting it but are also usually healthier than people who have no idea at all that they have problems. I have often said that my patients are for the most part healthier than the people they leave at home. Of course, people who are prejudiced and speak pejoratively of those seeking help are themselves sick and most in need of treatment.

I do not know the various state laws, but I do believe that it is unethical to probe into a person's life and hope that it is, or soon will be, illegal to ask about a person's psychiatric treatment. I believe that personal privacy ought to be a respected privilege in a free society.

Q: I am one of a group of women who meet once every two weeks to kind of talk things over. I guess you could call us a consciousness-raising or even a therapy group. How do you feel about groups like this?
A: Groups such as yours can be very valuable. Therapy groups permit ventilation, encourage mutual support, and enhance insight. Therapeutic groups permit members to learn how they interact, and this can be very helpful in relating to people generally. But the groups must not be used exploitively. This means that members must not use other members sadistically or vindictively. Unfortunately, some groups are taken over by leaders who are destructive and sessions are neither compassionately supportive nor therapeutic.

Of course, some very vulnerable people have emotional difficulties that may be ameliorated in group therapy but only if the group is led by a professional—usually a therapist trained in psychoanalysis.

Q: Do you believe in E.S.P. or that certain people really do have special mental powers—can bend keys and so forth without touching them physically?
A: No and No! I believe there are a lot of people who desperately want to believe and a lot of clever people and sleight-of-hand artists as well as con men who take advantage of gullibility and suggestibility.

As to E.S.P., I think that much that passes for it is the result of very keen observation, which often takes place very rapidly and almost unconsciously, so that the observer himself is unaware of having seen or learned something that is later attributed to a sixth sense. Also, some people have a special talent for both memorizing and putting together miscellaneous facts very rapidly. These and coincidence, I believe, explain those E.S.P. phenomena that are not the direct result of just plain chicanery and deft magicianship.

Q: Is it true that psychiatrists have their own emotional problems or even more than most people?
A: Being human, psychiatrists, psychologists, and psychoanalysts have the same problems that all other people have. Some have more. Some have less. Some of the best people working in mental health have been drawn to the field largely in response to their own problems. Awareness of problems and a willingness to do something about them—that is, undergoing analysis themselves—makes them so much better at the work they do.

Q: A friend of mine has been having psychoanalytic treatment for years. Why does this kind of treatment take so long?
A: The length of treatment varies from person to person depending on many factors, including age, motivation, nature of presenting problems, the goals desired, and so on. Serious treatment involving desired change and growth on a deep emotional level must take considerable time. Habits and problems that have existed for years take years to understand, to resolve, and to change. Relief of symptoms is most often much more quickly attained than changes in personality and ways of relating to oneself and others which caused the symptoms in the first place. Psychoanalysis is essentially an education in oneself. To learn about oneself on a deep emotional level is not easy or simple, since each of us is a member of the most complex species on this planet. This kind of education takes struggle and time, as do other educational endeavors of a much less complex nature.

Q: My family doctor advised me to see a psychoanalyst. I am a very anxious person and a chronic worrier and I do

think I can use some help. But my life is the way it is and I
don't want to upset everything by opening up a Pandora's
box. Am I wrong to feel this way?

A: The "everything" you don't want to upset probably
contains a number of items that are upsetting you—hence
your chronic worrying and anxiety. Psychotherapy does involve re-evaluation and if necessary rearrangements in life-
style that will make a more comfortable and happier life
possible. Fear of upsetting familiar ways and patterns is not
at all unusual because we are all afraid to enter unfamiliar
territory. But some of our most familiar "everythings" are
highly destructive to our well-being and in fact need to be
upset so that we can save ourselves. The qualified analyst
has no interest in causing upset for its own sake or changing
any situation that is constructive or has constructive possibilities. As to Pandora, treatment involves revealing and resolving problems, but it almost always results in finding
assets and resources in ourselves that we didn't know
existed or that have remained muted and quiescent for too
long.

Q: I have been in psychotherapy for a short time with a
man who has a Ph.D. in psychology. A friend of mine has
recently told me that M.D.s (psychiatrists) are more highly
qualified to do therapy than psychologists. Do you feel this
is true?

A: No. I have known unqualified psychologists and psychiatrists. The possession of the M.D. or the Ph.D. is not
the crucial criterion or guarantee of ability in this highly specialized area. I feel that the most important criterion is training by a good psychoanalytic institute (from my point of
view these institutes are recognized by either the American
Psychoanalytic Association or the American Academy of
Psychoanalysis), and this always includes personal analysis
of the student analyst. Of course, some therapists are more
talented and more dedicated than others, which is true of all
fields. Also, not every therapist is suitable for every patient.

Some people are better suited for the treatment of particular people while others do better with still others. But these variables aside, the criterion of maximum importance is psychoanalytic training.

How Do People Know They Need Psychiatric Help?

This is a very common and worthwhile question that I've been asked many times.

It is of prime importance that you get an expert consultation to determine if help is necessary and, if so, the kind of help that is appropriate for the particular problem. Be wary in this regard of well-meaning friends, relatives, and even family doctors. Some are discouraging for personal reasons. Many have their own chronic problems, which they prefer to keep buried. Others are afraid of angering or embarrassing you. Still others like to play amateur psychiatrist. Listen to yourself and, if you feel the desire despite what anyone else has to say, see an expert for a consultation. I feel that in this field as in others the best expertise rests with those people who have had maximum training. These are both psychiatrists (M.D.) and clinical psychologists (Ph.D.) and social workers who have been trained and have graduated from psychoanalytic institutes recognized by either the American Psychoanalytic Association or the American Academy of Psychoanalysis. My own feeling is that the person you consult ought to be a member or "fellow" of either or both of these organizations—a graduate of a recognized analytic institute with considerable training beyond. This initial consultation is extremely important because it will largely determine what, if any, course of action to take. Several visits may be necessary for this determination but again—much will depend on the qualifications of the expert you consult with!

I would advise professional consultation if one or more of the following fifty conditions or problems is prevalent:

1. Insomnia and unusual sudden and sustained restlessness.

2. Gross weight loss or weight gain despite negative physical findings.

3. Psychosomatic symptoms, including undue digestive disturbances, asthmatic attacks, migraine headaches, irregular heartbeats, and the like (plus consultation with a good internist).

4. Chronic destructive relationships, especially sadomasochistic ones.

5. Inability to keep a job.

6. General underachievement.

7. Phobias or fears, the causes of which are unknown.

8. Compulsions or having to perform certain acts or rituals without control or knowledge.

9. The inability to say no and general difficulty in asserting oneself.

10. Addictions—including food, alcohol, drugs, and tobacco.

11. Sexual difficulties.

12. Chronic boredom and inability to "find oneself."

13. Unusual difficulty with making decisions.

14. Chronic or severe anxiety.

15. Depression.

16. Excessive attacks of guilt and an overwhelming inappropriate sense of responsibility.

17. Chronic frustration.

18. Undue shyness.

19. Excessive jealousy, envy, and overprotectiveness (of spouse or child).

20. Hyperirritability and chronic fighting, especially over nonexistent issues.

21. Inability to express anger and/or other feelings.

22. Inability to have pleasure and to enjoy leisure.

23. Withdrawal and inability to sustain friendships.

24. Chronic bad judgment leading to frequent legal entanglements.

25. Accident and surgical proneness.

26. Any loss of mental function: memory, ability to think clearly, orientation in time, place, or person.

27. Sudden and pronounced change in personality and behavior.

28. Overtalking and overactivity.

29. Suicidal and/or murderous preoccupations.

30. Obsessive ruminating and worrying about issues, people, things with no basis in reality or in realistic responsibility.

31. Feelings of worthlessness and inadequacy, despite realistic reassurance to the contrary.

32. Heightened suspiciousness and fear of people.

33. Dread of new situations and undue and unusual fear of change.

34. Inability to accept aging process.

35. Heightened and sustained cynicism and bitterness.

36. Hallucinations: hearing voices or seeing things that aren't there.

37. General feelings of discontent, unhappiness, and lack of self-fulfillment without being able to find appropriate reasons or rationale.

38. Poor frustration tolerance.

39. Preoccupation with illness and death.

40. Preoccupation with possibility of sudden disaster of either personal or general nature—war, world destruction, illness, loss of job, death in family.

41. Sudden and inexplicable attraction, preoccupation, and infatuation with a person or persons much younger than oneself.

42. Marked decrease in ability to function.

43. Marked perfectionism in many areas of one's life leading to chronic sense of disappointment, sadness, and hopelessness as well as periods of resignation and relative lack of desire.

44. Inability to keep expectations relatively limited and realistic, leading to a sense of hurt and disappointment.

45. Chronic feelings of abuse by others.
46. Inability to spend money or to be kind to oneself.
47. Chronic feelings of martyrdom and always finding oneself in a martyred position.
48. Disturbed relationships owing to vindictive forays and undue despotism and arrogance toward others.
49. Seeming sudden loss of one's sense of humor.
50. Fascination and satisfaction with tragedy exclusively.

Peace Without Pills

Let me say right off that I am not always against the use of pills. Chemicals or drugs certainly do have a place in medicine, and some of them represent enormous progress in the alleviation and even cure of certain sicknesses. But please note that I say they have a "place in medicine." This means that their constructive use ends where medical expertise does not exist. In simple terms, pills prescribed or taken without judicious medical expertise and authority often have destructive effects and can even lead to death. Yes, I believe in the adage that a "doctor who treats himself is treating a fool." This applies to both laymen and to qualified physicians. Unfortunately, some physicians—licensed doctors— have also been so inundated by cultural pressures that they, too, prescribe medicines injudiciously and even carelessly. This applies especially to the use of "psychiatric drugs," which are taken indiscriminately and in huge numbers by the general population with and without medical sanction.

"Psychiatric drugs" do have their place. Psychiatrists and qualified psychotherapists certainly take no joy from sustaining or prolonging emotional pain. Indeed, medication can be most helpful in alleviating the pain of severe depression, severe anxiety, and even severe emotional disturbance. Used correctly, it can aid in the long-term goals of psychotherapy; it can curtail the need for more drastic treatment such as electroconvulsive therapy, and it can even save lives. But psychiatry is a highly specialized field, and the use of drugs in this area must be combined with psychiatric knowledge. This does not mean that general practitioners should not prescribe these drugs. It does mean that they should do so with the benefit of expert psychiatric consultation. This is no different from obtaining consultation from a specialist in any area of medicine.

Now I don't want to get into a technical description of the "psychiatric drugs" as regards either their biochemistry or their physiological effects. I just want to describe them in the most general terms as they affect people's emotions.

For many years, long before so-called modern drugs came into being, sedatives and hypnotics were used to mitigate anxiety and to treat insomnia. Many of these drugs fell into the category of what are known as barbiturates. They are still in use, and many people now as well as then have become habituated to them and have overdosed and killed themselves with them. They are useful but their use must be limited to strict medical control. Use in combination with alcohol can be deadly. Habituation to these pills, sometimes called "downs," can lead to experimentation with "ups" (amphetamines) and to strong physical addiction to hard drugs such as heroin, morphine, and Demerol. One of the main disadvantages of the old-time drugs was that in addition to a tranquilizing effect they also made the patient sleepy.

The modern drugs, used in proper dosage, can relieve anxiety and great tension with a minimum of drowsiness, so that the patient can feel better and still function. These drugs are largely divided into the categories of tranquilizers and energizers. Members of these groups are used to combat anxiety, depression, anti-hallucinogenics and psychotic symptoms such as hallucinations (hearing imaginary voices and seeing imaginary visions) and delusions or irrational beliefs. Some of these drugs are relatively mild and others are extremely potent. Of course, they all come in graduated doses. Some are useful in short-term treatment and have an immediate effect. Others are used over a period of months and even years, and their effect depends on the maintenance of a constant level of the drug in the patient's bloodstream. All of them are capable of both physiological and psychological side effects that may be harmful. Overdose and death seem to be less common than they were with the old-time drugs, and graduation to addicting hard drugs seems to be minimal. But psychological dependence is common.

Why do so many people so readily turn to pills for peace? This amounts to vast numbers of people even when we exclude those who indiscriminately medicate and overmedicate themselves for all kinds of imagined and real medical conditions. The number remains huge when we exclude people who use dangerous combinations of "highs" and "lows" and nonbarbiturate hypnotics (sleeping pills) in an effort to abandon reality. Unfortunately, this latter group comprises a considerable population, too.

We Americans have come to regard various aspects of the human condition in extreme terms. This applies to our concept of peace of mind. For many people, the slightest inner stress, disharmony, frustration, tension, disgruntlement, conflict, struggle, or anxiety produces fear and a quest for immediate relief. Very often, we become more anxious in response to a discovery of anxiety in ourselves than the initial anxiety warrants. In other words, we have become afraid of even the slightest inner turmoil and respond to inner stress with panic and hysteria, creating painful, vicious cycles. Without awareness, we make demands on the human condition that simply cannot be fulfilled. We demand that inner peace should reign supreme at all times. Since this claim is constantly thwarted, we feel cheated, angry, and frightened. We feel frightened because feelings of disharmony are interpreted as gross aberrations when they are compared to the models of ideal peace we have in mind. But the fact is that human moods are like the ocean's waves, currents, and tides. They are constantly changing in both quality and amplitude and can never be pinned down into any pure form. We are not vegetables, and sensitive and complex creatures that we are, we are constantly subject to stresses arising from ourselves, other close people, and the world generally. Our changeability is evidence of our aliveness and vitality and therefore any human mood, feeling, or attitude can only be human. Seeking pure peace is seeking death itself. Many people take pills in an effort to seek pure peace and in so doing are killing the most alive aspects of themselves. These people have forgotten that aliveness is comprised of all kinds of feelings and that inner peace consists of only relative comfort and is not stultifying inner deadness. We simply cannot produce sustained anesthesia without giving up the joys and beauty involved in full conscious aliveness. We cannot be fully conscious and alive without at times feeling turmoil as well as peace, frustration as well as satisfaction.

So many of us have come to confuse inner peace, which is relative, with inner deadness. This confusion leads to an unwillingness to face personal issues, to confront problems, and to make choices and decisions. In many cases tranquilizers have become substitutes for healthy struggle leading to free choice and personal growth. Yet, without the ability to make choices, even though pain may very well ensue, there can be no real freedom and the escape from choice obliterates one of the most valuable aspects of being human. Then why do so many of us use pills to deaden appetites and feelings, conflicts and issues, and the need to make choices? There are many reasons too numerous and complicated to take up here. Suffice it to say, some of us are afraid to face our illusions and life's imperfections. Some of us can't give anything up and choice always involves some surrender. Some of us fear our feelings—especially love and anger. Many of us have come to rely on the mistaken belief that we are too weak to tolerate frustration, struggle, or anxiety when, in fact, we are not that fragile at all. Anxiety cannot be avoided in making choices, in establishing personal values, in growing wise, in attaining real and relative inner peace, and in doing anything creative. Of course, I am not talking about overwhelming anxiety or tension. But every creative person, including most women who have given birth, describes a certain amount of tension preceding the birth—whether ideas or babies were the result.

Tension and anxiety—seeming to be the very opposite of inner peace—often lead to inner peace if we don't tranquilize them away. This sounds paradoxical, but it isn't. Anxiety is often a signal that something is going on in us that we haven't yet faced and that is attempting to surface. Allowing real feelings, desires, and ideas to surface not only results in growth of aliveness but also permits us the peace that is lost when we try to repress aspects of ourselves. For example, if I'm angry and don't know it because I push my anger down, the possibility of my anger surfacing makes me feel inner turmoil. Instead of drugging my feelings away, allowing that anger to surface will rid me of the fear of anger and permit me to be whole and peaceful with myself. This in microcosm is what happens in psychoanalytic treatment.

In expert hands and used judiciously, pills can be useful where anxiety and depression have become so overwhelming that inner peace has been for the moment utterly destroyed. But even in these cases pills are no substitute for insight. They may remove pain temporarily so that the struggle for personal knowledge can ensue. But they never take the place of personal knowledge. Therefore, therapists sometimes prescribe pills so that the patient can function as psychotherapy goes on. But ultimately we must learn about ourselves, our feelings, and our problems. We must come to realize that inner peace is relative and that we are capable of sustaining inner turmoil. These are the factors that really free us and make it possible for us to seek and to sustain what inner peace is possible and realistic in being fully alive and human.

Q: Please tell me, are you against the occasional aspirin, nose drops, antacid, or tranquilizer?

A: I am against any pill or medication taken against or without medical advice. This does not mean that the doctor has to be called before each aspirin or antacid is used. But he should have been consulted about them and frequency of use in the first place. The fact that a drug can be bought without a prescription is no guarantee that it is harmless either physically or psychologically. Likewise, ease of availability is no guarantee against its being habit forming.

Part Three

FEELINGS

OUR EMOTIONS ARE the result of deep reactions to people, events, and ourselves and they find different modes of expression in each of us. Some people react through dramatic presentations and lusty or kinetic activity. Others respond with physical symptoms or illness. The variety of expressions is as numerous as there are people.

Many times we get into difficulty because somewhere during our development we learned to hide our feelings from ourselves. However, the energy generated by these emotions has to be released. The emotion discharged often cannot be associated with the source. Thus, we are confronted with irrational fears, phobias, anger, jealousy, envy, and depression. Each of us has to learn our personal style of reacting so that we can become more openly responsive without distorting our feelings.

Chapter Eight

HAPPINESS

*Stress and Happiness • Love and
Romance • We Like to Be Liked*

HAPPINESS, TO ME, is *feeling good,* just that, *feeling good.* There are other ways of putting it: being at peace with oneself; feeling fairly comfortable; enjoying a relative sense of self-acceptance; being pain- and tension-free for the most part. Yet as simple as it seems, this stuff of happiness is often most difficult to find, and sustaining it for reasonable lengths of time can be even harder. While happiness is not the whole of life, it is, of course, an enormously important facet of human existence. Indeed, there is little else that makes life more worthwhile. Unfortunately, too many people find it impossibly elusive and some hardly ever experience it at all.

Fantastic experiences, magnificent accomplishments, tremendous good fortune, enormous assets sometimes bring moments of brilliant glory, feelings of great exhilaration, and sensations of exquisite triumph. But these moments of great stimulation, heightened sensations, and ''highs'' usually have little or nothing to do with *happiness* or *feeling good.* Indeed, they are often precursors of serious and even disastrous emotional depression. At best, their relationship is usually casual and even accidental. Feeling good is seldom the result of mountain-peak experiences. Feeling comfortable and happy frequently and for sustained periods of time usually happens in less rarified and in less heady atmospheres. In other words, happiness flourishes in the atmosphere of just plain everyday stuff. It is best nourished by ordinary, much less than glorious, human existence. In fact, it is found much more frequently in times of struggle than in times of triumph.

Q: I remember an article in which you said that happiness for you was a state of feeling relatively comfortable with yourself rather than monumental highs or periods of great exhilaration. I agree with you. May I ask if you agree with me that there has been too much concentration on achieving happiness and too many books and articles written on the subject?

A: Now it is my turn to agree with you. I think you are absolutely right! Happiness cannot be achieved by any head-on attempt to achieve it. There are no easy rules or lessons to be learned and no act of "simple willpower" helps. If internal emotional conflicts and problems block happiness they must be resolved and this usually involves professional help. If severe emotional problems are not blocking the way then what helps most is involvement with people and activities that are meaningful to us. Involvements that make us tap our inner human resources and thus lead to personal growth usually produce periods of relative happiness (and these are what we are humanly capable of—permanent absolute happiness doesn't exist) without even tackling the subject of happiness head on.

Stress and Happiness

Survival has involved almost impossible odds throughout the ages. Today, however, we have come to expect more from life than survival. We want to be successful at our work, recognized by our colleagues as contributors to society, sexy mates, wonderful parents, good children, ecology-minded (and at the same time possessing all the things this industrial age has to offer), well-read, fashionable, and, of course, thin! If we attain it all, can happiness be far behind? Unfortunately, it can be almost entirely obliterated if our self-esteem is based on cultural values that few achieve outside of the cinema or T.V. Our obsessive striving to fulfill illusory goals almost invariably prevents us from enjoying life and the healthy struggle that is part and parcel of being alive.

Reality in just about all areas of our lives is almost always helpful and constructive, even though it may at times be painful. I find facing the truth, knowing the worst, knowing what is ahead of me, far less threatening than circumventing reality by constructing illusions that deep down I know are false. Repression of reality eventually causes anxiety and contributes to emotional depression. Knowing the truth is like being in the eye of the storm. I feel calm and clear-headed.

I don't mean to suggest that people who have real troubles (serious illness, out of work, troubled children) should keep a "stiff upper lip." The situation calls for appropriate irritation and sometimes angry and sad feelings, too. However, once these emotions have been tasted we can go beyond them and help ourselves out of an emotional slump by taking some self-protective action. The following suggestions may be helpful in dealing with reality and with facing inevitable stress in our lives:

1. Keeping physically healthy and fit as much as is feasibly possible. This contributes to feeling good about oneself and to a sense of sureness and confidence, making it easier to deal with people and activities generally on an emotionally healthy level.

2. The struggle to accept and tolerate anxiety in the recognizable form of physical symptoms (palpitations, headaches, gastric upsets, and so on) as well as emotional symptoms (untoward fears, disproportionate worries, insomnia, ruminations) is very important. Anxiety begets anxiety. Getting anxious about being anxious produces a snowball effect. To the extent that we accept anxiety we

limit and prevent anxiety. This also gives us an opportunity to explore our fears objectively, to face our situations realistically, and to grow constructively. This is the antithesis of being inundated by metastatic anxiety. Interestingly, this is largely the substance and work of professional psychotherapy.

3. It is often helpful to make a realistic assessment of the stressful situation. Validate reality. Rarely is the situation of crisis proportions. Refuse to become demoralized by excessive anticipation of disaster.

4. Separate wants from needs, limitations from assets. Concentrate on those elements with which you can do something constructive.

5. Do not sustain relationships with people who patronize or denigrate you, your family, or your work.

6. We must not hate ourselves for past mistakes or blunders. Time spent ruminating over "what I should have done" is time and energy spent in the service of developing self-hate, wallowing in it, and leaving us paralyzed and helpless.

7. We must not blame those close to us with whom we share a common stressful burden. Mutual recrimination and attempts to lay blame on each other destroy morale and the benefits that mutual support makes possible.

8. One must be able to share confidences with at least one other person. This includes sharing angry as well as warm and loving feelings.

9. Sustaining a capacity for the enjoyment of food, sleep, and leisure activities without becoming compulsive or overindulgent has beneficial effects.

10. Make decisions and choices after a good struggle with the pros and cons without capitulating to inner tyrannies. Once you have decided, don't continue to agonize over the abandoned choices.

11. Do not hesitate to seek professional assistance if you are unable to handle stress well enough to get on with your life or if life seems to be much struggle and little or no happiness.

Love and Romance

The Language of Lovers

When I speak of the "language of lovers" I mean a language that applies to people who love people and who love the state of being human as well as people who are "in love" and love each other. This "language," and I use this term very broadly, may be used by all people who have a genuine desire to enjoy a relationship—any kind of relationship—with another or other human beings. People who desire really constructive relationships are, in fact, "lovers" of people, even though they may not be lovers in the conventional sense. As we go on, however, it will become increasingly apparent that the "language of lovers" is especially applicable to people who are engaged in a sustained loving relationship.

The "language of lovers" is based on a desire to communicate ideas, thoughts, and feelings, and especially feelings involving each other. This means having a strong desire both to understand the other person as well as to make oneself understood by the other person. Lovers are at least as interested in understanding their partners as they are in getting their points across or in being understood by their partners. This, of course, involves listening as well as talking—and I mean listening to more than words.

Listening in the broadest and deepest sense really means using ourselves to perceive and to observe all the ways we have of communicating. Lovers learn to observe and to understand the subtle meanings of body actions, especially hands, facial expressions, ways of dressing, and even smells and skin tones, as well as countless other subtleties that pass between partners. The fact is that people do express their feelings and underlying moods and emotional attitudes in the way they dress, the particular activities they desire at different times, their appetites for food, and other things. Many people smell one way when they feel free and easy and good and quite another way when they are anxious and depressed. Sweat glands and other glands quickly respond to mood and state of mind, as do skin tone and color. Lethargy indicates sadness or the beginning of emotional depression in some people, while in others it indicates a state of relative contentment and relaxation. Learning the nuances and subtleties of emotional communication is really the essence of getting to know each other. The more *open and perceptive* we are about receiving emotional messages, the more possibility exists for mutual understanding and the possibility of greater intimacy.

Of course, all this is predicated on the desire for ever-increasing closeness and the belief that increased mutual understanding and closeness increases the possibility of happiness. This is not to say that listening—even the best listening—is all of it. One must also speak, and the most important speech of all is that which conveys feelings. Since language is still the principal way we convey how we feel, we can readily see how destructive *imposed* silence can be. Talking openly is indeed of prime importance, but only if such talk is used to convey how we feel about all issues and especially about ourselves and each other. Speech is usually the best way to convey likes, dislikes, and desires of all kinds, and getting to know each other's desires in many areas is an important tenet of lovers. Of course, lovers of long-standing can often convey feelings and desires without words or by the most subtle gestures or facial expressions, but these must not be relied upon. New lovers, particularly, must talk, and even in talking they must be open, patient, and willing to struggle to understand each other because even when we talk and use the same language we don't always mean the same things and there may well be initial misunderstandings.

Lovers are interested in touching in all ways and through all the nuances and uses of love language. This takes time, patience, struggle, and, at least occasionally, frustration, too. The language of lovers is not an instant fabrication, but even more than with other languages takes much time and work. In this—probably the most soul-satisfying language of all—there are some extremely important dos and don'ts. The don'ts may be seen on a practical level as blocks to effective communication and relating and the potential for happy satisfaction therein contained. Let me list and describe some important characteristics involved in our quest to learn this "lovers' language."

1. While lovers are eager for closeness they also respect individuality and individual needs, desires, appetites, rhythms, feelings, and moods. They want closeness but not mutual imposition and the creation of a two-headed monster.

2. Language is used to understand one's partner, to convey understanding of oneself and one's desires, and to help one's partner better understand him- or herself.

3. Language used to manipulate one's partner, to make him over in one's own image, to hide feelings, to impose one's will is the antithesis of lovers' language.

4. Language used to subvert, to blackmail, to punish, to score vindictive triumphs over one's partner leads to mutual disaster.

5. Partners interested in who is right and who is wrong, winning and losing, or in getting even, getting their fair share, or competing with each other are destroying the language of love.

6. In using the language of love, partners are not interested in mutual judgment and moral equivocation. They are interested in mutual help and in the extension of mutual education and the solution of problems. They permit—indeed encourage and support the expression of—all feelings, especially angry ones, and they then sit down to a "love session," in which they try to help each other understand the basis of these feelings.

7. Lovers do not in any way use each other as exploited stepping-stones to self-aggrandizement.

8. Partners in this language do not use sullen silence as a weapon, nor do they harbor or sustain grudges. These are absolutely poisonous to lovers' language.

9. Every attempt is made to build common interests, areas of mutuality, and an understanding of each other's values and respect for them. These loving partners come to value the same and similar things, activities, places, and people and to share feelings and ideas openly about them, even as they permit individual proclivities and activities.

10. "Lovers of people" try as much as possible to understand and to accept the limitations, conflicts, confusions, and complexities inherent in being human. They therefore try to minimize grandiose illusions and exorbitant expectations as regards the world, people generally, and especially each other.

11. Lovers do their best to love themselves—truly to love and take care of themselves—and to stand up against any self-hate whatsoever. This is the best guarantee against projecting hate and blame onto their partners.

12. Lovers learn that their language is always enhanced by caring for and about each other and also by sharing fun as well as problems.

The language of lovers is never ideal, nor does it even approach perfection. How can it? People are not perfect. There are many times when we will falter, when personal pride, confusion, and prejudices will cause a communication breakdown. But where underlying love is present, these too can be used constructively, because we can learn and produce growth from problem areas if we are willing to struggle. Is the struggle for mutual understanding worthwhile? Of course it is! Indeed the language of lovers is the stuff of anti-hate and anti-war on any level. It is a language that springs from the depths of our humanity and contributes so much back to our humanity. It is a language designed to give us much needed closeness, warmth, and happiness, and it can grow as we can—all the days of our lives.

Q: I'm a liberated man. I'd like to sound off about the notion that women are more romantic than men. I don't think so. I am more romantic than any woman I have met. I was more romantic than my first wife, and, though I have not remarried, I'm looking forward to seeing someone "across a crowded room" whom I will fall madly in love with and marry. Which sex do you think is more romantic?

A: I like a man who wants to learn what women are all about and so will read magazines geared to the ladies. Through my clinical experience I have not found that women are more romantic than men. In the past, being romantic was considered a feminine characteristic. That is, the culture encouraged women to daydream about the man in shining armor, riding a white horse, who would come along and sweep them off their feet. Society has also led women to believe that they must receive hearts and flowers on Valentine's Day, and that little surprise gifts and thoughtful gestures are their due.

Now that we are taking a more liberated attitude toward what were traditionally male and female characteristics, men are allowing themselves to recognize their "softer" feelings, their more romantic feelings. Eventually, we probably will see no difference in romanticism between men and women. I hope the ladies will accept this "new romanticism" in men and encourage it by being liberated enough themselves to send flowers and to extend all the little romantic gestures that were once on the "ladies only" list.

I'd just like to add a brief note here about your "across a crowded room" statement. Let me caution you about this type of reaction. Sometimes this may be used as a defense against meeting and falling in love with a real person. We have to be careful not to let our romantic illusions destroy real and constructive possibilities.

Q: Do you believe in love at first sight?
A: I believe that many people are in love with love; that instant chemistry does exist and so does instant infatuation. I believe that complicated relationships involving love take time and mutual emotional investment.

Many people are vulnerable to "love at first sight" because of a great need and eagerness to be in love. These are the people who are in love with love. They usually have an idealized fantasy of the person with whom they can fall in love and easily project this image to any person who resembles this prototype. While it is true that chemistry or physical attraction is often immediate between some people, this aspect of love is only love's beginning and must not be confused with the entire complex process. Instant infatuation or worship of one's own projected fantasy of an ideal lover only occasionally develops into a sustained love relationship. This is so because disappointment usually follows idealized, exaggerated romantic expectations.

Sustained love is not instant and involves long-term relating largely because it takes considerable time for people to get to know each other; that is, really to know each other without fantasy aberrations. It also takes time for people to share common experiences and to share mutual growth and change. More than anything, it takes time for people to care about each other and, from my point of view, mutual caring or emotional investment in each other is what sustained, mature love is all about.

Q: Since I've been a child I've periodically heard the expression "gift of love." I've wondered about it. How does one really show love for someone else? I mean beyond the "I love you" and other affectionate gestures. What do you think?
A: I think we give love whenever we make people feel better about being themselves, regardless of how we do it. Self-esteem is one of the greatest emotional assets. When we help someone to raise his or her self-esteem, we are certainly producing and giving a "gift of love."

We Like to Be Liked

We like to be liked.

It makes most of us feel comfortable and secure; it brings on warm and even sweet feelings not unlike those of early childhood. Being liked is equated with being accepted, cher-

ished, cared about, and taken care of and protected. When
we felt liked as tiny children, we were given an enduring
message about our importance to our family and to the human species, and that message provided self-esteem and a
deep sense of personal security and self-confidence the rest
of our lives. It made it possible for us to develop from children into healthy, independent adults. But if the message is
obscure, or if it is delivered poorly or if it isn't delivered at
all, we never become healthy adults. Unfortunately, some
of us, born of insecure, disturbed parents, never get the message. Some of these parents confuse overprotection with liking, and overpermissiveness with good care. Some of them
are too self-occupied to convey any feeling at all, even
though they go through the mechanical motions of child
care. These are parents who do not treat children as if they
like them, and there are those who dislike and even hate
their children. They exploit, manipulate, and vilify and hurt
whomever they are in close contact with.

To the extent that we have felt liked as kids we will have
self-esteem and a sense of being independently grown up as
adults. This means that as adults we enjoy being liked and
feel warmly disposed toward the feeling. But—and this is
all-important—we will not feel obsessively dependent on
being liked. Our well-being will not hinge on whether or not
we are liked. We will not go through life in an obsessive
quest to be liked. We will not efface ourselves, automatically conform, and do just about anything at all, however
much it ultimately is hurtful to us, in order to be liked.
Those who suffer low self-esteem, who have not, for whatever reason, felt liked as children (and this feeling may well
be repressed and unconscious in adulthood) place unusual
importance on being liked. Many spend entire lifetimes in
an effort to be liked. This effort largely represents the desire
to be liked by parents, to compensate for the feeling of less
than total acceptance by parents when they were children.
Often, the quest for being liked becomes highly exaggerated
and quite destructive. They want to be liked all of the time
by everyone. All kinds of popularity contests must be won

and won constantly. Any kind of even seeming rejection can produce awful hurt for weeks and months. Destructive relationships are entered into repeatedly in an effort to find the perfect loving parent substitute, and each disappointment brings grievous self-hurt. Claims and tests are made on friends, lovers, mates, and children to prove their love. These tests are always failed and lead to disturbed, hurtful relationships. But the worst hurt is the self-blackmail and the lack of regard for real needs and self-enrichment as the quest to be universally liked or loved demands total time and energy. This virtually guarantees a continuation of low self-esteem, dependence on other people in order to be happy, and failure to become independent and truly self-nourishing. Again, all of this is relative; it exists in all of us to a degree.

Most of us are likable. But this does not mean that we are liked by everyone all of the time. Some people like us, some don't, and some are indifferent. Shifts take place so that some who did, do and some who did, don't. Some people like some aspects of us and don't like other aspects of us. Much depends on the feelings and moods of the particular people in question and these, too, shift from time to time. Some people are so preoccupied with being liked themselves they have little of themselves left to invest in liking others. Some of these people like, or at least think they like, only people whom they think like them.

Being universally liked has been made much too much of in our society. This may well be evidence of much low self-esteem and immaturity in our population.

Yes, it is nice and feels good to be liked. It is crucial among family members. Of course we also dislike one another at times and should show it. People who really like each other give each other the right to express angry feelings and the truth of how they feel. They do not gloss over with phony sweetness. But being liked is not all that important and its role in bringing happiness has been grossly exaggerated.

Being ourselves, honestly ourselves, almost always makes us more likable. Phony acts almost always have the reverse effect. Therefore, the less we are preoccupied with being liked and the less we manipulate in order to be liked, the more we are liked. The more we like ourselves, the more we can be ourselves; the more we can be ourselves, the more we are liked by others—relatively, not universally, absolutely, or always!

Those of us who feel disliked and who are preoccupied with being liked and with constantly winning popularity contests do not like ourselves. Those of us who are always in quest of perfect partners, perfect love, and are obsessed with being loved rather than with being loving do not like ourselves. Those of us who obliterate our own feelings and needs in order to conform and to be liked do not like ourselves. Liking ourselves is crucial. Without real love of self (never to the exclusion of others) we can never realistically evaluate or appreciate love from others. However much we are liked and loved by others, we will doubt that love's authenticity, because as long as we don't love ourselves we will not believe anyone else can love us. For those of us obsessed with being loved, love of self must be improved. Often this can be done only with professional help to seek out the roots of early poor self-esteem.

Q: Is it so bad to want to be liked by people? My daughter says I won't take a stand on anything because I am afraid of antagonizing someone. Maybe she's right, but isn't she missing out on much if she is not liked?
A: It is nice to be liked and sometimes it's even useful. But the compulsive need to be liked by everyone all the time robs us of knowing who we are, what we really feel, what we want, and our own inner vitality generally. It makes "yes, nothing people" of us and eventually fills us with self-contempt and misery. Being liked, popular, and admired are terribly overrated commodities in our society. Some people are amazed at how well they can get along being liked only sometimes by some people and how much better they feel about themselves. This is, in fact, the most important issue—how much we like ourselves. When we

like ourselves sufficiently we can spontaneously and fully participate in life and relate to people without a crushing and constricting concern for being liked.

Q: I want to ask you about my wife. She is really a very sweet and fine person. She is liked by just about everyone we know. As a matter of fact, she goes out of her way to be liked. She admits that it's very important to her. But periodically she puts her foot in her mouth. What I mean is this. We go to a party or gathering and she blurts out something that is unbelievably hostile. Later on she wants to bite her tongue but it's just too late. She swears she has nothing at all against the person she inadvertently hurt, but out it comes. Why does she do this?

A: People who have a more than usual need to be liked have great difficulty showing displeasure, let alone anger. They fear that an expression of anger will lead to being disliked. They have unfortunately convinced themselves that being universally liked is the only way to feel safe and secure in this chaotic world. As a result surface sweetness often masks a good deal of repressed anger. This anger comes out unexpectedly and inappropriately. This means that hostility may be displaced from its original object to someone who has nothing at all to do with evoking anger in the first place.

The only cure to these inappropriate "angry slips" is giving up the quest to be universally liked. This permits anger to be felt and expressed appropriately so that unexpected and inappropriate expressions from a hidden storehouse don't take place. Of course, this is not easily done. Giving up the image of utter sweetness and lovability can be most difficult. But it can also be an immense relief to all concerned. The fact is that none of us is that sweet. We are nearly all capable of lovability and sweetness, but this does not preclude getting irritated and angry, too. All feelings and characteristics are part of being human.

Q: My husband tells me that I gossip a great deal and to tell you the truth I think he is right. But why do I do it? I've tried to stop but I just can't and always find myself gossiping with friends all over again. Is it because I'm really a bad person? I have a lot of friends and I think I'm a pretty good person otherwise. What do you think?

A: I think that gossiping has nothing to do with being either good or bad. We all gossip at times. For most of us, people are after all more interesting to talk about than any other subject. But compulsive, chronic gossiping usually involves one or more of several unconscious needs. Some people gossip in order to make contact with other people. This is their way of reaching out and touching and is sometimes evidence of insufficient deep involvement with other people. Some people gossip as an effort to dilute boredom, which largely comes from lack of development and use of one's own inner resources. These people have insufficient involvement with activities that could provide interest and satisfaction. A great many gossips do it as a means of expressing repressed anger. This anger may be at the individual gossiped about or may be displaced to that individual from another person with whom the gossip is really angry. Most compulsive gossips do it as a form of entertainment for friends in order to be liked and admired. They really think that they are putting on a kind of show and feel they need to do this as a form of gift giving in order to sustain the friendship. Of course, this is an indication of feelings of poor self-worth and insecurity. Other people gossip as a means of "putting someone down" in order to raise themselves up or as a means of attempting to dilute feelings of inferiority. Getting over this compulsive activity often necessitates psychotherapy in order to get at the roots of this kind of psychological symptom.

Q: I have a girl friend who is very promiscuous sexually. Do some people just have more sex drive than others? If this is so, would hormonal treatment help? I'm afraid she may get into serious trouble one day because she seems to wind up in bed with just about any man, including many she hardly knows.

A: Some people have more drive than others in sex and in other areas of their lives, too, but this has nothing to do with compulsive sexual acting out. Hormones are not the answer in this case and hormone treatment for any condition at all can be dangerous and must be given with utmost care.

Sexual promiscuity is often the result of a desperate need to be liked and an inability to say no. Many promiscuous people are inordinately frightened of rejection and will comply with any request at all in order to be found acceptable and worthy. People with very low self-esteem often feel enormous and inappropriate gratitude for time spent with them. They believe they have nothing to give other than sexual gratification. If they don't give it they feel they are giving nothing at all and in this way they are cheating whoever deigns to spend time with them. Help in this area must be sought from a competent psychotherapist rather than through hormonal treatment.

Q: I strongly suspect that my sixteen-year-old daughter is sexually active. What bothers me most is that I have the feeling that she isn't really enjoying it at all. I think she and probably some of her friends, too, are mostly involved in order to feel they belong and for status. What can I do? I feel hurt.

A: Many adolescents act out sexually on the basis of compliance and conformity. Indeed, their need to conform often leads them to other activities that are unquestionably destructive, including taking drugs and smoking. This is especially true of adolescents who have poor self-esteem, who are compliant, or who react to a need to conform by rebelling. Of course, they view their acting out as growing up and the most conforming are particularly susceptible to peer pressure. Therefore, who their peers are, where they live, and the kind of schools they attend are of prime importance. Unfortunately, we live in a society in which popularity and being liked have taken precedence over self-worth and self-care. A great many girls and young women consent to sexual involvement only because they are terrified of rejection. We must all learn that rejection is common in life and need not be devastating if we can cope with our own hurt pride. This frees us from blackmail and permits us to act as we really desire to act rather than in compulsive, compliant ways.

It is of paramount importance that you discuss these issues with your daughter. The goals of the discussion are to find out if she is, indeed, acting out compulsively as a self-blackmailing device; to clarify the issues I mention above; to make certain that she understands principles of pregnancy and contraception; to convey information about dangers of venereal infection (without terrifying her); and mainly to convey your understanding, your caring, and your support. This can be done only in a warm, loving, nonjudgmental atmosphere. Moralizing, recriminations, and harsh judgments will make things worse. A dialogue involves a warm exchange and not a stern lecture. You must keep in mind that her welfare must take precedence over your hurt feelings if your talk is to be constructive.

Q: I'm eighteen years old, fairly attractive and I have dates pretty much. But I'm not nearly as popular as a few other girls I know. Do you think I'm wrong to be concerned? My mother says that popularity isn't all that important, but I don't know. I think she's just trying to make me feel good.
A: Your mother is on the right track. I think the need to be universally liked, admired, and popular runs rampant in our society. I think it breeds compulsive conformity, compliancy, loneliness, and boredom. I think it is the enemy of individuality, spontaneity, a strong feeling of self-identity and self-esteem.

Popularity is a highly questionable asset and has been greatly oversold to young people by parents, the media, and advertisers. I have not known it to bring self-realization or happiness. It is addictive and as with all addictions is a slave master requiring more and more proof of its existence. It is never an adequate substitute for the satisfactions inherent in a few, meaningful relationships, let alone from one mutually satisfying relationship. Its obsessive quest often leads to deep loneliness. This is so because energy and time used in its pursuit destroy the possibility of meaningful relationships in which caring and a mutual expression of feelings are exchanged. Lack of this exchange eventually produces a chronic, deep yearning for closeness and a sense of emptiness however much popularity is in evidence.

Q: I have a friend who absolutely worships movie stars. I think most of her life is taken up with fantasies about these people whom she sees as just about perfect. What is this kind of thing about?

A: All of us have unconscious and not so unconscious idealized versions of ourselves. Karen Horney called this phenomenon of seeing ourselves as superhuman, glorious personages the idealized image. Projecting this image constituting all characteristics we see as perfect to movie stars is relatively easy. Not really knowing them helps, inasmuch as knowing any human being close up immediately puts us in touch with their human limitations. We also tend to identify them with idealized roles they play, publicity about them, and general adulation of them stimulated by their agents and the media. People who have a poor sense of personal identity, have low self-esteem, and live a large part of their lives in their imaginations are particularly suggestible and subject to this kind of projection. Unfortunately, this kind of process often adds further to the belief in an unreal world inhabited by unreal "perfect" people. People like your friend often use this kind of distant worship to live vicariously, and in so doing make little use of their own lives and real possibilities.

Q: I have a friend who is twenty years old, and all she really cares about is being a celebrity. She is desperate to be famous enough someday so that people will recognize her and point her out no matter where she goes. What kind of problem does she have?

A: Our society is celebrity conscious to an enormous degree. Fame is extolled beyond almost all other achievements. Being known is equated with success as well as with mythical everlasting happiness. Being a celebrity for many people immediately confers every conceivable kind of expertise. I believe that television is largely responsible for this phenomenon. On talk shows actors and actresses are regularly asked questions about areas about which they know nothing. Unfortunately, many of them answer with inappropriate authority. Much that happens on T.V., from award-presentation shows to golf tournaments, paints a picture of a heavenly world that only famous people can enter. Your friend and countless other people have been unduly influenced by this manufactured myth. But some people, including your friend, are particularly vulnerable to these dreams of glory. These are people who feel that their lives are particularly shoddy and impoverished. Many people obsessively seek outside confirmation of their existence because they lack self-esteem and a sense of who they really are. Unfortunately, no amount of outside adulation adequately compensates for feelings of inner impoverishment. Likewise, there is no special heaven on earth, even for those who are instantly recognized on the street or elsewhere.

Chapter Nine

SEXUALITY

What Is Sex Appeal? • Flirting • The Most Asked Questions About Sex • A Sex Mental Health Quiz

What Is Sex Appeal?

I BELIEVE THERE is a universal sex appeal. That is, there are people who seem, for a sustained period of time, sexually appealing to just about everybody. But you may be surprised to find out that these people do not necessarily fit our society's usual criteria and standards for beauty and attractiveness. Of course, society's standards, fashion's dictates, the media, all play a role in influencing us. In effect, they tell us who and what (manner of dress and the like) to find attractive; we are brainwashed at a very early age. But people who attempt to comply, and even those who successfully comply with all the standards, do not necessarily come across as particularly attractive. Indeed, many are seen as rather exhibitionistic and little else. Of course, our experience, especially our early background with mothers, sisters, fathers, brothers, friends, and prototypes we consider ideal, has much to do with individual taste and attractions. Character structure also plays a very important role. Sex, after all, is never separated from the rest that goes on in us and is almost always an extension and mirror of how we relate generally.

Thus there are those who are rather dependent, who find independence in people sexually attractive. There are those who are shy, who are drawn to gregarious people. Those who felt vulnerable and hurt in childhood are often drawn to those who seemingly need our help and protection now in adult life. There are creative people drawn to people who provide admiration and support of further creativity. Some people who feel that their own lives are dull, mechanical, and prosaic are sexually attracted to people who project the illusion of glamour and mystery or who seem to be exotic. Some outgoing, effusive people are drawn to highly reserved people, and each finds the other challenging and sexually attractive. However clichéd it may sound, there are many who have not resolved early feelings for parents and are attracted to people who represent good mamas and good papas, and yes, there are many who are masochistic enough to seek out sadistic partners and vice versa.

I feel that those who are essentially healthy and relatively problem-free will find people sexually attractive whose main appeal is to their mental health rather than to that which is sick in them. They will be attracted to people with whom they can communicate, really exchange feelings. They will find people sexually attractive who like and care for themselves and who are capable of caring for others also. They will be drawn to cooperative partners rather than to competitive partners. They will be drawn to people with whom they have enough in common to be able to grow together rather than being so diverse in aspirations and interests that they will grow apart.

Of course, we develop a self-image at a very early age, and we also develop an image of the person we see as our sexual ideal. Different people, because of early influences, will be drawn to different physical attributes. These certainly play a large role in providing the initial chemical spark that draws people together. But they don't play as much a role as character influences in sustaining a sexual relationship. They also don't play as large a role as healthy mutual emotional investing—caring for and about each other's well-being—over the long run, and they don't account for universal appeal.

So what does make some people universally sexually appealing? I think it's the very important message these relatively rare people convey. The message is one of acceptance and openness. An invitation is sent out and in effect it says, "You needn't fear rejection, hurt, perfectionist and harsh judgment, being absorbed, exploited, used, ridiculed." These people convey the impression of self-acceptance, emotional health, and personal well-being, and they somehow let us know that they will find us humanly acceptable. They also make us aware of their own healthy spontaneity, vitality, and aliveness (not to be mistaken for noisy, synthetic affectation), and this helps stimulate us and put us in touch with our own vitality; it immediately makes possible a flow of feelings, an open emotional exchange to take place, and this is the stuff of real sustained sexual appeal.

Can a person's sexual appeal be enhanced? I'm talking of the deep, sustained variety. Yes, but from my point of view it is not easy. What it really involves is self-acceptance and the development of one's own proclivities. This never fails to attract people. We cannot accept others if we don't accept ourselves. If we reject ourselves we will reject others. Deep down we know this, even though we may be drawn to relationships neurotically. When we like ourselves—really like ourselves—other people feel that we can like them, too, and this never fails to attract! To the extent that self-realization takes place, we are attractive sexually and otherwise because self-development, vitality, and openness never fail to come through. A patient of mine recently said that she knows she is sexually appealing when she feels good about herself, and I believe it!

Flirting

Birds, fish—so many creatures, and people, too—all flirt. I've watched birds and fish execute elaborate rituals designed both to test and to interest others in potential relationships. For people, too, flirting may be considered the initial steps taken to establish contact. These *steps* may or may not go on to include sexual teasing and sexual availability. Some flirting is in itself a form of achieving sexual satisfaction. This means that some people are sexually satisfied by flirting and going no further. Some flirting has almost no sexual overtones at all. This sometimes goes on between highly intellectualized people who are content to charm each other with exchanges of cerebral statements and mutual esteem.

From my point of view, flirting is a way of making contact, of stating, "I'm interested," and asking, "Are you?" It's the opening sequence in all kinds of relationships, ones that are superficial, fleeting, or of minimal consequence, and ones that may turn out to be of lifelong duration. Flirting is a signal that, in effect, states, "Let's begin." Begin what? In some cases just touching and in others holding, sustaining, exchanging. And yet in all flirting there is at least some exchange of feeling and of interest. Flirting often takes place in advance of verbal exchange and may take place and conclude without an exchange of words taking place at all. Flirting—the process itself—can be so subtle as to go unnoticed by either outside observers or the participants themselves. Yes, sometimes we flirt without conscious intent and on occasion by gesture or glance convey emotional questions and answers to each other without conscious awareness. Casual observers sometimes know that we are flirting and attempting to evoke contact and interest while we keep it a secret from ourselves. Some flirtations are anything but subtle. They are blatant and everyone knows what is going on. But there are also blatant flirtations, in which no one comprehends, until to everyone's surprise a marriage has taken place. This is often true of teenage hostile bantering in which all kinds of derisive remarks, shows of lack of interest, and the like are used to cover up great interest and are also used to guarantee continuing contact. A single flirtation can go on for half a second, for example, a glance on a subway train. There are many flirtations that go on for a lifetime, sometimes sporadically but as a continued serial play each time the flirting couple meet.

Flirting is used to make contact or to exchange feelings; it can be an outlet or substitute for deeper relationships or for mutual support. There are couples who have an unexpressed and often unconscious agreement, which in effect goes like this, ''We shall flirt and in this expression of continuing mutual interest we shall reassure each other that we continue to be attractive people.''

Nearly all people flirt. Nearly all of us from a very early age have at least some consciousness of some aspect of ourselves we can present to other people as a form of attraction in order to make contact. Some of us do it with looks, with attire. Some with particular motions and expressions. Some of us do it with hand gestures, with eyes, with a look around the mouth, with a way of moving around a room. Some of us do it with words. Nearly all of us know the limits of acceptable flirting, of the social proscriptions involved, of what is and isn't appropriate and acceptable. Yes, we are all flirts and most of us go on flirting all of our lives. Perhaps, in part, flirting serves the purpose of a relatively noninvolving, innocuous emotional safety valve as well as a stimulating device for people who have relatively good long-term relationships. They may flirt with others but go home and make love to each other, a practice largely condoned by society and usually mutually agreeable as long as the flirting remains relatively light, casual, and subtle.

I believe that we learn to flirt from our parents. It is seldom taught consciously, that is, through actual lessons or instructions. We continue learning through siblings, other relatives, and friends.

Some extremely shy people cannot flirt and are unable to initiate relationships. This may lead to extreme loneliness and unhappiness. Some of these people come from homes in which parents were extremely restrained and did not show or permit demonstrations of any kind of flirting activity; some can be helped to learn to flirt by actual instruction by well-meaning confreres. But there are also people who are incapable of initiating contact on more than a social level. In effect, they cannot flirt with serious involvement of any kind: career, school, job, or whatever. Some feel that they have nothing to show of interest or to give anyone, and that they don't deserve to receive anything either. These people need professional psychotherapy to put them in touch with their own assets and to make flirting in all areas of life possible.

The Most Asked Questions About Sex

Q: Does the fact that I sometimes have love dreams about other women mean that I am not normal?

A: It means no such thing. "Love dreams" both of a sexual and nonsexual nature involving members of the same or the opposite sex are exceedingly common in both heterosexual and homosexual people. These dreams are very often indications of a desire for closeness and warmth. We often express these desires sexually because sexual feelings are strong enough to convey messages to us about our feelings that we may otherwise keep hidden.

Q: My husband is eager for what I consider abnormal sex. He keeps assuring me that nothing that gives pleasure is abnormal. Since I do not enjoy it, what should I do?

A: Re-examine and redefine your concepts regarding what is normal and what is abnormal. Many people eventually practice a great variety of sexual activities which, if they are not destructive physically or emotionally (sadistic practices with an unwilling partner), are abnormal only in the eyes of the beholder—or in this case the practitioner. Some people are terrified of being "bad," of letting go, and of engaging in any practice, sexual or otherwise, that smacks of too much freedom and gives too much excitement, fun, or pleasure.

Q: My mother once told me that I shouldn't have sex during my menstrual period. Is this right or is it just a hangover from Mother's era?

A: It's a hangover. Many women enjoy sex during their periods and suffer no harm at all. It is largely a question of individual taste and desire.

Q: Why has my sex drive decreased since I've been on the pill?

A: This may be because you lack confidence in the efficacy of this method of contraception. For many women, desire is enhanced. Since the pill affects hormonal balance, I suggest you consult both your internist and gynecologist about this problem.

Q: Sometimes my husband is so upset if I don't have an orgasm that I feel it is better to pretend I did. Is this terribly wrong since I know what I'm doing and it gives my husband such pleasure? I do enjoy sex. It's just that I can't achieve climax every time.

A: What is wrong is that you both feel obligated to respond simultaneously and with the same intensity. Your husband's pride in his ability to make you respond is hurt if you don't, and you, in turn, are afraid of making him feel inadequate through imagined inadequacy on your part. It may be a great relief for both of you to talk this matter over and to rid yourselves of the need for consistent mutual orgasm or the pretending that is used as a substitute for it. Mutuality of desire as regards time, place, and frequency is never perfect. The mutual desire for orgasm and response in general is never perfect. The most loving couples, including those who have highly satisfactory sex lives, are often arrhythmic. Therefore, it is exceedingly common that people do not share orgasm or intensity of feelings sexually or otherwise, each and every time. If your husband cannot accept this reality, it may well be an indication of considerable confusion about his masculinity and at least some psychotherapy would be helpful.

Q: Can a woman my age (fifty-four) have a satisfactory sex life with a man of thirty-two? Yes, I am "hung up" about our age difference.
A: Much depends on the people involved. There may be no difficulty in terms of the actual mechanics of sex, but the kind of relationship that ensues eventually reflects how they relate to each other generally. Therefore, questions of importance would include: mutuality of interests, values, experiences, insights, level of intellect, and so on. If, despite your ages, you have much in common, then a satisfying relationship is conceivable. But young men who are attracted to much older women often suffer from serious personality and emotional problems that sometimes don't show up till later. (These problems often affect their ability as sexual partners.)

Q: My seventy-one-year-old husband's sex drive shows no signs of diminishing. At my age—sixty-eight—I find it trying and tiring. Will my husband's sex drive ever stop?
A: I don't know, but he sounds like a man of considerable vitality and this is a wonderful characteristic indeed. Perhaps your difficulty comes from embarrassment. Some women feel that it is indecent to engage in—let alone enjoy—sex at an advanced age. Of course, this is a Victorian hang-up and patent nonsense. If you feel this way and can give up this idea, both you and your husband can go on to enjoy all possibilities, sexual and otherwise, whatever your ages.

Q: How many times a week should a couple have intercourse?
A: As often or seldom as they feel like it. There is absolutely no standard or norm except those we insist on imposing on ourselves. Frequency is highly individualistic and

variable among different people and with the same people at different times in their lives.

Q: Is there a right age to tell children about the facts of life?
A: Yes, when they start asking, which they invariably will do, provided they are not unduly inhibited by a household that is constricted, prudish, and punitive. There must be an atmosphere of healthy freedom, with the right to be curious. It is usually best not to force gratuitous information upon them for which they are not ready. This leads to confusion, as do misinformation, stork stories, and other lies. Age has little to do with it because different children mature at different times. In a household where people can feel and talk freely, parents are nearly always tuned in and aware of what information their children are and are not ready for.

Q: My husband would like me to be more aggressive sexually, but I cannot. Is something wrong with me?
A: I assume that you mean assertive rather than aggressive. If your husband expects you to be sadistic, there is nothing wrong with you, but he may have problems. But if you can't ask for or indicate what you want and what pleases you sexually, or if you can't allow yourself free participation and pleasurable indulgence, then you have a problem. This may be related to superficial inhibition, but it is often an indication of confused notions of goodness, saintliness, and a general inability to take good and loving care of oneself. This kind of self-effacement and self-neglect is best treated by a competent, psychoanalytically trained therapist.

Q: Is there a difference between a vaginal and clitoral orgasm, and which is better?
A: This has been an area of much controversy over the years. Having read the literature and having questioned many people, my own conclusion is as follows.

There is only one orgasm and it is almost always initiated

by clitoral stimulation. However, an orgasm may be felt locally—in the area of the clitoris or in the area of the clitoris and vagina—or "globally," that is, as a fully bodily and emotional response. The local orgasm, usually a result of clitoral stimulation without intercourse, is often more intense, but less satisfying; when it is over, you may feel something is missing. The global orgasm, usually the result of intercourse with or without accompanying clitoral stimulation, is often less intense, but provides a sense of greater fulfillment. No one has determined to what extent any of these responses is either physiological, or psychological, or a combination.

Q: Does the size of the male organ have anything to do with sexual satisfaction?
A: Very little, since the vagina adjusts in size accordingly and since the sense of fullness is more important than nerve stimulation because the vagina is particularly lacking in pleasure-producing nerve endings. Stimulation of the clitoris has little or nothing to do with the size of the male organ and is best effected otherwise. However, the size of the organ may have psychological effects on either or both partners.

Q: Approximately how long does it take a man to recover from an orgasm, that is, so that he can have another one? Same question for women.
A: Anywhere from several minutes to several days. This varies from man to man and can change at different times in a man's life. However, most men don't usually desire another orgasm for at least several hours. Much depends on state of health, age, sexual experience, and mood.

Women vary in this regard, too, but their ability in this area is more dependent on psychological factors than physical ones. Physiologically, women can have many orgasms in rapid succession, though many women prefer one orgasm at a time and with intervals of hours to days in between.

Q: What is frigidity? Discuss physical causes.
A: Frigidity is a woman's inability to respond sexually, either relatively or absolutely. It is almost never due to physical causes, though there are rare cases of hormonal imbalance or anatomical difficulties involving the clitoris. Sometimes the clitoris is covered over or bound down by excessive tissue and freeing it surgically helps a great deal. But nearly all cases of frigidity are due to great sexual misinformation, confusion, fear, or emotional difficulties.

Q: What is impotence?
A: Impotence is the inability to achieve or to sustain an erection so as to make satisfactory intercourse possible. This condition, too, is almost always psychological in origin.

Q: What do you think of the theory that female sex response can be enhanced by strengthening the pubococcygeal muscle in the pelvis?
A: I think it can be helpful in effecting more stimulation to the clitoris. It can also help psychologically because the woman in question feels that she is helping herself in her sex life.

Q: Can too much discussion and anxiety over sexual performance take the whole spontaneity and meaning out of sex?
A: Absolutely. We ought to be more concerned with participation and refuse to be involved with performing sexual feats of any kind. However, it is valuable to discuss likes, dislikes, and preferences openly—but not during lovemaking.

A: I have been dating one man steadily for seven months. He displays no affection whatever. He never hugs me. He has held my hand only twice. The only time he kisses me is when we are saying goodnight. I have never dated a man who seems to be so completely indifferent. Are some men just not interested in sex?

A: There are men who are asexual, but this is an extremely rare condition. Unfortunately, it is also a very difficult condition to treat. Of course, there are also men with a vast array of sexual problems who attempt to solve them by at least some minimal contact with women. But there are also a great many men who are shy, easily embarrassed by any potential clumsiness on their part, sexually inexperienced, and terrified of rejection. Warm and gentle reassurance sometimes goes a long way. It may be a good idea to have an open and gentle discussion at an appropriate moment.

Q: My husband used to stare at the posterior of a friend of ours so obviously that it was embarrassing. He's doing better since I mentioned it to him. He says it's because it's so big. It's not *that* big. Does a man stare this way for any reason other than sexual?

A: Unlikely, but to stare does not mean to act out in any way. Many men look, but most of the lookers reserve any activity for their wives or lovers. Some men stare not because it's actually that big but rather because it *seems* that big. This may be purely a function of a man's imagination. On the other hand, it may seem so because the woman moves or acts in a way that is subtly seductive or provocative. Some women do so without full conscious awareness and some men respond to this stimulus also without full awareness.

Q: I know a young woman who has recently been raped. I have two questions. One, is it true that the average, well-intentioned woman would fight back? Two, does a woman who has been raped really suffer all that much emotional trauma? Of course, I'm all for prevention of rape, but haven't its ill effects been exaggerated?

A: Since you did not sign your letter I don't really know whether you are a man or a/woman. I would judge that you are a man and a rather naïve man who knows little about women.

One—most women and indeed most men, if terrified enough in any circumstance, will not fight back. The fear of death prevents fighting back and often brings on an attack of paralysis and utter submission.

Two—the acute and sustained emotional trauma following rape is enormous. There is little else that is as effective in creating rage, demoralization, revulsion, and emotional pain as rape. Few women are ever completely able to get over the trauma of personal violation and the experience of physical exploitation, however short-lived the experience.

I recently heard a paper delivered by Dr. Martin Symonds, a New York psychiatrist and psychoanalyst who has long studied the psychological effects on victims of violent crimes. He pointed out that in addition to personal trauma, what makes matters much worse is the attitude of neighbors and so-called friends. Initial sympathy soon turns into avoidance of the victim to the point of near ostracism, as if she suffers from a contagious disease. Thus, the victim of crime and especially of rape who most needs friendly support often finds herself operating in a vacuum.

Q: I keep hearing about women who use headaches and fatigue as excuses for avoiding sex, but what about the reverse problem? Can a woman suffer from headaches and fatigue because of sexual frustration?

A: Sexual frustration can certainly produce much tension and anger. Repressed anger is a common cause of headaches and chronic tension causes fatigue. Many people also perceive lack of sex as general inattention and deprivation of love and affection. These sometimes produce even more dissatisfaction than deprivation of actual sexual activity itself. Some men who are less ardent sexual partners than their wives remedy the situation somewhat by being adequately affectionate and attentive. This includes being physically attentive with kisses, embraces, and general physical closeness even when sexual culmination does not take place.

Q: I know a man who never fails to touch and to feel other women at parties. He just can't keep his hands to himself! The fact that his wife is there doesn't seem to stop him at all. Why does a man do this?

A: The fact that his wife is there may be the major motivating factor. Some men who are still largely little boys unconsciously have to rebel against mama in order to feel manly. Unfortunately, their wives are in the position of being surrogate mamas whom the little boy slaps by touching other women. Other men vent hostility at their wives and attempt to manipulate and to embarrass them by touching other women. Still others do it because of confused notions about masculinity and as an attempt to feel and act what they consider manly. Some do it to insult and provoke other women's husbands. Many do it as a general insult to women, for whom they unconsciously have contempt and whom they equate with nice objects to be touched and enjoyed as desired. These men are male chauvinists as well as markedly immature. Some do it as a means of attaining sexual stimulation and as a substitute for more complete sexual involvement with other women.

Q: I am very much in love with my husband and we have a very good sex life and a lovely family. But I find myself attracted to other men and do have temptations. I don't intend to do anything about it and I find my present life-style just fine, but is it normal for a woman in such good circumstances to find other men desirable? Does this mean I am oversexed or that something is perhaps chemically wrong with me?

A: Love, a good life, and devotion do not preclude attraction to people other than mates. A chemical or hormonal imbalance is not necessary for a woman to find men other than her husband attractive. Many women repress feelings, desires, temptations, and conflicts, but many women do in fact find various men attractive. This is not evidence of irresponsibility or lack of love or maturity. It is part and parcel of the natural and human attraction members of one sex have for the other. This attraction goes on regardless of whether it is admitted or not and regardless of which standards or lifestyles we choose to live by. Human beings are not saints or angels. They may choose to do nothing about their temptations, but to expect not to have temptations at all or to expect them to go away altogether is expecting too much of people.

Q: Is it possible to be sexually attracted to someone you know is not good for you, someone you don't really like and in fact dislike, someone who even treats you badly?
A: Yes, and this is particularly true of people who dislike themselves. They are often most attracted and stimulated by people who will inevitably, in one or another way, cause them humiliation and even grief. Some of these people readily lend themselves to sadomasochistic relationships. Many of them are actually repelled by and contemptuous of people who respect them, even though they may consciously find these people likable and worthwhile. The unconscious feeling here is, "How can I respect and be attracted to anyone who finds an inferior person like me attractive?"

Q: Is it true that women reach the peak of sexual desire and satisfaction in their mid-thirties? I'm thirty-eight. I'd hate to think that it's all downhill from now on in!
A: I think that we are too interested in peaks and pinnacles in our society. I find that desire and satisfaction are highly individual matters. People are the most complicated entities on earth. Their sexual lives are derived from much more than biological function or chronological age or development. How they feel about themselves and others, particularly sexual partners in their lives, at any given time are crucial factors. When depressed, for example, most people experience little or no sexual satisfaction regardless of age.

Sustained, satisfying sexual activity can take place at almost any age if the right ingredients are present. These include good physical and mental health, general satisfaction in most areas of life—social, emotional, professional, creative, economic, and so on. Again—having the right partner is no small matter in this regard.

Q: Is it usual to have sexual fantasies—about a man I don't even know—sometimes during intercourse with my husband? Sometimes I pretend that two strange men are making love to me—that's my favorite fantasy. Does this mean I don't really love my husband? I think I do but I feel so guilty not telling him about my secret thoughts in bed.

A: It is not only usual but extremely common to have all kinds of sexual fantasies in and out of bed with and without one's loved one. It is not evidence of absence or lack of love. Telling about them and destroying the secret may also destroy the stimulating effect and excitement they evoke. A thought is not an action and few fantasies are translated into action. Indeed, most people are content with the effects of their fantasies and have no desire to act them out even where guilt is not a factor. Interestingly, some sex therapists encourage people to have fantasies like yours in order to help achieve and sustain strong sexual feelings—for their loved ones.

Q: My husband believes that our sex life would be better, more exciting, if I'd agree to read dirty magazines with him before we go to bed. I've always refused because I think these magazines are degrading to women, and frankly they embarrass me. And now he has a new request: he wants us to see an X-rated movie that's playing in town. What should I do? Give up and give in?

A: What are you giving up? If you feel that you are really giving up personal dignity and belief perhaps you should not give in. If you are giving up prudery, constriction, repression of a desire to see "those dirty things" perhaps you may want to give in. Pornographic material can sometimes be exciting and instructive. Some medical schools are now using pornographic films to instruct students. Sometimes if what is learned through pornography is applied to one's own sex life the desire for pornography is diminished. Unfortunately, some pornography diminishes the dignity of both women and men and a great deal of it is just plain boring. May I point out here that I do not consider interest in pornography evidence of perversion. Likewise, I have never seen evidence that in any way indicates that interest in or viewing pornography leads to sexual crimes.

Your husband's desire to include you in what he finds sexually entertaining, curious, and perhaps stimulating may indicate a desire for still more closeness to you. That he wants to share this potential for sexual excitement with you seems to be the antithesis of the destruction of dignity.

Q: I'm twenty-seven. I've been going with a wonderful thirty-six-year-old man for almost a year. He's a really solid, sensitive, responsible, good guy. I guess everybody would see him as a great "catch" and he wants to marry me. Trouble is he doesn't turn me on. I'm just not physically attracted to him even though there's nothing wrong with his looks. I know the difference—because I have been and am attracted to other people. My question—can physical attraction develop later?
A: Anything is possible, I suppose. But my own clinical experience dictates otherwise. Physical attraction is, I believe, usually there or not there—it's not an acquired taste. I believe that chemistry between people is a highly complex dynamic that is the result of a lifetime of conditioning, personal development, and experience. It cannot be turned off and on at will regardless of how good a catch a potential partner may be. I also believe that sex between married people is too important an area to be overlooked for other considerations.

There are people who block out sexual response because

they are afraid of commitment and sustained involvement. After they take the risk of closeness and living together and become relaxed, sexual desire for each other may be forthcoming. If you believe these or other factors may be in operation, it may be worthwhile to try living together for a period of time before excluding the possibility of a more permanent commitment.

Q: I recently read a book about women's sex fantasies. I understand there is also a book describing men's sex daydreams. Do women think about sex as much as men seem to? If there is a difference, is it because they are physically different? Is there anything wrong with me if I don't seem to think about sex very much and don't have the fancy daydreams other women seem to have? I have been married for ten years and our sex lives seem to be okay; at least neither of us has any complaints.

A: A recent authoritative psychological study involving a large sample of men and women indicated that sex occupied first or second place in most men's "on-the-mind" priorities. With women, sex was seventh or eighth on the list— house, children, clothes, responsibilities, and the like coming first. Nevertheless, I believe that however large or authentic the samples and the observations, vast variations exist and they are all within the normal range. So, there are normal men who think about sex relatively rarely, and normal women who think about sex a great deal. Some women hardly fantasize at all. Others have a great many elaborate daydreams. I believe that differences, where they do exist, are not determined by either anatomy or physiology but by cultural and familial background and training. I think that physical differences have a negligible effect, and this applies to whatever variations we may find between men and men, women and women, and men and women.

Q: Tell me the truth once and for all, are all men really promiscuous and simply can't help it?

A: Much depends on what you mean by the word "promiscuous." For me the term means compulsively seeking sex from random partners. This compulsion is always based on poor self-esteem and anxiety related to a poor sense of identity. It exists among both men and women and among both homosexual and heterosexual people. It is not universal, that is to say, the vast majority of people, including men, are not driven sexually and are not compulsively promiscuous.

Of course, both men and women are capable of physical attraction to any number of people, and this includes people for whom they may or may not have deeper affection. What they do about such attraction largely depends on mores and individual values and choices. The healthier the person is, the more he or she is able to exercise choice rather than compulsion in the sexual as in all other areas of living and human activity and encounter.

Q: At age nine, I was sexually molested by an uncle, who's since died. Now, at twenty-eight, I'm engaged to someone I love very much, yet I have no desire for or interest in a sexual relationship with him. He knows about this childhood incident and has suggested I see a psychiatrist, but I'm hoping that with time, my problem may disappear. Can a marriage work in spite of a sexual block?

A: No. At least it is extremely unlikely, and your fiancé in urging you to get help is already indicating that this area of your lives is important to him. It is also important to you.

These kinds of problems do not just disappear. Your having been molested may be only a small part of your difficulties. While it undoubtedly was traumatic, chances are that other factors are connected to your difficulties. Indeed, you may be using the incident to simplify the problem, which is usually a complex one.

I urge you to consult with a psychoanalytically trained psychiatrist who can evaluate your problem and help you with it. This kind of problem may be related to misunderstandings about sex and men as well as to fears of strong feelings and great closeness. It must be remembered that these problems are highly individual and usually are rooted in the early lives and familial relationships of the person in question.

A Sex Mental Health Quiz

I receive at least several letters each month asking me about sexual feelings and attitudes and whether or not they are healthy or "normal" from a mental-health or emotional point of view. I think that the questions that follow will bring some important attitudes about sex to light. These sexual attitudes never exist in isolation. They are invariably connected to how we feel about ourselves, other people, and life generally. I believe that for the most part our sexual attitudes are the results of how we relate to ourselves and to other people generally rather than the reverse. This means that while sexual problems can create other problems, they are often indications that other problems exist and are usually the results of other problems. For example, a person who feels guilty about being joyous or happy will have difficulty enjoying sex at least as much as she would experience difficulty with satisfaction in any area. Since sex offers the possibility of the very closest kind of relating, it is, of course, an area of great importance and will invariably reflect both the joys and woes inherent in close relationships. But it should be remembered that while sex is an extremely important area of human existence (it is, after all, the way we continue the existence of the species), resolving sexual problems without regard for underlying difficulties can be helpful but doesn't offer universal solutions.

Great variation is characteristic of human sexuality. To date, no one sexual life-style has proved to be superior to any other. While we have much in common, we also, unlike other creatures on earth, are highly individualistic in terms of attraction, intensity of feelings, preferences, and frequency of desire. The question of frequency of sexual intercourse is, I suppose, the question about sex most frequently asked. No norm has ever been established. What may be considered frequent and satisfying to one person or couple may seem paltry and teasingly frustrating to others. The same is true of duration of foreplay, kinds of foreplay, different positions, duration of intercourse, methods used to achieve orgasm, frequency of orgasm, and so on.

1. Do you recall a good deal of sexual curiosity, exploration, and experimentation as a child?

A history of early sexual interest and activity is usually evidence of a healthily developing child and a potential for future sexual drive of satisfying proportions. I hope you don't look back with guilt or recrimination. "Playing doctor" in multitudinous ways is an indication of a good imagination which can be put to constructive sexual creative use later on in life. "Playing doctor" with members of both sexes and with brothers and sisters, too, is exceedingly common. It must be remembered that we are not born with knowledge of cultural mores and prohibitions. This kind of knowledge or acculturation is learned as we grow up. Inability to recall childhood sexual experiences is sometimes due to guilt and strong inhibitions as well as to a prudish attitude to sexual feelings.

2. Are you aware of sexual feelings, urges, desires, and preferences?

Don't take these for granted! Asexuality is a very serious condition and is extremely difficult to treat. There are a number of people whose sexual feelings are almost totally repressed, deadened, and virtually obliterated. People who suffer in this way not only are deprived of the pleasures sex can bring but also always suffer from serious emotional problems in other areas. Being sexually alive is evidence of vitality in other areas, too. Knowing one's sexual preferences is often a valuable sign of being in touch with one's feelings and preferences in other areas of life as well.

3. Do you have any history of adult sexual contact and satisfaction?

Don't take this for granted! So many men and women have never had any sexual satisfaction, and there are also a number who have not had sexual experience as adults on any level. Many suffer from very poor self-esteem generally and have confused ideas about femininity and purity. Many people, even today, suffer from paralyzing inhibitions and deep-seated emotional conflict and guilt about sexual function and potential satisfaction. Having had pleasurable sexual experience at any time in life offers a considerably better prognosis in terms of resolution of sexual problems that may exist.

4. Do you have heterosexual feelings, that is, feelings and desires for the opposite sex?

This is an indication of a fair degree of sexual development and is directly linked to healthy sexual identification and self-acceptance. This, in effect, means being happy being a woman. A strong sense of sexual identification—being a woman and being attracted to men, or a man attracted to women—is crucial to a satisfying sexual relationship with a member of the opposite sex. Problems in this area stem from intense self-rejection, rejection and contempt for gender by parents, and inadequate emotional growth in the area of sexual development.

5. Do you have a variety of sexual fantasies and dreams, and do you accept having them with equanimity?

This is completely in keeping with being a person. Lack of fantasies or guilt about having them may be an indication of excessive repression and inhibition and inappropriate and confused notions about sexual feelings. Studies have indicated that most people have a great many sexual daydreams as well as night dreams and many of them are of a highly creative and erotic nature. They are often used as stimulating devices preceding actual lovemaking.

6. If you are a woman, how do you feel about menstruating? and about your body?

Abhorrence and hatred for this basic physiological function are at least to some degree evidence of rejection of one's femininity. Healthy acceptance in this area offers a good prognosis and self-acceptance as a woman generally. I feel this is particularly applicable to becoming and to being a mother. Good feelings about one's body and its functions offer the possibility of good feelings sexually and specifically in using it for conceiving, developing, and giving birth to a baby. This is linked to healthy satisfaction and the ultimate pleasure derived from the sense of creative accomplishment involved in becoming and being a mother. Abhorrence for one's body and its functions must create repercussions in one's sexual life. This kind of poor self-esteem unfortunately deprives a woman of good feelings about motherhood, and sometimes she unwittingly conveys these feelings to her daughters by attitudes and things she says of which she may be unaware.

7. Do you find people other than your partner sexually attractive? Do you feel hurt if your partner seems attracted to another?

This is perfectly normal. It is evidence of long-standing interest (from early childhood on) in the opposite sex. It in no way indicates lack of love or lack of sexual attraction for one's mate. "Never looking at anyone else" is, by the same token, no evidence of love or overwhelming passion for one's lover. More often than not, it is an indication of inhibition, prudery, and lack of spontaneous human curiosity and interest.

8. As an adult, do you enjoy a fairly active (to your satisfaction) guilt-free sex life, which includes some degree of pleasure for you and your lover?

If you do, you are fortunate indeed. So many people have little or no sexual contact or satisfaction and what pleasure they manage to achieve is unfortunately mixed with feelings of guilt and unhappiness. It cannot be stressed too much, that no sexual relationship is ever ideal or perfect. Relative satisfaction and varying degrees of contentment at different times are characteristics of good sexual relationships. Quests for impossible sexual goals and exorbitant demands invariably lead to confusion, frustration, mutual anger, and misery.

9. Are you aware that people are arrhythmic for the most part and that adjustments and accommodation to each other's disparate and individual needs are necessary for a mutually satisfying relationship?

People, however much they are in love, are sexually attracted to each other, and care about each other's needs do in fact have different sexual appetites at different times. Expecting two people to synchronize their desires perfectly is expecting the impossible. Insistence on equal desires, responses, and satisfactions is a sure way to destroy a potentially good sexual relationship.

10. Are you aware that sexual boredom often has little or nothing to do with sex?

Knowing this is evidence of maturity and sophistication generally and can have healthy repercussions sexually. Seeking and sharing areas of common interest leads to self-development. Finding areas of mutual fun has good sexual reverberations. This is especially true of taking vacations together without the children.

11. Are you relatively free concerning experimentation and extension of your sexual experience with each other?

In so doing also make ample use of clothes, music or whatever turns you on. This helps to keep lovers feeling like lovers, however long they've been married and whatever their age.

12. Are you aware that sexual responsiveness as well as satisfactory sexual adjustment between people seldom occurs instantly?

People do not form full-blown relationships instantly. Relating is a developing process and this is just as true of sex as it is of any other human area. Many people need time to develop and to evolve their sexual response to the point of orgasm. This requires experience, practice, mutual trust, and the desire to be each other's student and teacher. Sometimes professional consultation with an expert is necessary, too. Above all, time and patience are necessary. Knowing this may prevent discouragement, hopelessness, and despair.

Let me close by stating that great lovers, no matter how much in love, are not mind readers. "He should know how without my having to tell him" is a common and highly destructive claim. There is no substitute for open and free communication, in which two lovers (not during sex, of course) talk over their mutual interest and desires in an effort to help each other and themselves to have sexual fun.

Chapter Ten

THE FEARS

What Makes You Afraid? •
Depression • *Anger*

What Makes You Afraid?

OF LATE THERE have been a great many articles published in newspapers all over the country about people who suffer from anxiety attacks and phobias, who are afraid to leave the neighborhood, their own houses, or even a particular room. Some people are incapacitated to the point of complete paralysis in just about all areas of their lives, and these may include social, sexual, and economic function. Each month I receive great numbers of letters from people who suffer a myriad of symptoms that are obvious evidence of emotional difficulty. We human beings are enormously innovative, and when we use our ingenuity to turn on ourselves, the variety of self-torturing devices is almost endless. These include incessant worrying and ruminations; phobias or seemingly inappropriate fears; inhibitions; compulsions; and anxiety attacks. Let me quote from two letters, which in their way typify so many of the others I receive.

"I have an unrealistic fear of sharp objects such as knives, scissors, etc. Sometimes this gets to a point where I collect them and carry them out of the house before I go to bed. This all started one night when I looked at a knife and wondered what would happen if I lost control of my will and hurt someone with the knife."

The second letter reads:

"My daughter, now twenty-one—bright, sensible—has periods of anxiety. She is provoked with herself about these attacks and my husband and I can temporarily help her by our love and discussions. After a day or so, she is better; but they recur. At the age of nine, while in an elevator with my son, my mother and myself, my daughter witnessed my mother's fatal heart attack. Can this kind of event cause periods of anxiety? She confided to me that riding in elevators bothers her and she is becoming anxious about driving any distance."

Anxiety attacks are common and can be among the most distressing conditons a person can have. They vary in degree from mild tension and disquietude to unrelenting, inappropriate fear, and from a sense of loss of orientation and identity to utter panic. Attacks can be short-lived and infrequent. They can occur almost without stop, forming an all-pervasive, chronic continuum. Many include concomitant physical symptoms, rapid heartbeats, excessive sweating, weakness, flushing, vomiting, headaches, light-headedness, dizziness, and so on. People suffering from frequent attacks may become fearful of leaving home, and anxiety may be elaborated and channeled into all kinds of symptoms, including seemingly inappropriate fears (such as the lady who is afraid of sharp objects). Indeed, many psychoanalytically oriented psychiatrists and psychologists, including myself, feel that anxiety underlies nearly all emotional or psychiatric disorders and disabilities. Anxiety attacks, whatever form they take and whatever elaborate symptom complex (such as fear of knives or elevators) they are converted into, can be useful as well as destructive. As evidence of underlying and deeper distress, they signal the need for help and provide motivation to change what needs changing in one's life.

In answer to the second letter—yes, people do sometimes suffer traumatic anxiety or neurotic reactions following accidents and fearful occurrences in their lives. But if these conditions continue they are almost always evidence of underlying difficulties of a more serious and long-standing nature. Anxiety attacks, whatever their form, including pervasive fear and "a sense of impending doom that seems to be hooked to nothing at all," are most often due to a fear of facing certain feelings and internal conflicts and the continuing attempt to keep them buried and out of conscious awareness. Potential emergence of unwanted feelings into full consciousness often brings on the anxiety attack. This happens because many of us have an idealized version of ourselves that is at variance with the feeling we are attempting to disown. In practice, I have found that repressed anger and its threatened emergence are the most common causes of severe anxiety attacks. Many of us are afraid to admit, let alone to express, angry feelings early in life for fear of alienating the very people we depend on. Later on we come to put much too much stress on being loved by everyone in order to feel safe. This concept of always being loved does not include angry feelings and sometimes also eliminates all kinds of other powerful yearnings, such as sexual feelings or yearnings for power. This causes intolerable conflicts of all kinds. Also, simple feelings of anger, when repressed, tend to snowball, so that when they finally emerge they take frightful forms of what seems like murderous rage or as symbolically expressed by the fear of knives or whatever.

Obviously what is required is a re-examination and a healthier and fuller means of feeling and expressing anger and other emotions. This is never simple, but it is certainly possible! Giving up saintlike images of ourselves and accepting our humanity and human feelings, especially anger, produce a long-standing cure. The mother's love undoubtedly helps her daughter a great deal because it helps her to accept herself. But unfortunately "she is provoked with herself." She needs her own love and acceptance most of all. This acceptance must include all the feelings she is attempting to escape from and especially those that make her feel "provoked with herself" or ashamed of herself in any way at all. To do this alone is often impossible, because she does not consciously know what these feelings are or how to bring them into conscious awareness where she can cope with them. She needs help to do this. People suffering from chronic attacks of anxiety can be helped, but it is imperative that they seek the right kind of professional help and the earlier the better. From my point of view, that kind of help *does not*—I repeat, *does not*—include T.M., primal scream, electroshock, or behavior modification. Proper investigation of these symptoms, where they are coming from and what they are all about as well as a resolution of the problems causing them, is best investigated by a psychoanalytically oriented psychiatrist or psychologist who at very least has been analyzed her- or himself so as to be conversant with these all-too-human problems on a personal, experiential level. Behavior modification treatment and medication may alleviate symptoms, but I feel that underlying causes require deeper treatment.

Q: Could you in one word tell me what prejudice is mainly due to?
A: Fear.

Q: One day when my daughter was a baby, I didn't fasten her high chair securely, and she fell and injured her head so badly that she was in the hospital for several days. Now my girl is a healthy five-year-old, but whenever I see that faint scar on her forehead, I'm overcome with guilt. How can I forgive myself?
A: What you must forgive is the fact that you are human. This means that you are less than perfect and that you have quite human limitations and like all of us a capacity for mistakes.

It may sound strange, but you probably have a considerable problem with unconscious grandiosity. Yes, it is grandiose to believe that you can be the perfect guardian and preventer of mishaps of any kind. You must accept your humanity.

Your humanity may also include feelings of hostility that
are repressed. Believe me it is not unusual for parents to feel
hostile to their children, however much they love them.
This, too, is part and parcel of the human condition. But if
we see ourselves as perfect we tend to repress that hostility
and then react to it with untoward guilt, fear, and overprotection. We also become so fearful and guilt ridden that we
actually desire something bad to happen and contribute to
the event. But accidents do occur! Your guilt at this point
serves to whip you to attain more perfection in yourself.
Stand up against it and for your humanity. Having limits and
kids who get hurt and kids who get well are part of being a
regular person. That your daughter grew up to be healthy is
a much more important reminder of what a good mother you
are and has much greater significance than anything that a
small scar symbolizes.

Depression

Emotional depression runs rampant in the United States. Indeed, it is surely the most prevalent symptom we must cope
with at this time. Depression, of course, includes a very
broad spectrum, which ranges from periods of short-lived
moodiness to chronic, very painful periods of near total despair. Many depressions take forms that are not readily de-
tected, and these include periods of more than usual
disability, accident proneness, inability to hold a job, inability to enjoy normally fun experiences, insomnia,
overeating, lack of appetite, hyperirritability and temper
tantrums, crying spells, loss of sexual interest, more than
usual sexual interest, and so on.

Depression hits everyone—people of all ages and both
sexes, children and the aged, and people in every socioeconomic bracket. No one is exempt and neither success nor
failure as a parent, lover, professional, business person, or
artist are preventatives. A great many of us have very serious depressions in our lives and suffer periods in which any

kind of functioning is a great hardship. For some of us, so-called normal functioning is impossible. Most people suffering from depression are not treated. Indeed, the majority of cases are misdiagnosed or undiagnosed. Many minor depressions are ignored until a cumulative effect produces severe incapacitation. Some cries for help are greeted with derision and even chastisement by embarrassed relatives who just want to wait for it go away. Some desperate people feeling utterly lost, hopeless, and helpless attempt suicide. Many depressed people are treated with what I consider poor treatment. Some are given useless vitamin shots. Many without any investigation as to cause, origin, or purpose of the depression are immediately and heavily dosed with tranquilizers, energizers, antidepressants, and in some cases a combination of all three. Some are immediately given electroconvulsive treatments without any attempt at less drastic treatment first. There are some attempts to talk people out of their depression. Some people receive excellent treatment involving psychoanalytic psychotherapy, in which the cause and purpose of their depression are investigated and put to constructive use for healthy change in the individual's life.

Nearly everyone "recovers." But some people will be about the same as they were before and subject to further depressions. Some will be worse off—full of more self-doubt than ever before—and will go through life depressed about having been depressed and fearful of another severe depression. Others will have learned much about themselves, will change and grow, and as a result of being depressed will be better off than ever.

As with all human phenomena, depression is not a single, simple mechanism. It has been called "an adult temper tantrum" and may well be that, but if so, it must be viewed as a very complex tantrum. Depression just about always has multiple roots or causes and also serves several purposes. Emotional or psychological "symptoms" are always also symbols and as such are a kind of language in which we attempt to deliver a message to both ourselves and to others. Unfortunately, our messages are too often ignored by all concerned, especially by ourselves. In any case, while a precipitating event *seems* to cause a depressive reaction, there are invariably long-standing causes that play a greater role, even though they may be hidden from immediate conscious awareness. As someone once said, "It is not the straw that breaks the camel's back but the load underneath." Here then are some of the more prevalent aspects usually found in combination when we investigate a depression.

1. Repressed anger that is turned in on oneself.

2. Self-hate—in which we see ourselves in the worst possible light in all aspects of our activities.

3. An attempt to anesthetize and to deaden ourselves so as to cope with emotional pain, which might otherwise produce suicide.

4. Disappointment, frustration, and rage owing to thwarted ambitions, unfulfilled expectations of self, of life, of loved ones.

5. Pain of real loss, especially of a loved one.

6. An attempt to manipulate those around us to satisfy our needs and desires.

7. Effects of hormonal changes and physical illness.

8. A scream and a message to ourselves that we have neglected ourselves and our needs in favor of spurious activities that have in no way produced real self-fulfillment.

Obviously, it is of paramount importance to recognize a depression. Proper treatment, and I consider analytic treatment the best, is invaluable. But can depression serve a constructive purpose? Indeed it can! However, this is so only if the messages of depression are not ignored. They must be taken with appropriate seriousness and dignity. They must be carefully and correctly interpreted in terms of the individual's life and personal frame of reference, and they must be heeded and acted upon.

A depression is a signal that change is indicated and as such can initiate the most constructive period in a person's life. It can clear the air and help rid oneself of years of accumulated anger and hurt. This can clear the way for feeling and expressing feelings of warmth and love that may have been blocked for years. It can lead to a re-evaluation of expectations of life, self, and others, making more fruitful relationships possible as well as providing satisfactions inherent in everyday life that were hitherto blocked by cynicism and bitterness. It can provide an opportunity to understand and to rid oneself of self-hate and to enhance compassion—the most therapeutic instrument of all—for oneself and others. Mostly as a result of depression, we can hear and heed our inner cry for self-realization. We can struggle to understand how we have cheated and neglected ourselves in order to fulfill unreal, idealized, perfectionist images of ourselves. This gives us opportunities to give our real selves sustenance.

Q: What exactly is a nervous breakdown in layman's terms? What kind of treatment is necessary?
A: Frankly, there is no such thing. Nerves have not broken down and no demonstrable organic changes in the brain or spinal cord have taken place. People generally call any emotional condition that results in an inability to function as usual for a period of time (from weeks to years) a nervous breakdown. This includes periods of severe anxiety, depression, irrational behavior, and acute flare-ups of psychosomatic illnesses (gastrointestinal disturbances, certain rashes, bronchial asthma). I have always felt that an "emotional breakup" would be a better term because these reactions usually represent the breakup of old patterns of behavior. From my point of view these very painful "time-out-of-time" reactions may serve as valuable signals that much has not been in order for a long time. This means that there are conflicts that have never been resolved; hidden fears that have not been faced; feelings that have not been expressed; yearnings and desires that have never been given adequate respect; proclivities and potentials that have not been realized; and so on. This period, therefore, can be used in the service of oneself—not to go back to inner conditions as they were prior to the breakup but rather to change and to grow in the direction of constructive health.

Treatment depends on the particular individual's history, personality, and condition. Consultation with a psychiatrist trained in psychoanalysis is best, and from my point of view psychoanalytic psychotherapy is usually most helpful not only in getting over painful symptoms but, more important, in effecting constructive lifelong changes.

Q: A close friend is going through a severe depression. I've been willing to listen to her gripes for quite a while, but after six months it's the same story over and over. Each time I talk to her, *I* become depressed. How can I be supportive without getting dragged down, too?

A: Depressed people do tend to repeat themselves ad nauseum and to wear out themselves and those who listen to them. You sound as if you need replenishment yourself. We can be of little help to others if we don't take care of ourselves. Perhaps it is time to dilute your contacts with your friend for a while. I do hope that she is in treatment with a competent professional therapist. Depression is a very serious illness, and while a friend's support is helpful, treatment on a professional basis is imperative and maybe lifesaving.

Q: My sister-in-law is always unhappy—more than unhappy—miserable! She has as good a life as anyone else—some ups and some downs—but she is always miserable even when things are looking up and good things are happening. Is it possible that there are some people who really prefer misery to happiness? Maybe she really likes to be miserable.

A: No. Some people *seem* to prefer misery, but all people really prefer to be happy. Those people who are always unhappy cannot extricate themselves from the habit of misery, and this is due to complex problems requiring professional help. Many of these people suffer from serious and chronic depression, which goes untreated because they manage to function despite deep and unrelenting unhappiness.

Q: So many people that I know personally seem to go through serious depressions. Is emotional depression as prevalent as it seems? If so, what is this all about?

A: Yes, most experts agree that depression is the most prevalent symptom of emotional disturbance in our society. Indeed, there are very few people who escape at least some incapacitation owing to serious depression one or, more times in their lives. There are many people who are chronically depressed and some who have been depressed for so long that they do not remember feeling otherwise. Some people suffer from intermittent depressions at certain times of the year and in cycles.

Depression is characterized by any number of symptoms and ranges from virtually no impairment of function to complete paralysis. Some of these symptoms are lack of appetite, insomnia, overeating, constant fatigue, "sleeping all of the time," extreme sensitivity and vulnerability, weeping, self-denigrating thoughts, suicidal thoughts, accident proneness, extreme pessimism, moodiness, despair, hopelessness, loss of sense of humor, an inability to be happy, overwhelming sadness, extreme weight gain or loss, or a slowing down of all physical movements.

There is often a precipitating event that initiates a depression, usually involving hurt pride, such as loss of a job, failure in an examination, a divorce, or whatever. Sometimes it involves loss of a loved one, in which a mourning period evolves into a serious and chronic depression. This is more likely to happen in very dependent people. Sometimes there is no precipitating event at all.

The underlying cause of depression is almost always connected to self-hate. Depression cannot occur (and we must differentiate here from appropriate sadness) in people who are truly self-accepting, loyal to themselves, and compassionate to themselves. Unfortunately, too many of us predicate loyalty to self and acceptance of self on accomplishment and performance of all kinds. We live in a complex society in which all kinds of achievement and status have taken the place of real self-love and self-care. It is a highly competitive society of exorbitant and rising expectations. These include expectations of ourselves, others, the human condition, and the world generally. Failed expectations usually result in self-hate and depression.

Obviously, where at all serious—any depression that lasts more than a few weeks or causes any serious symptoms—psychiatric help is indicated. Depression is, after all, a dangerous illness. It destroys happiness and function and in some cases produces death through suicide. But it can also cause a constructive turnabout in one's life. Using it as a signal that a re-evaluation is in order, many people go on to reconstruct their lives on a more realistic and constructive basis. This involves reducing expectations and learning loyalty to self—just on the basis of being human.

Q: I recently had a wonderful baby girl but became depressed shortly after giving birth. Is this a common experience?

A: It is not at all unusual to suffer a letdown following the exhilaration accompanying such a momentous event. Some new mothers respond to the added stress and responsibility of taking care of a newborn infant with depression.

There are, however, some women who, following delivery, sustain moderate to severe emotional disturbance. Some doctors feel that these reactions have their origin in hormonal imbalance or other physical repercussions. Others believe that they are entirely emotional in origin and connected to unconscious conflict stemming from early traumatic family relationships. In any case, they are highly treatable by competent psychiatrists.

Q: I have a friend who was divorced recently and is now quite depressed. She wanted the divorce and still wants it and at first felt very good about it, even ecstatic. But this was followed by her current mood, which is almost like someone in mourning. Is this very unusual?

A: Not at all. As a matter of fact, this kind of reaction—ecstasy followed by depression—is quite common. People have unrealistic expectations about both marriage and divorce. This produces initial euphoria followed by disappointment and depression. Many people react to divorce with a period of mourning, despite the fact that they prefer to be out of the marriage. This is in large part due to a sense of loss of a cherished dream as well as a reaction to the death of a relationship. Many people are particularly depressed after a divorce because of unconscious feelings of guilt. These stem from conventional prohibitions against divorce. Divorce is also seen and felt as a personal failure, as a rejection by another human being, as proof of poor judgment in choosing a partner, and as a loss of prestige in moving from a married to a single state. These factors, loneliness and the necessary changes in living conditions and social life can cause considerable depression and require a period of adjustment. This is particularly true of people who are unused to being alone and self-sufficient. If depression following divorce is severe or prolonged, psychotherapeutic help is certainly indicated.

Q: I got divorced four months ago and I am quite depressed. I don't understand it because I couldn't stand to be married to him and I certainly would never go back. In fact, I am truly happy we are parted and I knew it was over for the last three years or more (we were married for eight years). But why should I feel so bad now, especially when I felt so relieved and good when it finally happened—only a few months back?
A: Several possibilities and factors exist, and your reaction is very common among divorced people. These often exist on a relatively unconscious level.

1. Sadness and a sense of loss owing to the death of an important relationship as well as to the end of all kinds of hopes, desires, fantasies, and illusions connected to that relationship.

2. Guilt and self-hate caused by a sense of failure—"not having been able to make a go of it."

3. Disappointment in self, in him, in marriage.

4. Conflicts about how to go on with one's life, buried feelings regarding morality and being a good girl, leading to guilt and anxiety.

5. Disappointment with new-found freedom, which initially produced excitement and happy expectations but which soon gave way to the current problems of reality.

6. Loneliness, especially difficult for dependent people.

7. Disappointment born of expectation of instant adjustment to both a new single status and a cultural life-style that may have changed radically since the time one's marriage took place. This adjustment takes time and includes new attitudes of friends and relatives to one's newly acquired single status.

Q: I'm wondering about the worrying I do. Sometimes it seems as though it is for a good reason and other times it seems like plain foolishness. How can a person tell the difference and can anything be done?

A: I'd rather call it appropriate and realistic concern if the reason for mulling over something is a good one. For example, if a woman finds a lump in her breast, it is appropriate that she should be concerned and her concern may indeed save her life. If she preoccupies herself with fearful thoughts about the lump and does nothing about it, this process must be defined as obsessive worrying. The same, of course, is true of the woman who is told again and again that her breast examination is negative but nevertheless goes on worrying about nonexistent lumps. I find that there are two good ways to tell the difference between appropriate concern and worrying.

1. In appropriate concern, proper and possible action is taken quickly and usually relieves the concern. In obsessive worrying, action is postponed, and when something is eventually done the worrying goes on anyway.

2. In appropriate concern we can put the issue out of our minds for a while and occupy ourselves with other things. Comfortable postponement is possible. In compulsive and obsessive worrying and ruminating the issues cannot be

postponed or removed from one's mind. It goes on and on and makes attention to other real and pressing matters almost impossible.

Obsessive worrying is often a way of avoiding issues, conflicts, and feelings we don't want to face. We use worrying as smoke to cover up the real fires that need attention. When these real issues are finally confronted and settled, especially unexpressed feelings of all kinds (particularly anger), the worrying to displaced areas usually disappears. There are, of course, some people for whom worrying has become a way of life. They have chronically avoided the real issues in their lives and have also come to feel that without worrying catastrophe will take place. These people use worrying magically to ward off "the slings and arrows of outrageous fortune." For many of these chronic worriers psychotherapy is necessary to help them stop this tragic dissipation of time and energy.

What Could Have Been

Nearly all of us have played the game of *what could have been* at various times in our lives. My own feeling is that this game, especially in the form of questions, is most prevalent among women. Some of the common questions are: What could I have been if I never got married? What would have been had I married Joe instead of Bill? What if I never went ahead and had a family? What could I have been had I been born a boy instead of a girl or if I had different parents or if I was brought up in a city rather than on a farm? What could I have been if I had gone on with school? What if we had not lost that money ten years ago? What if we had become rich? Why do I always think of what could have been?

In my psychoanalytic practice I have always followed up these questions with explorations as to their real meaning. It is interesting to note that when women have elaborated they invariably assumed that *what could have been* would have turned out to be infinitely better than what actually took place. Indeed, it seldom occurred to them that their lives may have turned out better than the *could-have-been* turns in the road would have. It also became apparent to me that pre-occupation with *could have been* became particularly prevalent and took on excessive importance when the individual in question was seriously depressed. I have also realized for some time now that the game of *could have been* is particularly prevalent and strong in chronically unhappy people. This is especially so for people who feel that they willy-nilly fell into the various patterns of their lives or were pushed into their current situations without having made active choices of their own. Unfortunately, the *could-have-been* game does not usually lead to mobilizing one's resources and desires and striking out in a self-chosen, constructive direction. In fact, this game is a rather deadly one and insidiously contributes to a sense of self-depletion and futility. This is so because the underlying purpose of the game is self-deprecation as well as deprecation of the here and now of our lives. If each here and now is destroyed in favor of a mythical could-have-been life, it becomes obvious that this process is a destroyer of our well-being, our self-esteem, and our happiness. Indeed, it has become my opinion that with rare exception ruminating of this kind is a very destructive and highly prevalent form of self-hate that often masks considerable emotional depression. Of course, some of us play the game only on occasion, and we do not suffer from serious depression. But even then, I suspect that the game derives from a darker mood and is not really a joyous, playful activity. I also believe that any kind of self-recrimination about the past is potentially addictive and can become a chronically destructive process, eroding our morale and the good of our lives.

In addition to its function as a form of self-hate, the game is deleterious in another way. It is often used as a diversionary tactic, focusing our attention and energy away from the possibilities and choices that may exist in our lives now, in the changeable present. Yes, often when we are afraid to make choices and to effect changes we focus on the unchangeable past so as to divert ourselves from making changes now. Knowing this is very important because when we find ourselves recriminating about the past or ruminating about what could have been we might make a considerable effort to focus on NOW and *what could be.* If we are pulled back to the past and if we continually have nostalgic feelings for the past, I believe this must be taken as further evidence that we fear current issues in our lives and particularly desires and possibilities of change. Unfortunately, many of us find it easier to weep about missed opportunities than to take advantage of the opportunities that currently exist. Of course, this promotes a continuance of the process because the missed opportunities of today will be agonized over tomorrow, thus perpetuating the process.

It is important, even urgent, to realize that hindsight is easy but almost always destructively demoralizing. We make our decisions as best we can and then we must go forward, not backward.

It is important to realize that *only—yes, only—*here and now exists. The past is gone and the future is not yet here.

It is important to realize that we are only human. We are not clairvoyant. No human being can predict the future or can know what could have been.

It could have been better and it could have been a lot worse, too, and it could have been a mixture of both.

It is urgent to realize that we can't have it all; cannot have experienced it all. There are priorities and choices; there are limitations; there are rewards and there are always prices to be paid. It is impossible to know how it could have been— only how it was.

It is most important to know how *it is now.* To give the here and now the attention and energy it deserves, we must refuse to play destructive hindsight—could have been— games. We must focus on now and investigate current priorities, options, choices, and decisions. We must abandon destructive nostalgic games, whatever form they take, and act either in favor of maintaining our current situations or in changing them. But whether or not we change, we must not recriminate about the here and now.

Anger

When was the last time you got angry? What did you do about it? How did you feel about it?

If you can readily remember the last time you were angry chances are you're way ahead of the game. Some adults repress anger so quickly and automatically that they may have to reach far into their childhoods to answer my first question.

A direct angry response is immediate to the situation or person that provoked it and conveys the message verbally as well as emotionally. Many people, especially children, also respond physically by throwing things, hitting something, banging their heads and kicking their feet. By maturity, however, all this honest pouring out of emotion has too often been "successfully" and totally blocked. Cultural or societal forces, family patterns related to the handling of anger, and our own personal psychologies about general relating patterns (such as the inappropriate need to be universally liked) have profound effects on how we handle anger. If you're one of the lucky few adults who respond to anger directly, you probably have, at least in part, modified it since childhood (no more head-banging, I hope). If you're like the majority of us you probably have, without conscious awareness, chosen to divert or pervert anger, at least to some degree. I describe these "perversions" in detail in *The Angry Book*, which I wrote some years ago in response to what I consider one of our most prevalent emotional problems.

Anger that is blocked must eventually find release. It is in the manner we choose to release it or to withhold it that we get into trouble with ourselves and other people.

What do we do when we get angry? Too many of us convert the response (I call this perversion of a normal, human, healthy emotion) to one we believe will be a civilized one, acceptable by society. The ultimate perversion is no anger at all. Over years of successful conscious and unconscious training "not to care," "to forgive and to forget," to "talk about it when I've cooled off," some people have reached the point where anger is automatically pushed aside into what I call "deep freeze." We cannot freeze one emotion and expect to remain healthily responsive as far as our other emotions are concerned. When we deaden anger we inadvertently also kill off spontaneity, love, and creativity. We may not know it, but we isolate ourselves from ourselves and from others. Have you known anyone who goes about cold, distant, sullen, and silent for weeks and even months and years at a time? Fortunately, most of us never reach the deep-freeze stage. We are usually content with converting anger into a more common variety of symptoms: headaches, fatigue, anxiety, depression, overeating, overdrinking, self-sabotage. Diverting anger from original sources to various business, family, and social situations or to particular people creates one of the most difficult climates for constructive and happy relating. Most of us have experienced having had difficulty with a supervisor, teacher, or parent and have returned to the "safety" of home and have begun haranguing and blasting a wife or child for a minor mishap. This type of diverting is easily recognizable. It is, however, the more subtle diverting or "perverting" that is insidious and most damaging. A mother may unconsciously pick on her son and be generally hostile to him because of resentments and anger toward her father or husband. Continued inappropriate response to her child destroys communication, acceptance, self-esteem, and it eventually has disastrous consequences for all concerned. This child will grow up to be a repressed, angry adult and will probably continue the cycle.

Self-sabotage is a particularly hazardous manner of diverting anger. This includes accident proneness, overeating, overdrinking, headaches, and fatigue. The ultimate displacement of anger from its original source onto ourselves is self-hate, depression, and, in some people, suicide. Destructive emotional symptoms are intimately connected to a buildup of buried angry feelings that have been denied an outlet. Incapacitating ruminations, self-recriminations, and explosive temper tantrums are evidence of impending emotional explosions. These "explosions" cannot take place in people who have not stored their anger for a great period of time.

The list of "perversions" is a long one. Some of the common ones include aggressive driving, burned dinners, forgetfulness, chronic lateness, chronic fatigue, destructive gossip, sadism, masochism, sexual teasing, smoking, overworking, and so on. Yes, overworking can be a perversion of anger. Many of us attempt to work off anger rather than to feel it as it is, let alone to express it. People will go to almost any length to avoid expressing their feelings.

How do *you* feel about your angry feelings? I feel good when I let loose and confront a situation that calls for anger with strong feeling. Unfortunately, anger is the most misunderstood, maligned, and mishandled of all our emotional expressions. Our culture has erroneously and damagingly taught us that feeling angry and expressing angry feelings are bad, the opposite of love. It associates anger with loss of control, irresponsibility, irrationality, craziness, and even murder. This attitude overlooks the fact that severe emotional explosions and violence are characteristic of repressed anger. How many times have you read about the nice quiet young man next door who never, ever got angry who one day suddenly murdered his whole family? This is, of course, an ultimate expression of the perversion of anger and does not happen if anger is healthily felt and expressed.

For me, anger is a warm emotion. It shows interest, involvement, caring, and love. Yes, love, because most of our anger centers around family and the people we love the most. When we stop loving it is usually because of great blocks of anger that inhibit the free flow of love. There is little as beneficial to human relating as the ability to voice displeasure to clear the air and to repair misunderstandings rather than to stew in chronic, cold silence. The other day I had the privilege of witnessing this precise anger/love flow when I was visiting my niece and her two-year-old daughter. Little Sara was playing with a friend when her mother came along and disturbed her play. Sara became incensed, stamped her feet, pushed her mother away, shook her head vigorously, and shouted, "No! No!" She was angry and showed it physically, emotionally, and verbally. Needless to say, she got her message across to her mother, who allowed her to finish her game peacefully. At that time, little Sara was able quite unselfconsciously to go over to her mother and spontaneously hug and kiss her. Her mother received her with open arms, harboring no resentment over her earlier rejection, and Sara was able to extend love freely because she had been able to express her anger. For adults this is not so easy, but it is a struggle worth engaging in.

If we seriously want to change our ways of handling anger we must learn to recognize angry feelings when we have them. Sometimes people need help with this and have to be told that they are indeed entitled to be angry. This is very much like the mother of a toddler who can recognize that his stubbornness most of the time probably means that he is hungry, that he just hasn't learned to read himself and to express that need yet. Encourage those close to you to express their anger and ask them to help you with yours. It is sometimes easier for us to recognize anger in someone else. When you see your obese daughter going to the cookie jar after she's been told to clean her room, you know she's angry. Tell her. Once the anger is released, accept it as a warm emotion and try not to harbor resentment. Accepting anger from those closest to us will encourage them to accept our anger as well. Try to remember the intimate tie between anger and love. Love cools when resentment blocks it on an unconscious level. Anger when felt fully is short-lived. Expressing anger rids us of resentment and permits love to flow freely and consciously.

Q: My husband is a nice, rather mild-mannered, gentle, considerate man with very good manners. But when he drives he becomes a veritable Mr. Hyde. He gives no quarter. He has temper outbursts. He curses and finds fault with just about all other drivers, and he speeds, too. What is this crazy car behavior all about?

A: Many people who are "crazy" on the road are discharging repressed anger. They may also be expressing feelings displaced from other people and areas. For example, there are a number of people who are compliant Milquetoasts at work and tyrants at home. Some people are mild at work and at home and tyrants on the road. Unfortunately, many people feel their automobiles are extensions of themselves and the most powerful aspect of themselves. They therefore need and use the car to express feelings they cannot otherwise express because without the protection and strength of the car they feel weak and vulnerable. Unfortunately, this kind of confused displacement and misidentification can lead to tragedy. It is especially dangerous when men use their cars to support childish macho images they have of themselves.

Talking this out with your husband may be helpful. Real change takes place when anger is handled and expressed at its source rather than in the car on the road. But to do this a change in the perennial nice, mild, gentle image may be necessary. The fact is that none of us is so nice that we never get angry. If we continue to repress anger long enough to sustain an image of being a "nice guy," explosions of anger are inevitable. When they happen on the road all kinds of nonaccidental accidents often become tragic realities.

Q: Sometimes I have unbelievably terrible fantasies. I think of my children dying and my husband, too. There are times they are suddenly there and I find myself in tears and quite a while passes before I can stop them. Can you tell me what this can be about?

A: These fantasies are quite common. Recurrent fantasies sometimes indicate the presence of underlying, unresolved problems and feelings. They are also a way of discharging and ridding ourselves of feelings that we don't want to experience or to be aware of. Fantasies involving death of loved ones are exceedingly common and often come from one or more of several sources. These are sometimes used to express repressed anger at loved ones. The more we repress, the stronger the mood of the fantasy tends to be. These kinds of fantasies are also used to torture and to punish ourselves and as such are expressions of self-hate. They are often the result of some supposed transgression, which turns out to be quite human. For example, some of us feel we deserve punishment for sometimes feeling that we would like to be free of having our children altogether, even though this is a normal feeling. Another function of this kind of fantasy is to enact a drama in order to test how we would feel minus loved ones and also, at times, to compensate for feeling bored. If torturous fantasies become chronic, professional psychoanalytic therapy can be very helpful.

Q: When I'm angry about something, I believe in saying so and putting the issue behind me, but my husband is just the opposite: when a problem arises, he fears it could cause heartbreak and wants to drop it before things go too far. If I bring up a subject that troubles me, he refuses to listen, and, should I insist on talking about it, he becomes livid . . . so I've been letting my anger build up inside. What's a better way to deal with this conflict?

A: Repressing anger is a sure way to make things go too far. Repressed anger leads to a vast number of difficulties, including psychosomatic symptoms, anxiety attacks, depression, explosive rages, chronic sullenness, communication breakdown, sexual malfunctions, unconscious mutual sabotage, and the repression of other feelings, including warm and loving ones.

Issues that produce anger are the most important to discuss. Clearing the air invariably has an ameliorative effect all around. However, it is most constructive to discuss these issues compassionately. There is a vast difference between warm open anger and vindictive, sadistic tirades. The latter are almost always counterproductive.

If your husband cannot be reached otherwise, it may be wise to bring in a third party you both respect. These include a minister, doctor, good friend, or professional therapist. It is important in these sessions to clarify issues and to help each other rather than to dwell on who is right and who is wrong. The third party should be used as a conduit for open communication and not as a judge of guilt and innocence.

Your husband may view discussions of these kinds as proof that your relationship is less than perfect. He must be reassured that no relationship is perfect. Differences always exist and there is always a need for clarification of ideas and feelings.

Q: I have a friend I dearly love, but she is a gossip. She will periodically say things about people that are hurtful and later on wishes she had bitten her tongue instead. She says she just doesn't know why she does this. She promises herself to keep her mouth shut and then bang! she talks and gets in trouble all over again. Why?
A: Much gossip takes place as a form of entertainment and some people use it in order to be admired—like telling a joke. It is also used in place of giving a gift and as a way of trying to be liked. But one of the most common uses of gossip is to hurt as part of a process of discharging repressed anger. Most gossips are unaware of these motives, which largely remain out of conscious awareness. Awareness on a fully conscious level helps the gossip rid herself or himself of this compelling impulse.

Q: I'm one of those people who always think of what to say after it's too late. I know a few people who almost invariably say something nasty to me. I usually answer them back but not really the way I want to. Later on it occurs to me what I really would have liked to say but then it is too late. Why can't I be fast in this kind of thing like some other people I know?
A: You probably have a strong need to be liked, not to "make waves," to hide angry feelings from yourself and others. You probably repress strong angry feelings when they occur and block out any good answers that would effec-

tively convey these feelings. In this way you protect your "nice-person" image and let the words and feelings emerge only when it is too late and *safe*.

Repressing anger has a self-corrosive effect, and the attempt to be loved by everyone brings no reward at all. Some people can change themselves and gradually learn to risk saying how they feel—exactly how they feel. Others need psychotherapy in order to do this. The relief and sense of freedom can be truly exhilarating. It also brings sustained self-esteem as well as better relationships generally.

Q: I was in a bad car accident three years ago. I didn't get nearly as badly hurt as I might have. I am thirty years old and have driven a car since I was sixteen. I was a very good driver and the accident was not my fault. A man drove through a stop sign and hit me. I guess the worst part of it was the shock, the total surprise. I just haven't been able to drive since then, though I am absolutely physically fit. I can hardly get into a car even when someone else is driving. I keep imagining someone will suddenly drive into us. I've even dreamed of the whole thing again just a short time ago. I really hate to be handicapped this way. Am I crazy?

A: You are not at all crazy. You are suffering from what is sometimes known as a traumatic neurosis, which often follows unexpected shock or trauma. Reliving it is an attempt on your part to work it out of your system. You do this in fantasy as well as dreams. This kind of symptom often lingers because it is linked to other disturbing events in childhood, which are buried in the unconscious. Sometimes guilt for the accident keeps the condition going even though it was not the victim's fault. The condition is highly amenable to competent psychotherapy. This is one of the few conditions that are often aided by hypnosis. But do not engage in any kind of amateur therapy, hypnosis or otherwise. It is important to see a competent psychoanalytically trained psychotherapist.

Q: Is it my imagination or is it possible? It seems to me that when I'm in a bad mood—nervous and depressed—my eyesight is not as acute as when I feel good. I'm not talking about seeing double or anything like that—just seems to me I don't see as well.

A: Moods, states of relative well-being, tension, anxiety, depression, and state of mind generally certainly can affect one's senses and perceptive ability. This includes the eyes as well as all other organs of perception: taste buds, ears, nose, and so on. This is not unusual if we realize that it is all happening in one body and that moods, glands, muscles, and all physiological systems are intimately connected and interdependent. I would still recommend a careful eye examination with a reputable ophthalmologist just to make sure there is no direct eye problem present, even if an emotional response is there, too.

Q: I'm terrified of getting any dental work done or, for that matter, going to the doctor for any treatment, however minor. I've been in psychotherapy and it has helped me in just about all areas, but I still quake before any kind of treatment. I recently had to get a small mole removed from my forehead, and I thought I'd die of anxiety. Any suggestions?

A: Psychoanalytic treatment often helps in this area, and sometimes people have to uncover childhood fearful events and traumatic incidents in order to face medical interventions with greater equanimity. Some people do much better after they gain insight about their fear of helplessness.

On an immediate, practical level, doctors often help their patients considerably by premedicating them with light sedation or a mild tranquilizer. This helps both the patient and the doctor, but in many cases the patient must convey her sense of dread and fear to the doctor in order for him to do this. Some doctors are unfortunately unaware of the distress suffered by the patient who develops anxiety in treatment, however minor that treatment may be.

Q: I have to have a hysterectomy sometime within the next few months and I'm so upset I hardly sleep. It's an elective operation for a benign condition; I've been reassured that the operation is without danger and I believe it, but I'm still upset. I'm forty-three years old, have two wonderful children, and I certainly do not want any more babies. Why am I acting like such a baby? Help!

A: I don't think you are acting like a baby at all. A hysterectomy has a great symbolic connotation for just about all women and this certainly includes the most adult and has nothing to do with age or the desire to have babies. Contemplation of surgery is always appropriately anxiety producing and doubly so when highly symbolic organs are involved. You are certainly entitled to be upset without being upset about being upset. However much you are reassured, going into a hospital, away from home, into unfamiliar surroundings to undergo an unfamiliar process is upsetting. Having one's uterus removed is often felt as an attack on one's femininity and as a loss of youth, fertility, and attractiveness. Even though you may well know that fertility is all that will be lost, it is not easy to get over a sense of sadness, especially since the hospital is also a reminder of another time when the very same uterus was used to produce babies. Many women feel terribly angry because they have to undergo the operation and sustain this loss of a richly symbolic organ. But since they feel no one is at fault they find it difficult to experience, let alone to vent their anger, a reaction they feel would be irrational. This repressed anger makes them feel much more anxious than they would otherwise feel. It is often very relieving and helpful to experience the anger and to "let it out," however inappropriate this seems. This sometimes is possible only in a psychotherapeutic encounter. My own feeling is that several sessions with a good therapist before and after any major surgical procedure can be very helpful in feeling better and in healing better, too—both physically and emotionally. This is especially true where sexual organs are involved in either sex (prostate surgery in men).

Q: I've had gums and teeth problems for quite some time. My dentist recently told me that some difficulties such as this can be emotional in origin. Is this possible? I recently lost two of my teeth and I can't tell you how bad this makes me feel. I keep telling myself that it's only two teeth, but this doesn't seem to help. Perhaps my exaggerated feelings about this do mean that I'm more emotionally disturbed than I think.

A: The mouth has great symbolic as well as practical importance for all of us. It is, after all, used for eating and breathing, both of which are essential life functions. It is also used to kiss, to talk, to sing, to taste, and to demonstrate changes of mood and feelings by assuming different shapes, such as smiling, crying, and frowning. This powerful "organ" of expression is therefore felt as an intimate part of ourselves, and any injury or loss connected to it is bound to be felt deeply, both as a personal injury and as a threat to our ability to communicate. Loss of teeth is often felt as a sign of getting old, losing one's looks, becoming weak, and it generally makes people feel self-conscious and embarrassed. Much of this goes on unconsciously, but this does not mitigate the sense of loss and consequent sorrow that is felt.

Many people who are anxious and tense without full conscious awareness of their feelings clench and grind their teeth during sleep. Many of them repress anger during the day, and some grind and clench their teeth in an attempt to express their anger at night, when they feel it is safe—no one else will know. Others clench and grind in an attempt to continue to hold back their feelings at night, too. Analysis of dreams that take place during bad periods of grinding is sometimes quite revealing in demonstrating what it is the teeth-grinder is attempting to repress and/or express. Analytic treatment that leads to freer acceptance and expression of feelings can be helpful in dealing with this symptom. In any case, here again one can see the importance of the mouth both as an organ that expresses feelings to others and as a major recipient of unexpressed feelings in ourselves.

Interestingly, I have had a number of patients who have suffered from breakdowns in their mouths (teeth and gums) when they suffered breakdowns in communications with themselves and others. Since the mouth is used so much in communication, this is not really unusual. In some cases dental work was helped considerably as the person's ability to communicate improved and his/her feelings about himself/herself and others became clarified.

Chapter Eleven

THE EMOTIONS

*Self-Esteem and Self-Hate • Envy •
Jealousy • Loss and Mourning*

Self-Esteem and Self-Hate

SELF-ESTEEM IS HOW we feel about ourselves. We reflect our attitude through our behavior at work, play, and our relations with others. Those of us with a realistic sense of self-worth are indeed fortunate. Our actions and responses will largely be determined by our own values and opinions, and we can continue to feel self-assured even when we make mistakes or have a different point of view from the majority.

On the other hand, those of us with poor self-esteem will most likely distort behavior to achieve recognition. We may be arrogant, manipulate for compliments, suffer from various forms of self-hate (such as an inability to find pleasure and lack of satisfaction in the usual endeavors of life), and use other machinations in the service of creating an acceptable self for someone "out there." Sadly, people with poor self-esteem are starving for affection and understanding. Unfortunately, their behavior may invite only alienation.

Q: Every time I'm criticized, I crumble. This hurts my performance at work and keeps me high-strung at home. How can I learn to be less sensitive?

A: Your untoward reaction to outside criticism probably stems from lack of compassion with yourself. You must struggle for greater self-acceptance in all areas as well as reduced expectations of yourself. If you succeed in treating yourself better and seeing yourself in a better light, outside appropriate criticism may not only become tolerable but may also be used constructively to further enhance self-esteem.

Q: My husband isn't a bad guy. As a matter of fact he is very good! He's devoted to me and the children. He is a responsible person who can be counted on in most things. He is usually warm and loving. But when we go out with other people he is often unbearable! He becomes unbelievably arrogant. He's suddenly a know-it-all and really alienates friends. Some have even commented to me about this. What can this possibly be about?

A: Arrogance, in which we ascribe or arrogate to ourselves power, position, and expertise that we don't really have, is almost always a device used to cover up fear. Some people become arrogant only when particularly vulnerable areas of themselves threaten to be exposed. Other people virtually spend their lives in a state of secret terror and have made arrogance the predominant characteristic of their personalities. Arrogance in these people is sometimes confused with strength. It is actually a mask for fear and fragility, of which the individual may or may not be relatively conscious. The chronically arrogant person sometimes does not know he is arrogant. He is seldom aware of underlying fear until a direct confrontation occurs and often as a result a serious emotional collapse takes place. Yes, chances are that your husband becomes fearful and feels vulnerable in social situations. He covers up these feelings with arrogant bluster. The more arrogance, the more fear. Why he is fearful in social situations would necessitate much more information about him. We can only speculate. He may feel competitively inadequate with his social peers. He may feel jealous of the attention or potential attention to you. Part of his behavior may be an unconscious desire to impress you with his worthiness relative to other men who may be present. In any case, arrogance tends to diminish as people become more comfortable with themselves and others and become less fearful.

Q: I have a friend whom I truly love but who periodically gets what my husband and I call "know-it-all attacks." At these times she is overbearing and impossible and will argue with just about anyone regardless of how expert the other party may be. What makes a person so arrogant?

A: In one word—fear. Arrogance covers up fear and is usually directly proportional to the underlying fear a person has. People who are chronically arrogant are really very fearful people, although they let neither themselves nor anyone else in on it, posing instead as strong and all-knowing. Intermittent "attacks" such as you describe in your friend are often due to fear in particular social situations. When your friend feels comfortable she drops her arrogance or defensive mantle. When she feels threatened, perhaps by the presence of certain people (maybe the very experts she argues with), up goes the protective shield. Of course, this happens automatically without conscious awareness on her part.

Q: I am all for women's equality with men; after all, I am a woman. But don't you think that women are more emotional than men and that therefore men make more stable and better leaders? Women do have hormonal changes and periods, which men don't have.

A: Women are no more emotional than men and men also have hormones that affect them. I believe that personality and character structure determined by many factors, mainly upbringing, have much more of an effect on the emotions than hormones. Perhaps it would be better if some of our leaders did, in fact, trust their hearts more than their heads. In any case, I am convinced that neither sex has any particular predisposition for good leadership. Perhaps you should re-examine your belief about being all for women's equality. Neither men nor women are exempt from cultural brainwashing and sexist prejudice.

Q: I have a girl friend who is always putting herself down, often for no reason at all. She is really a lovely, bright person, but if you listen to her you would believe that she is an unattractive dope. Why does she do this? She simply can't take the smallest compliment without making bad remarks about herself.

A: This kind of self-derision may have one or more of several motives, usually unconscious, on the part of the person "putting herself down."

Some people do it because they really feel inferior and embarrassed by compliments. Their feelings of inferiority often come from great unconscious vanity and extremely high standards relative to which they feel grossly inadequate. Some people use personal self-effacement as a means of feeling safe from the potential onslaught of others, feeling that if they put themselves down, others won't. Some people do it as a secret (to themselves) means of manipulating others to compliment them and to insist on recapitulations and reassurances of their good points. Others do it as a form of self-glorified—"poor little me"—martyrdom, through which they make claims on other people for special consideration and understanding. Others do it as a form of superstition and "placating the gods," believing that this kind of false humility will protect them from dire uncontrollable events. There are people who are terrified of compliments, experiencing them as standards to which they must measure up lest they be rejected and disliked. This is especially true of people with low self-esteem who have a compulsive need to be liked by everyone with whom they come into contact in order to feel secure.

Q: I never get anywhere on time. It drives my friends and family crazy, but I can't seem to break the habit. What's it going to take to make me change?

A: What will help you to change is mostly the desire to change, which will motivate you to investigate and to use the insights you find that apply to you.

Any or all of the following may be present. They usually

remain on an unconscious level but prevent the chronic latecomer from coming on time until full conscious awareness takes place. Needless to say, chronic lateness is highly destructive to one's reputation, self-esteem, and just about all personal relationships.

1. Poor self-esteem so that the feeling is sustained that it doesn't matter whether one comes on time or not since one's presence is of so little importance anyway.

2. General ruthlessness regarding other people's time, energy, and needs, combined with lack of responsibility characteristic of lack of an appropriate conscience.

3. High degree of narcissism and preoccupation with the self to the exclusion of full conscious awareness of the presence of others.

4. Emotional disturbance causing poor orientation and lack of ability to use time effectively. This may stem from organic brain damage.

5. Grandiosity and failure to take into account human limitations, causing the repeated belief that one can do more than one can do in a given period of time.

6. Easily distracted, lacking organization, and even experiencing fragmentation, so that severe emotional disturbance makes simple tasks really impossible.

7. Extreme sensitivity to coercion and the unconscious belief that being on time or keeping a prearranged appointment is surrendering to coercion. People with this problem always have much difficulty with commitments, contracts, or agreements of any kind.

8. The need to rebel against authority. With this frame of reference, appointments are unconsciously seen as authority and coming late is felt to be a freeing, self-assertive maneuver.

9. Repressed anger and an unconscious need to retaliate, to tease, to frustrate, to get even, and to be vindictive. In this context, lateness is an equivalent temper tantrum.

10. The childish need and desire to test people—to see how much they will take. In effect, one says, "If you love me, you will take my lateness and perhaps other provoca-

tions.'' Some of these people will arrive at prefixed appointments later and later, in a test of how much provocation will
be withstood.

11. Hidden self-hate and the need to be self-destructive.

12. Coming late is often a maneuver to be in charge and
to be manipulative—to keep the other person waiting is a
way of being in control of that person.

Q: What about people who can't fix their own homes up
without a decorator? Don't you think there's something
really wrong with them? Don't they have taste of their own?
What happened to good old healthy self-reliance?
A: Of course, there is a difference between blindly com-
plying with other people's tastes and making up one's own
mind after getting expert consultation. Some people have
never developed their own taste or have so little regard for
their own preferences that they must depend on others to tell
them what is right. Others don't want to be bothered and
would prefer that someone else take over for them. There
are still other people who are so terrified of hidden dependency feelings that they must rebel in all areas of their lives
and can never avail themselves of genuine expert help. Self-
reliance is a wonderful characteristic, especially when it is
combined with constructive cooperation and exchange of
mutual skills. Depriving people of expert help does not increase self-reliance. Self-reliance is linked to self-esteem
and has its roots in healthy parent-child relationships.

Q: I know a man who is a terrible bigot. His hates include
just about everyone except himself. He makes Archie
Bunker seem like an open, accepting person. What makes a
guy like this tick? He doesn't have a good word for anyone,
even people who try to be nice to him. I must say fewer and
fewer people want to have anything to do with him. His wife
tries to get him to mend his ways, but like Archie and Edith it
just doesn't work.
A: I can't agree with you about hating everyone except
himself. He hates himself most of all. So much, in fact, that

he must project it to other people to keep himself from the despair he would experience if he allowed himself to feel it. Coupled with this method of putting his own self-contempt out of awareness is his attempt to feel superior by putting other people down. This kind of man needs acceptance from other people desperately but of course makes it most difficult for other people to give it to him. He feels rejected and this increases his self-hate, feeding the whole process. It also proves to him that he is right about people after all—thus increasing his cynicism.

Q: Do you think that some racial groups are genetically more intelligent than others and therefore almost always produce smarter people and the best students while others simply can't?
A: No. I believe that some groups have socioeconomic advantages. Some have greater encouragement and support for intellectual activity. Some are influenced by a value system that places great esteem on academic achievement. It is difficult and often impossible to achieve anything intellectually in a state of human deprivation and hunger. This includes hunger for food, hunger for warmth, hunger for caring, hunger for love, hunger for respect, and hunger for dignity. This kind of difficulty has nothing at all to do with genes or heredity and will invariably affect any group of people subject to brutalization, prejudice, isolation, and deprivation for a significant period of time.

Q: I have a friend, twenty-four years old, who wants to be a celebrity. I suppose I would like to be famous, too, but I don't think it's the most important thing in my life. But my friend talks of little else. He doesn't even quite care how he becomes famous. The important thing is that someday everybody will recognize and know him as a great celebrity. What makes a person crave this kind of thing so much?
A: Our society pushes the importance of fame or celebrity status way beyond any possible happiness or satisfaction it can bring. Some of us are more than usually vulnerable to

this distortion. Your friend's obsession with fame may entail several possibilities.

Let me first say that the victim of this kind of obsession is seldom conscious of its roots. Celebrity status is confused with sustained and endless admiration and love. These are particularly important to people who feel inadequate, unloved, and self-hating. Celebrities are viewed as people who live charmed lives, who don't suffer from ordinary pains and problems, and who are really part of a heaven-on-earth life. This fantasy is particularly appealing to people who feel that their own lives and surroundings are impoverished and shoddy. Fame is equated with expertise and with abiding respect. This has great appeal for people who feel useless and who feel they are incapable of attaining respect from others through the genuine acquisition of proficiency in any endeavor. People who feel that they have been unjustly treated as children and who continue to feel abused as adults use fantasies of fame in an attempt to make it up to themselves. For some, fame is seen as a way of getting even, as a way of scoring a victory over supposed detractors and persecutors. In short, fame becomes a substitute for self-esteem and is regarded as the magic ingredient that will make all wishes and expectations come true.

Q: My teenage son seems to be quite a snob. He is very critical of friends and lacks interest in them unless they are very bright, capable in all things, ambitious, and the like. What makes him this way? My husband and I are not at all like this.

A: The name of this game is insecurity, low self-esteem, and self-rejection. These are covered up by demands on other people and snobbism in an effort to identify with other people's qualities as a means of establishing one's own synthetic adequacy. This kind of snobbism is no different in adults of all ages. In both young and older people, intense shyness is often camouflaged by seeming lack of interest in other people. People are seen, for one or another spurious reason, as lacking qualities necessary for friendship. When basic insecurities are realistically dealt with, many of these so-called snobs begin to see people they formerly rejected as interesting and acceptable.

Q: I am an attractive, youngish woman. I always try to look good. Even though I make this effort on my own behalf, I feel very uncomfortable whenever someone says something nice about anything even remotely connected to me. Strangely enough, I find it easier to accept criticism. Why am I this way?

A: People who can't accept compliments comfortably are usually very self-effacing. They deal with considerable self-hate and anxiety by denying their very existence as people. They may secretly desire recognition and praise. But this desire remains secret, since any notice, attention, and especially compliments stress their identification as real people and threaten the self-effacing pattern they have established in order to feel safe. Paradoxically, many self-effacing people also have very high standards. Thus, no amount of praise is really good enough. It does not dilute self-hate, and it does not help to succeed in achieving impossible goals based on unrealistic standards. Criticism, especially of an adverse nature, is more acceptable since it fits in with self-hate and can be used to flagellate oneself further in a push to impossible goals. Compliments are appropriately enjoyed when we can combat our self-hate, raise our real self-esteem, regard ourselves as real people, and get over the fear of being seen as real people. That you recognize your being attractive and try to look good indicates that your self-esteem is not nearly as bad as that of other people who suffer from this highly prevalent problem.

Q: I'm a junior in high school and I'm interested in art. I'm thinking of someday teaching art history on a college level. We got into a pretty heavy discussion in class last week about artists and other creative people. Do you feel that artists tend to be sicker mentally than other people? Do you think you have to be emotionally disturbed or at least a bit neurotic in order to be creative?

A: I think that creative people have to be in touch with their deepest, innermost, and strongest feelings in order to be creative. Alienation from these feelings produces hackneyed works at best, which is not art. People who are in touch with their feelings are in a way extremely healthy, in as much as they benefit from inner vitality and spontaneity. This makes them highly individualistic, and they may seem somewhat eccentric to more conventional and conforming people. Some artists, like some other people who have no relationship to art whatsoever, have been mentally disturbed. But their artistic and creative ability was not due to their mental illness but was linked to their health and their creative vitality.

Experience with my own patients has invariably demonstrated that as people resolve their conflicts and problems they become more able to tap their resources in the service of both healthy living and creativity. To date, I have never met anyone who has become less creative or less artistic as a result of becoming less neurotic.

Q: Does anyone really know why some people are more creative than others?

A: Since various theories exist you can be sure that no one knows the answer with certainty.

Some "experts" believe that creativity is purely a matter of inheritance and that this is especially true of the unusually and vastly gifted. Others feel that creative people do indeed inherit creative genes but that they are really "mutational accidents" who happen along on occasion and who are radically different from the rest of the population.

I subscribe to the theory that all people are inherently creative, but that much blocking takes place as a result of selfhate, unresolved inner conflicts, fear of self-expression, fear of failure, fear of success, and other neurotic inhibiting forces. Unfortunately, many of us are so strongly conditioned to think, feel, perceive, and express ourselves in constricted, preordained roles that we cannot shake off in order to realize our potential uniqueness. I have known some creative people who have shared the common background of having been brought up in families where individual proclivities and unique expressions of self were encouraged and even cherished. I have also seen an increase in creative ability in people as they progress in psychoanalysis and shake off worries about what other people will think and whether they are good enough. As people become free of old learned and established inner dicta and conventional shoulds and should nots, they show an increase in spontaneity and sometimes become aware of and in touch with talents they never knew existed. Once people let go and start creative processes going—priming the pump, so to speak—one creative activity leads to another and the process continues to develop and to give personal satisfaction all of one's life.

Q: Please help me stop terrible thoughts that come into my head from I don't where! I am a saleswoman, working in a very pleasant atmosphere; I have a pretty nice friendship with a young man and I'm generally a content person. Sometimes, however, right out of the blue I get these awful thoughts, like embarrassing things that happened ages ago, accidents that nearly happened, thoughts of terrible things happening to me or someone I care for. Once these things start, they blow up to giant proportions and I get into a terrible mood. I cry a lot, can't eat, and am just plain miserable. This can last from half a day to several weeks. Then one day it just stops and I'm fine again. Could you please tell me how to stop this—I really would be grateful!

A: What you are experiencing is exceedingly common in many people. It is a form of self-hate, which only you can stop. It is not easy and requires investigation and understanding on your part. Try to look back at all the times that you have experienced the onset of terrible thoughts. Then think back a little further and try to remember what preceded the onslaught. You may come away with a pattern of similar events that brought forth this self-punishment. The entire phenomenon is highly personal. We each must search out our own behavior patterns and see what brings forth attacks of self-hate.

Q: Why do I constantly rehash and torture myself about mistakes I've made in the past? I just go on and on with my second-guessing to the point where I exhaust myself. Sounds crazy, but here I am a fully grown woman feeling like a bad little girl.

A: Rehashing, second-guessing, and self-recriminating are very common forms of self-hate. As with nearly all self-hating devices, there is almost always a hidden, unconscious demand for one or another kind of self-idealization or perfection. Falling short of the demands produces self-hate and punishment designed to push one on to continue the futile search for perfection.

Self-torture about past mistakes is usually based on an unconscious demand for perfect decisions and perfect performances in all matters in life. There is also the unconscious demand that one be able to predict the future, since only perfect predictability of the future can guarantee perfect decisions and no past mistakes. Of course, these inhuman goals are unattainable and, unless they are understood and abandoned, punishment for being a "bad little girl" will continue. This not only produces exhaustion but also makes it very difficult and even impossible to make decisions. Fear of a wrong decision and anticipation of self-punishment that will surely follow eventually have a paralytic effect. Real humility, compassion for self, acceptance of the limitations and fallibilities inherent in being human are the antidote. Psychoanalytic help may be necessary when self-hate has become an ingrained way of life.

Q: I hate being the center of attraction for any reason, even at my own birthday parties. Is something wrong with me?

A: Several possibilities exist and these often go together.

1. You may have confused notions about modesty and may place inordinate value on it.

2. You may suffer from considerable self-hate as well as lack of self-esteem.

3. You have adopted a self-effacing role to make yourself and your existence as little noticed as possible as a way of being liked by everybody and removing any potential threat to your well-being.

4. This may also be a way of masking an enormous desire to be noticed, admired, talked about, and above all to be the very center of attention. This need would conflict with self-effacement and therefore every attempt would be made to keep it hidden from consciousness, since conflict produces anxiety.

Q: I have a close and very attractive girl friend who is attracted only to men who are of a different nationality and of a different ethnic background. The fact that she may have just about nothing in common with them is just about meaningless to her. If they are of a different race she is even more attracted. Of late, she will simply not go out with any man of her own ethnic background. Is this just an "opposites attract" kind of thing, or can it have some deeper meaning?

A: There's nothing unusual about being attracted to and curious about people who, at least on the surface, seem different from ourselves or exotic in any way at all. But obsessive and blanket rejection of people who, at least on a superficial level, remind us of ourselves must have deeper meaning. This kind of behavior may be evidence of strong rebellion against prohibitions and conventions learned early in life and an attempt to free oneself from what is felt as an overwhelming and stifling conscience. Some people who feel this way go out of their way to do what they think is "far out" because they are terrified by their strong but hidden need and compulsion to conform to conventional standards. It may also be evidence of considerable self-hate; thus, the rejection of any reminder of self and the attraction to anyone who seems to promise the possibility of escape through identification with what seems foreign.

Q: Can a woman be a male chauvinist?

A: And how!

My own experience has indicated that more women are male chauvinists than men. Not only that—they are more chauvinistic and often so in areas that really count. They may be more subtle than men, but they are often more prejudiced, too. They put not only themselves down, but nearly all other women as well. It is not accidental that books that preach total subservience to men and the pure marvels of living totally for and vicariously through husbands are selling in the hundreds of thousands—to women. I am certain also that it is no accident that I find it infinitely more difficult to refer women to women physicians than to refer them to men. Most men readily accept a physician of either sex. Women almost invariably prefer to see male doctors, and a great many absolutely refuse to see women doctors regardless of superb qualifications. Most, unfortunately, do not realize that this preference springs from their own chauvinism and self-hate.

Women have the possibility of humanizing their children—that is, teaching them that being human is a wonderful thing. *Human* includes all characteristics, possibilities, and potential, regardless of gender. This means self-acceptance as a person regardless of sexual identification and is all-important to mental health and to future family health. But how can women make this great contribution if they themselves are prejudiced and chauvinistic?

Q: I am a forty-year-old housewife and mother, and I think I'm known for being very responsible, mature, and level-headed. But I still have half a dozen dolls, given to me when I was a little girl. I don't play with them, but I would never get rid of them. I am not a doll collector and have never had a desire to acquire any others. But I am sentimentally attached to these dolls and must admit I get pleasure out of holding and looking at them on occasion. Do you consider this a sign of sickness or some hidden emotional disturbance?

A: No. There is nothing wrong with sentiment. Your attachment to dolls of the past is not obsessive and is not at the expense of the present. Many people keep pleasant mementoes of the past, especially those that remind them of happy childhood days. They may have particular attachments to things given to them by loved ones. This kind of love of objects that are symbolic of childhood may be very strong in people who are always "very responsible, mature, and levelheaded." Sometimes we seek relief from the intense pressures of constant adulthood through cherishing objects of days when we were young and carefree.

Q: I have a physical complaint, aches and pains in my muscles and joints. They are not severe, are intermittent, and my doctor told me that it is a light form of rheumatism and very common. I feel better on sunny, bright days. Could this be my imagination or is there possibly a real reason for this?

A: Atmospheric changes can affect how we feel physically. This seems to be especially true of symptoms involving muscles and joints. But people's moods are often strongly affected by the weather and this, in turn, can have a physical effect. If you feel happier and more cheery when the sun is out you may also feel more relaxed. This may have a direct, good effect on your muscles and joints.

Q: When it's sunny and warm out I almost always feel a bit of a lift no matter how difficult things seem to be for the moment. The opposite is true of cloudy, gloomy weather. I guess bad weather makes me gloomy, too. I've heard songs tell about the same effects on a person's mood. Is this a normal kind of reaction or is it a sign of being quite neurotic?

A: Reacting appropriately to weather is part of being alive and in touch with one's feelings. This is certainly evidence of health rather than neurosis. However, grossly exaggerated reactions to weather as well as to other uncontrollable conditions or occurrences in one's life are often indicative of emotional difficulties. These may be an extension of neurotic claims that an individual makes, in which she or he feels that not only the weather but also life in all of its ramifications ought to be sunny at all times. Some people also have unusual difficulty with any aspect of life that is uncontrollable, and this is extended to weather, airplane delays, accidents, sickness, taxes, or whatever.

Q: Do you think that people who choose cats as pets rather than dogs tend to have more emotional problems?
A: No. I've met all kinds of pet owners and non–pet owners and feel that choice of pet is not a very reliable test of mental health. There are some people, however, who become more involved with pets than with people. This is sometimes a clue to intense loneliness; sometimes to bitterness and cynicism toward people; sometimes to fear of people.

If You Lie About Your Age

Everyone lucky enough to survive birth *must* get older. Clothes, cosmetics, and hairdos can make people look better, but they cannot stop the aging process—only death can do that. So it is that getting older is the very stuff that life is made of.

Unfortunately, however, a great many people have been caught in an extremely destructive trap: they have become ensnared by what I call "the youth-cult sickness." These people have been subtly and blatantly taught by books, television, movies, advertisements—and even by their own mothers—that young is the only way to be; that young is good and old is bad. Consequently, these individuals invest too much pride and have too high an emotional interest in staying young. Thus, each passing day is an assault on their self-esteem. To them, getting old brings on enormous, often unconscious (hidden), self-hate and self-rejection.

If you are to live and live happily, self-acceptance is of prime importance. This means accepting yourself as you are at any given moment, at any given age. Self-acceptance does not preclude improvement and growth. On the contrary, it is self-rejection, self-hate, and the denial of reality that make healthy growth impossible. The compulsive need to cling to youth is such a fruitless and frustrating endeavor that it invariably leads to malignant hopelessness and resignation. It robs us of energy that can be used for more rewarding interests. The compulsive need to cling to youth is a vicious cycle: the more time and energy we spend on trying to stay young, the more hopeless we feel; and the more hopeless we feel, the older we seem.

It is very sad when, for example, a woman won't admit her age or lies about her age. This is ample proof to me of that woman's self-rejection and self-hate. Evidently this woman has been caught in the need to satisfy a superficial vanity. Such vanity will make her older than she is, older than she has to be, older than the woman who freely admits her age. Whatever a woman's age, if that woman has relatively good health, she will have sufficient energy, reflexes, and physiological ability to pursue nearly all the activities she desires.

We must all age to live, and to any self-accepting person, living in the present is far more fulfilling than the superficial vanity feedback a mirror can bring. As we develop new insights and new maturation with regard to ourselves and the people of the world we live in, we will become more and more vital. With new interests and new involvements will come still more interests, and our emotional vitality will increase, whatever our chronological age. Time spent growing in this way will leave little time to concern ourselves with getting older.

Envy

I think of this poison as agitated discontent.

Envy in this context means wanting what one believes someone else has, believing that one is unjustly deprived in not having it, and usually hating the person or persons who seem to have it.

Envy is surely one of the most prevalent and corrosive poisons found in human relationships. It is equally destructive to oneself and to one's relationships. It eats away at one's well-being and demeans and destroys real accomplishments, self-esteem, satisfaction, and pleasures in meaningful pursuits and fun associated with anything owned—material or otherwise. Anything the envious person attains turns to ashes as soon as he gets it. Envy is highly malignant and eventually invades and permeates all aspects of living, so that nothing and nobody is ever good enough and morale is destroyed. It creates a state of insatiability and anxiety resulting from ever-escalating, inappropriate yearnings and desires, which usually are perceived as necessities and as always owned by undeserving people.

Few people are aware that envy can exist on an unconscious level. It is not at all unusual for envious people to be totally unaware that they suffer from this deadly poison. Lack of awareness in no way militates against maladaptive aspects of this poison. The misery associated with self-hate and disturbed relationships is prevalent in both conscious and unconscious envy. Indeed, of the two, unconscious envy is more difficult to root out and to treat; often its victim denies its existence, despite the obvious ravages of its onslaught.

Living with an envious person is living with a person who is chronically and deeply dissatisfied and unhappy. *Doing* something for that person usually brings few results and virtually no sustained satisfaction. If the envy is directed at the partner, many of the other poisons will also be present and life may well become a chronic state of hell for all concerned—unreasonable rage, nit-picking, complaining, self-pitying, blaming others, debasing and demeaning others, and jealousy are almost always accompanying poisons. These serve to create still greater unhappiness and still more agitated discontentment or envy.

Envy has its roots in an illusion of unjustified deprivation.

Some highly envious people may actually have been deprived as children, especially in terms of emotional needs. But more often than not, lack of self-esteem, the roots of which are multitudinous (overprotection, negligence, disturbed households, and parents) exaggerate the feelings of being abused and deprived. These feelings feed envy and the ensuing self-corrosion and disastrous relating experience feeds these feelings, creating a vicious cycle from which extrication becomes most difficult.

It must be understood that envy is basically an externalization. This means that one's wants, needs, sense of esteem, and general frame of reference are always in someone else's hands—mainly the person or people of whom one is envious. For example, a woman works hard and receives a master's degree, but has short-lived satisfaction because she envies a friend who receives her doctorate. Now she must have a doctorate—and more. In fact, her friend has determined the direction she must take and has been used with many other friends to design dictates, which are in no way her own goals.

The antidote consists of any move, treatment, and attainment of insight, usually through great struggle, that enhances real self-esteem. This almost always involves an understanding of the reality of the human condition and its very real limitations. The antidote is aided enormously by redirecting expectations to human proportions and smashing illusions about what life ought to be.

But nothing is possible until the victim becomes fully aware of suffering from the disease. This must be accompanied by increasing and full awareness of the destruction produced by the poison to oneself and especially to one's relating partners and to the relationships themselves. Subtle hints by friends, relatives, and therapists are usually uselsss. Most often, direct and unrelenting confrontation is necessary. Envy must not be looked upon as a sin or treated by either condemnation or condescension. But it must not be neglected either. It must be confronted head-on until the victim of this corrosive trait knows full well that he or she has been poisoned and that the process must be curtailed because it feeds on itself and hurts everyone in its presence.

Jealousy

Jealousy is surely one of the most common human emotions. Just about all of us feel jealous at one time or another in our lives. Frequency, quality, and intensity, however, may vary enormously in different people and also in the same person at different times in his or her life. Jealousy—the threat that something is being taken or may eventually be taken away from us—may be felt so mildly as hardly to be perceived on a conscious level. Jealousy may be felt on a conscious level as merely a vague feeling of disquietude or mild anxiety. On the other end of the scale, jealousy may be felt as life threatening and may bring on feelings of murderous rage and even psychotic behavior. Jealousy can permeate an individual's life so that it takes over the central core of his or her existence and affects all other feelings, thoughts, and actions. But even jealousy of a less obsessive, chronic, and malignant variety is destructive to personal happiness. Jealousy is surely the champion in its ability to hurt and to destroy close relationships and the potential happiness that may otherwise have come of them.

At this point it is important to put to rest what I consider the six most common myths about jealousy and to clarify some basic issues.

1. Jealousy has no priorities or exemptions as regards ethnic, racial, cultural, religious, professional, or socioeconomic groups. Doctors, lawyers, poor people, the superrich, Anglo-Saxons, Latins, French, Indians, Scandinavians, Chinese, Catholics, Baptists, Moslems, and Jews are equally subject to attacks of jealousy. Different groups may have different views about the emotion. Some may find it more acceptable (even praiseworthy) than others. But members of all groups suffer jealous attacks and their consequences.

2. Jealousy may coexist with love or may be present where there is little or no love at all. But jealousy is never evidence of love, nor is it an emotion born of love. Indeed, love of another human being involves caring and giving to that person. Jealousy involves a neurotic preoccupation with self, the fear of self-depletion, and the need for constant proof and reassurance of being given to or being fed by one's partner. Thus, jealousy often destroys the capacity to love and the ability to give, leaving only an insatiable appetite to take and to receive. Lack of jealousy is not evidence of lack of love. Both jealousy and love may be lacking in a relationship, but love certainly has a much better chance of flourishing in a nonjealous atmosphere.

3. Jealousy is equally prevalent and powerful in its effects among members of both sexes as well as in heterosexual and homosexual people. It is not evidence of masculinity, femininity, or sexual drive. It is often linked to self-doubt about one's lovableness, attractiveness, and ability to perform sexually.

4. Jealousy is not confined to any age group and may occur at just about any time in a person's life, from infancy to very advanced age. I have seen terrible attacks of sexual jealousy leading to paranoid accusations and even violence in people in their eighties. This is understandable if we realize that these attacks stem from feelings of sexual inadequacy linked to lack of self-esteem and a sense of worthlessness, which may have been relatively hidden for years. Emotional maturity (having little to do with chronological age), that is, development as responsible adults with good self-esteem, especially as regards belief in one's lovableness and sexuality, and the ability to give to others as well as to receive—mitigate against jealousy attacks.

5. Nobody is "born jealous" or has any kind of inborn proclivity to being more jealous than other people. But there are psychological factors that we acquire as we grow up that predispose us to jealousy. I've already mentioned *poor self-esteem*, and this is an important factor, but I shall go into some of these a little later on.

6. Jealousy is not confined to the most passionate or most emotional people. Indeed, it has little or nothing to do with real strength of feeling or a synthetic show of strong feelings or with degree of reserve or exuberance. The shy, the gregarious, the withdrawn, the highly emotional, the supersensitive, the calloused and blunted, the supercharged, and the undercharged contribute equally to the ever-changing population of the jealous among us.

Acute or short-lived attacks of jealousy are linked to temporary feelings of low self-esteem. The person in question seldom knows this. He or she may or may not realize that feelings of jealousy are irrational, but the real reasons for jealousy remain essentially unconscious. These attacks often occur as a result of business reversals, school failures, fear of new responsibilities, fear of advancing age, or whatever. Some people experience attacks of severe jealousy at about the time of each decade birthday, which has strong symbolic significance. Attacks are often linked to fear of impotence in men and fear of undesirability in women. Sexual jealousy is most prevalent and strongest among people whose self-acceptance is largely based on personal sex appeal and attraction and on their ability to function well sexually. This sexual basis for self-acceptance is, unfortunately, fed by the culture we live in. Sometimes the jealous person, in addition to other problems, is sexually attracted to others than his or her sexual partner largely as a need to feel his or her own attraction. This increases jealousy because the person in question becomes convinced that the partner is likewise attracted to other people. This kind of projection, based on jealousy and self-hate and self-rejection, is often transmitted to both the partner and to the imagined transgressor, who is often secretly envied for being more attractive, stimulating, and lovable than oneself. Thus, a mere glance at another person by one's lover or mate can bring on severe attacks of self-hate projected out as fear of loss and rage. Short attacks usually pass, as the stimulating agent (business reversal, birthday, or whatever) loses its power or becomes resolved. But this is not true of people who suffer chronic severe jealousy to the point of paranoia and violence.

For the chronic sufferer, no amount of rationalization of their great love or possessiveness, which is due to the "my woman" macho myth in men or the "my man" great-love myth in women, brings relief. These people suffer from an essential disbelief in their own lovableness, in their sexual attractiveness, and in their sexual ability. No amount of reassurance in these areas has any lasting effect because the essential problem is much deeper and exists on a completely unconscious level, which makes it particularly powerful and permeating. The essential fact is that these people are secretly severely dependent on their sexual partners for any sense of personal adequacy and are terrified of the possibility of abandonment. They live in constant dread because their very low self-esteem makes it impossible for them to believe that they should not, in fact, be abandoned for a more adequate and superior partner. This is, of course, lived out on a conscious level as chronic, severe jealousy. But what makes the problem more difficult is the fact that this sense of unlovableness, severe dependency, and fear of abandonment is a carry-over from childhood and one's relationship with one's parents. In effect, the chronic jealousy sufferer has not grown up emotionally and has never resolved these childhood issues, which are carried into chronological adulthood and transferred to one's lover and mate. Cure or help is possible, but this almost always requires dealing with these problems at the root level on a psychoanalytic basis for which expert professional help is necessary.

Loss and Mourning

There are many losses of all kinds, which inevitably occur in all of our lives, and there are various ways we react to different kinds of losses. How we react is often a measure of mental health and maturity. For many of us, certain losses are followed by ritualized behavior dictated by culture, custom, and religion. Some rituals are designed to promote at least some degree of healthy expression of feelings. Other emphasize symbolic changes in the mourner's status, helping to alleviate guilt while marking the ending of one era and the beginning of another. "The king is dead, long live the king" is a fairly typical expression of the latter process and is also an expression of the popular statement "life must go on." But even the well-known Irish wake and the merriment that goes on often cannot alter the continuing feeling of deep loss and in some people continuing despair. The ritualistic Jewish *shivah* period of mourning and the long Italian mourning period often have little effect on the continuing severe effects some people suffer as the result of loss of a loved one.

I should point out that over the years I have seen many people in consultation whose severe emotional reactions to loss in no way involved the death of a loved one. Yes, some were reacting to the breakup of an important relationship, and this comes closest to appropriate mourning following the death of a loved one. But others were reacting to loss of power, prestige, money, and in some cases illusory dreams of what they thought life was supposed to be like by a certain age or place or position. To feel sad about the loss of money or an election or a house one has loved is appropriate. But for some people these kinds of losses are followed by severe emotional reactions, including serious depression, incapacitating anxiety, serious psychosomatic illness, and even psychotic behavior, including attempted suicide. These so-called inappropriate reactions to loss nearly always have one thing in common—enormous *self-hate*. This self-hate is the result of a blow to one's neurotic pride or sick image of oneself. For example, the man who sees himself as being so omnipotent as never to suffer a business loss is the very man most vulnerable and prone to enormous self-hating attacks when these losses occur. Though these kinds of losses may have practical implications, the severe reaction is never due to the imposition of new limitations, loss of luxury, or a necessary change in life-style. They are always due to the symbolic emotional attack on self-esteem, on neurotic vanity, on the neurotic need for perfection, everlasting youth, and good looks. The reactions themselves are often severe and therefore completely evident on a conscious level. But the underlying self-hate and the reasons for it may be totally out of the conscious awareness of the sufferer. These severe reactions occur only in people whose demands on themselves, on the human condition, and on the world they live in have always been inappropriate. Obviously the woman who believes that she will never lose her looks or her sexual attractiveness is exceedingly vulnerable to these kinds of reactions. Psychoanalytic treatment is usually necessary in these cases in order to change a value system that made the reaction possible in the first place.

But what about the loss of a loved one—the death of a child, a husband, a parent—and subsequent feelings or emotional reactions?

People do not make great emotional investments easily. Perhaps this is because feeling, caring, identifying, empathizing, and the entire complicated process involved in deep relating may well constitute the most important thing we do in life. Investing emotion or deeply relating to another human being represents at least some degree of exchange or sharing of selves. It is our way of extending ourselves through another human being. Small wonder that we suffer a sense of great loss when a loved one dies because emotionally we have indeed lost that part of ourselves we have invested in the other person. And yet this in a way is compensated for by the continuing influence and memories both conscious and unconscious of the lost person, which continue to live in us. The emotional chemistry of human relating has been researched and theorized about for centuries by both scientists and artists, and yet much of it eludes us. This is probably because we are dealing with the most complicated process that exists on earth and that in great part distinguishes us from most other life forms on this planet. I say "most" because we know very well that other creatures also relate and suffer loss and mourn.

People who do not react emotionally to the loss of loved ones (and reactions are not always public) are usually very sick emotionally. Some have been so hurt and emotionally stunted that they have been incapable of making emotional investments at all. Others repress, blunt, and deaden their feelings because to feel anything at all is intolerable to them. But some people, especially those whose emotional investments have been very neurotic, may react with chronic mourning and severe and even intractable depression. Rather than evidence of love, this is usually the result of severe and crippling dependency on the loved one. These people have often overinvested, which is to say that they have largely lost a sense of separateness and have so melded with a loved one as to feel a complete loss of identity and self with his or her death. These are often severely immature people who must do a great deal of developing and growing in order to survive. There are also people who use chronic mourning as a way of denying the death of a loved one. This is an unconscious attempt to keep him alive by becoming living memorials to him, showing the world his continuing effect on and through the mourner. There are still other people who use mourning as a self-imposed form of martyrdom through which they unconsciously seek self-glorification and attention. Small wonder some religions in anticipation of these kinds of reactions have prescribed and even dictated limits to mourning periods and activities. I might mention that I have also known people who use chronic mourning to cover up intense guilt connected to unconscious fulfillment of a death wish for the person who died. Of course, all of us have hostile feelings and even wish loved ones dead at certain times, but chronic guilt is always associated with deep neurotic conflicts.

Feeling a great loss is indeed appropriate to a great loss, and this includes anticipated loss of self. Going through a period of emotional reaction is entirely human and healthy. We all emote differently so this process may or may not include tears, talk about the person in question, screaming, a period of lack of desire to function fully, and so on. It always includes a feeling of loss and a yearning for what is lost, and at least to some small degree that sense of loss continues all of our lives. To feel this loss actively, however it is expressed or not expressed, is very important because the feeling is there and therefore must be felt since denial of it invariably leads to great emotional difficulty. It is also important to reaffirm to ourselves what is important in our lives, namely life itself—especially our own lives and those of loved ones. And it is important to feel what we feel and to free ourselves of these feelings so as to bury the dead emotionally as well as physically. This is not to say that we should forget them. We never can and never do. It simply means that yes, life does go on, and that the very process of feeling the loss—mourning—gets us through periods of inevitable loss and makes mourning itself finite. Yes, mourning must be finite, thus ultimately giving greater priority to life than to death for ourselves and our children.

Q: Can you tell me why a person would spend a great deal of her time thinking about death? The fact that I will one day die is on my mind a great deal of the time. Why?
A: Particular reasons for preoccupation with death have much to do with the individual in question. Much detailed information has to be known about a person to understand a particular psychological manifestation or symptom.

Many people preoccupied with death are afraid of strong feelings and afraid of feeling fully alive. They are, in fact, fearful of living in the fullest sense and use preoccupation with death to deaden themselves and to escape confrontation with life. Some people can give up morbid and compulsive preoccupation with death only after they are able to overcome serious inhibitions that prevent them from fully living. One of the deepest fears of death occurs in people who feel that they have not yet lived and will possibly die having missed the opportunity to live.

Q: Lately I've been dreaming a lot about dying. Does this mean I will probably die soon? I hope not because I'm only thirty-six, but both my parents died at very young ages.

A: I do not believe a dream is in any way a prediction of the future, even though dreams sometimes, in indicating what we desire for ourselves, become self-fulfilling prophecies.

Dreams do tell us much about our inner selves, including fears, feelings, and conflicts of which we may not be fully consciously aware. But the surface look of a dream must not be taken for granted because each item of a dream may be a symbol for people, places, events, and forces other than they immediately seem. Also, the same and very similar dreams may have entirely different meanings at different times in a person's life and may have vastly different interpretations for different people.

Your dream seems from what you say to have more to do with the fear of death and a preoccupation with death connected to early loss of your parents than a desire for death, let alone a prediction of death. But dreams such as yours sometimes indicate a feeling that something (a hidden talent, a strong desire, a hope, a problem) is dying in us. At times we desire that something in us indeed will die and be forgotten. At other times we may fear losing a part of ourselves and really desire resuscitation and development of that "something" we feel is slipping away. In any case, the interpretation of a dream can be accurate and of value only if the analyst knows the dreamer, the dreamer's history, the dreamer's use of symbols, and the thoughts and feelings of the dreamer relative to the dream.

Q: Does it seem crazy to you that I should feel angry at my husband for dying and leaving me alone? I loved him so much and now he's gone. For over a year I was so depressed I thought I couldn't go on. Now I feel angry, and I suppose this is terribly self-serving.

A: There's nothing wrong with being self-serving. I think your anger at being left alone is quite understandable, because his dying, even though this was not his choice, did, in fact, leave you alone and deprived of a loved one. I think this is a very common reaction and I admire your insight and openness about it. Most people hide this anger and resentment from themselves, and as a result it becomes self-corrosive and prolongs their depression.

Q: I recently entered a hotel for older people and I've been quite happy here. Everyone has been very warm and friendly to me and I've made some good friends in a short time. One lovely woman I met and whom we all liked died suddenly about three weeks ago. Nobody has said anything about it. It's as if it never happened and as if she never existed. I can't understand the callousness and insensitivity of such seemingly warm and caring people. Could you explain?

A: People who are afraid of death, who feel close to death, who feel the whole issue is terribly painful sometimes enter into an unspoken agreement to avoid talking about it. In a peculiar way this may be a life-affirming action. I'm sure it has nothing to do with insensitivity. Actually, her friends and yours, too, may be sensitive and sensitized and may care so much about their loss that it is too painful to talk about.

Q: My brother passed away suddenly several years ago. At family gatherings, his absence is very strongly felt, the more so because all of us consciously avoid talking about him—I think we're afraid to stir up the old grief. Yet this attitude casts a shadow over the proceedings, and I wonder if gently introducing the subject might ease the tension. Any suggestions?

A: You are absolutely right. Suppressing talk and feelings about a lost loved one aggravates and sustains grief. It also prevents mutual support when it is most needed. Additionally, it puts us out of touch with fond and enriching memories and in so doing denigrates the dead by pretending they never lived at all.

"Stirring up the old grief" is the best way to get rid of it. The therapeutic effect of open ventilation and emotional expression cannot be exaggerated. That is why mourning adequately is so very important.

Talking it out may at first be painful but not nearly as painful as isolated sitting with one's own grief. Sharing feelings—all kinds—is the essence of human intimacy and is, in itself, evidence of love and respect for ourselves and the persons who are no longer with us whom we loved in common.

I feel you will find that open talk will do more than relieve tension. It will also relieve guilt, which sometimes occurs when a family member dies suddenly. Thoughts and feelings about neglect and what could have been said and done but weren't can be exchanged and clarified. This is extemely important for those who are still alive because it rids them of self-hate and enhances compassion for self and others. Little else is of more significant therapeutic value than compassion.

Index

addictions, 27

adolescent(s): and adjustment to college, 48–49; alcoholism in, 41–42; boys' idealization of girls, 43–44; and "college-application anxiety," 48–49; and conformity, 52, 223–24; depression in, 51; and divorce, 28, 77–78; and family problems, 53–54; and fear of rejection, 43–44, 48–49; loneliness of, 52; and name-changing, 42; and popularity, concern with, 52; and preoccupation with appearance, 53; problems of, xi–xii, 51–56; problems with opposite sex, 43–44; rebelliousness of, 15; self-destructive behavior of, 52; and sex, ignorance about, 53; sexual activity of, and low self-esteem, 223; sexual role-playing of, 52–53; shyness, 54; snobbery, 287–288; and unrequited love, 53

adoption, problems of, 33–35

age differences in relationships, 9–10, 234

age, peak, of sexual desire in women, 241–242

aging: acceptance of, 168, 295–96; and sex drive, 234

Alanon, 41

Alcoholics Anonymous, 41

alcoholism, 22, 41–42; in teenagers, 41–42

alienation, and infidelity, 20–21

alone, need to be, 73, 114–115, 119

American Academy of Psychoanalysis, 187, 195

American College of Plastic Surgeons, 137

American Institute of Psychoanalysis, 187

American Psychiatric Association, 42

American Psychoanalytic Association, 187, 195

American Psychological Society, 42

analytic therapy, 11–12. *See also* psychoanalytic therapy, psychotherapy

anger: blocking of, 271–72; cultural attitudes about, 268; and death fantasies, 272–73; and driving fantasies, 272; and driving a car, 271–72; expression of, 119–20, 270–71; expression of, and need to be liked, 221; and gossiping, 222, 273–74; and men's fear of commitment to women, 111–12; related to loss and mourning, 307–308; repression of, 221, 254, 268–79; repression of, and hysterectomy, 277; repression of, and